THE THIN WOMAN

In late twentieth-century Western Europe the concept of 'anorexia nervosa' has taken up a prominent place in the pathologization of certain aspects of women's experiences. 'Anorexia nervosa' has become the name, and an 'explanation' for, the extreme distress that many girls and women experience in relation to food, embodiment and identity and for the seriously self-destructive behaviours that accompany this distress. *The Thin Woman* locates 'anorexia nervosa' within a complex social and discursive context and explores how everyday discourses about gender, subjectivity and embodiment are imbricated in the problem of anorexia.

In Part One, psychoanalytic and post-structuralist theories are discussed in relation to the category of 'woman' and in relation to our understanding of science, knowledge and truth. Part Two takes an historical perspective to examine how the diagnostic category of anorexia nervosa was first constituted at the end of the nineteenth century and how it has subsequently been constituted within the various academic and clinical discourses that claim to know this problem. Part Three focuses on Helen Malson's original research with women diagnosed as anorexic. It contrasts the 'expert' discourses of Parts One and Two with the voices of the women themselves. Gender, subjectivity, embodiment, control and the paradox of self-production/destruction are the strands that are clearly interwoven in the everyday discourses and discursive practices in which anorexia is constituted.

The Thin Woman offers new insights into anorexia nervosa for those with an interest in eating disorders and gender. It will also be useful to those interested in feminist post-structuralist theory and discourse analytic research.

Helen Malson is a lecturer in psychology at the University of East London and has previously authored a number of journal articles and book chapters on the subject.

WOMEN AND PSYCHOLOGY
Series Editor: Jane Ussher
Dept of Psychology, University College, London

This series brings together current theory and research on women and psychology. Drawing on scholarship from a number of different areas of psychology, it bridges the gap between abstract research and the reality of women's lives by integrating theory and practice, research and policy.

Each book addresses a 'cutting edge' issue of research, covering such topics as postnatal depression, eating disorders, theories and methodologies.

The series provides accessible and concise accounts of key issues in the study of women and psychology, and clearly demonstrates the centrality of psychology to debates within women's studies or feminism.

The Series Editor would be pleased to discuss proposals for new books in the series.

Other titles in this series:

THE MENSTRUAL CYCLE
Anne E. Walker

POSTNATAL DEPRESSION
Paula Nicolson

RE-THINKING ABORTION
Mary Boyle

THE THIN WOMAN

Feminism, post-structuralism and the social
psychology of anorexia nervosa

Helen Malson

London and New York

First published 1998
by Routledge
11 New Fetter Lane, London EC4P 4EE

Simultaneously published in the USA and Canada
by Routledge
29 West 35th Street, New York, NY 10001

Typeset in Baskerville by Routledge
Printed and bound in Great Britain by TJ International

British Library Cataloguing in Publication Data
A catalogue record for this book is available from the British Library

Library of Congress Cataloguing in Publication Data
Malson, Helen M.
The Thin Woman: feminism, post-structuralism, and the social
psychology of anorexia nervosa/Helen M. Malson
(Women and Psychology)
Includes bibliographical references and index.
1. Anorexia nervosa – Social aspects. 2. Leanness – Pyschological
aspects. 3. Women – Socialization. I. Title. II. Series.
RC552.A5M345 96–39930
616.85' 262–dc21

ISBN 0–415–16332–3 (hbk)
ISBN 0–415–16333–1 (pbk)

For Paul and Otto

Words are far older and fickler and more experienced than the writers who suffer under the delusion that they are 'using' them. Words *have been around*. No one owns them, no one can prescribe how they ought to be read, and most certainly not their authors.

(Adaire, 1993: 26)

CONTENTS

CONTENTS

PREFACE

Medicine, psychiatry and psychology have presented us with particular ways of understanding eating disorders and more generally of understanding ourselves as individuals and as women. They present us with particular perspectives which are by no means the only ones from which we can understand our own and others' experiences. From a mainstream perspective, 'anorexia nervosa' is viewed as a clinical entity, as a legitimate and relatively unproblematic category of a medical taxonomy of diseases and disorders. And this stance brings with it a number of (often unspoken) assumptions about the nature of women's experiences and about the causes of women's distress. It is assumed, for example, that 'anorexia nervosa' is something that exists 'out there' as a 'disorder' that we do or do not suffer from; as a clinical entity whose typifying characteristics can be accurately and objectively documented and whose (universally applicable) causes can be discovered through scientific enquiry. 'Anorexic' behaviours and experiences are viewed, then, as pathological, as distinctly different from the 'normal' 'healthy' experiences and practices of non-anorexic girls and women. They become separated from their social context and from the everyday experiences of ordinary girls and women. Hence from a mainstream perspective the object of enquiry is the disorder, the anorexia, not the varied, complex and socially contextualized experiences of the individual girls and women who have been diagnosed as 'anorexic'.

Throughout this book I shall be questioning this notion of 'anorexia' as *individual* pathology and asking whether there might not be better ways of theorizing our own and/or others' experiences of eating and not eating, of losing and gaining weight, of being fat or thin. I shall be arguing that we need to radically rethink our approaches to understanding these (and other) experiences. We need to be developing new frameworks within which to theorize and research our own and others' experiences. When it appears that increasing numbers of girls and women are being diagnosed as anorexic, and when so many girls and women suffer considerable distress in relation to eating, food and body-image, we need to ask whether a medical or quasi-medical notion of 'anorexia' as an *individual* pathology should retain its powerful hold over our understandings of 'eating disorders'. For the notion of 'anorexia' as individual pathology precludes or at

least limits our attempts to understand 'anorexia' within its socio-cultural, political and gender-specific contexts. It produces an apparently objective
distinction between the experiences of those who are and are not diagnosed as
eating disordered. By presenting 'anorexia' as something located within the
pathologized individual, this perspective limits the extent to which we can
explore anorexia as a socially, discursively produced problem.

Mainstream medical, psychiatric and psychological perspectives bring with
them commonsensical assumptions about the nature of experience, of gender, of
the individual and about the relationship between individual and society. As we
shall see, such assumptions close down many of the questions that we might
otherwise address, so that even when issues about social context and gender are
considered within mainstream psychology, such considerations tend to be undertheorized. 'Femininity', for example, is frequently taken to be an unproblematic
category that may even function as an implicit explanation of girls' and women's
apparent 'propensity' to develop 'eating disorders'. The reasons *why* so many
girls and women diet or starve themselves or binge and purge are frequently left
unexplored. As Susie Orbach notes,

> No one is much disturbed by statistics that show that 80 per cent of
> women in countries like the USA, the UK, New Zealand and Australia are
> dieting at any given moment. The anguish and distress behind these
> figures are concealed behind an attitude that accepts this as the norm and
> sees the need for no further questions. Women like to diet. Women expect
> to diet. Women are accustomed to diet. Women have a tendency to fat.
> Women are vain. Women are always so self-involved.
>
> (Orbach, 1993: xxiii)

It is these kinds of (often unspoken) assumptions that we have to examine critically if we are to better understand the problem of 'anorexia'. We have to
re-examine our conceptualizations of gender, of identity or subjectivity, of
embodiment, and of the relationship between individual and society. Yet the
ways in which socially dominant ideologies of (for example) gender are themselves deeply imbricated in the problem of 'anorexia' remain relatively
unexplored within mainstream psychology. What I shall be arguing in this book
is that it is precisely these kinds of questions about gender, subjectivity and
embodiment, and about the individual–society relationship, that we need to
address if we are to understand better women's experiences of eating and not
eating, of losing and gaining weight, of being fat or thin, of being women. That
is, we need to develop new theoretical and methodological frameworks which
enable us to 'deconstruct' our current knowledges of 'anorexia' (and other 'disorders'), to go beyond the concept of 'anorexia' as an *individual pathology*, and to
explore critically the ways in which the discourses and discursive practices of our
society constitute and regulate our own and others' experiences. We need to
develop new perspectives within which we can theorize and research the

problem of 'anorexia' in ways that more fully locate 'anorexic' experiences within their socio-cultural/political and gender-specific contexts.

The limitations in current understandings of anorexia are also further compounded by the lack of effective treatments available for those diagnosed as anorexic. Fatalities are estimated at 10–15 per cent and research suggests that long-term prognosis is often poor (Hsu, 1980), whilst accounts of unsympathetic (even hostile) treatment are not uncommon (e.g. Pembroke, 1993; EDA, 1993). Whilst this book does not examine treatments *per se*, I have aimed to provide an alternative account of 'anorexia' that might in some way contribute towards the development of more effective and acceptable help for those diagnosed as anorexic. One of my aims in producing this account has been, therefore, to provide a critique of the current perspectives on anorexia. I have not adopted a 'traditional' psychological stance that would re-produce 'anorexia' as an individual pathology. Rather, I have wanted to take a stance, both theoretically and methodologically, that would enable a critique of 'scientific' knowledges of anorexia *and* which would provide an understanding of (gendered) subjectivity as fluid, contradictory and as socially embedded.

The book draws, therefore, on feminist, post-structuralist and psychoanalytic theory as well as on the current psychological literature on eating disorders. As I argue in Part I, this theoretical framework provides an understanding of (gendered) subjectivity in terms of multiple, shifting, often contradictory, subject positions produced and regulated within discourses. It provides, I think, an opportunity to research anorexia in a way that more fully acknowledges its socio-cultural and gender-specific contexts and makes it possible to re-conceptualize 'anorexia' and 'the (anorexic) woman' in terms of multiply produced discursive constructions. And by rejecting the notion of any absolute, objective Truth, post-structuralist theory also provides a framework within which to critique the (scientific) Truths both about 'anorexia' and about 'woman'. As Foucault (1972: 49) argues, discourses do not objectively describe objects existing beyond or anterior to them. Rather, from a post-structuralist perspective, discourses 'systematically form the objects of which they speak' (Foucault, 1979: 100).

Such a perspective seems particularly suited to a critique of 'traditional' knowledges of anorexia, but it must also be applied reflexively to my own work. The account that I have produced is no more objectively true than those institutionalized accounts that I critically analyse (see Part II). It equally forms the objects of which it speaks. My critique of current approaches and my analyses of the nineteenth-century discourses within which 'anorexia nervosa' first emerged as a disease entity (Part II), and of those discourses and discursive resources used by women today in talking about their experiences of anorexia (Part III), constitute an inevitably partial account of anorexia. It is conditioned by my own subjectivities, by my theoretical stance (see Woodiwiss, 1990), by the particularities of those discourses available to me and to others. Nevertheless I hope that it provides some insights into the ways in which the socio-cultural issues of gender, subjectivity and embodiment are imbricated in the discourses and discursive practices within which 'anorexia nervosa' is produced.

In writing this book I have relied on the help, advice, support and encouragement of various people. In particular I would like to thank Jane Ussher for her excellent supervision throughout my doctoral research on which this book is based and for her continued advice and helpful comments on earlier drafts of this book. My heartfelt thanks also to her and to Catherine Swann for their continued support and friendship. Thanks also to my family and friends, particularly to my parents and to Laurence, Alan, Carol, Mick and Anita. And to all those women who contributed to my research, especially those women I interviewed. It was a privilege to have shared in their experience. Thanks also to Barbara Lloyd and Gerry Webster for providing earlier inspiration. Finally I am particularly grateful to Paul Sutton whose support, affections and metatheoretical compatibility have sustained me throughout my doctoral research and throughout the writing of this book.

Helen M. Malson

ACKNOWLEDGEMENTS

The author would like to thank the following for permission to reproduce material:

Carfax Publishing Company, PO Box 25, Abingdon, Oxford OX14 3UE, for material from Malson, H. and Ussher, J.M. (1997) Beyond the mortal coil: feminity, death and discursive constructions of the anorexic body, *Mortality*, 2 (1), pp. 43–51.

Eldritch Boulevard Ltd/EMI Songs Ltd, London WC2H 0EA for an extract from 'When You Don't See Me', music by Andrew Eldritch and Andreas Bruhn and words by Andrew Eldritch © 1990.

The Journal of Community and Applied Social Psychology/John Wiley & Sons, Ltd for material from Malson, H. and Ussher, J.M. (1996) Body poly-texts: discourses of the anorexic body, *Journal of Community and Applied Psychology*, 6 (4) pp. 167–280.

Sage Publications Ltd for material from Malson, H. and Ussher, J.M. (1996) Bloody Women: a discourse of amenorrhea as a symptom of anorexia nervosa, *Feminism and Psychology*, 6, pp. 505–521.

Every effort has been made to obtain permission to reproduce copyright material. If any proper acknowledgement has not been made, we would invite copyright holders to inform us of the oversight.

TRANSCRIPTION CONVENTIONS

= indicates an overlap or the absence of a gap between two consecutive utterances.

// indicates an interjection. For example, 'I think yeah /H: mm/ I could be like her.'

(.) indicates a pause.

Italics indicate where words or phrases are stressed.

[. . .] indicates that part of the transcript has been omitted.

(inaud.) indicates where a part of the recording of the interview was inaudible.

( ) brackets surround words where the accuracy of transcription is in doubt because of the poor quality of the recording.

( ) brackets are also used to indicate where, for example, there is laughter.

{ } brackets surround explanations that are not part of the transcript but are added to clarify the meaning of an utterance. For example, 'It {anorexia} was about not having feelings.'

{ } are also used where extracts are quoted in the text to indicate where words have been altered.

Sounds such as 'mm' and 'uhr' are transcribed phonetically, as are colloquialisms, abbreviations, stutters and half-said words. Where utterances are not grammatical, punctuation is used so as to make the transcript as readable as possible.

INTRODUCTION

Pathology has always done us the service of making discernible by isolation and exaggeration conditions which would remain concealed in a normal state.

(Freud, 1933b: 585)

TALES OF THIN WOMEN

This book is about 'anorexia nervosa'. It is about the distress that many girls and women in contemporary Western society experience around eating and not eating, around losing and gaining weight, being fat or thin, around being a woman. But this book is also about questioning the ways in which we currently understand these 'anorexic' behaviours and experiences. It is about questioning the socially dominant 'mainstream' bodies of knowledge about 'anorexia' and about exploring new ways in which to theorize and research women's 'anorexic' practices and experiences. It is about 'making recognizable things which would normally remain hidden' (Freud, in Klein, 1968: 339), exploring what 'anorexia' has to say about being a woman in late twentieth-century Western culture.

Part of this book is based on an analysis of interviews that I carried out with women who had been diagnosed or self-diagnosed as anorexic. Amongst the many issues we discussed I asked them what they would want to say if they were going to write a book about 'anorexia'. These are some of the answers that they gave.[1]

K: I mean god if I was going to write a book I think I'd have to write a lot about the misery of what it's actually like because you even forget yourself. (.) Because for this time I got to my target weight and I'd been losing and (.) I'd been delighted at losing (.) until I just hit a point where I've been getting really down (.) again because you forget all of the (.) you know it's not an a solution (.) unless you you actually kill yourself.

LYNN: Um I think I'd write how I I've suffered with uh my life up to before I was (.) um stopped eating because I've always kept it to myself and shrugged it off as if it didn't mean nothing. And now I grew up I want to tell people what it, it's been like this. It's been this terrible. You know

1

(.) I want people to be *aware* (.) of of you know what I've been through and you know how horrible it's been.

LAYLA: I wouldn't know. How would I ever (.) can explain it. [. . .] To *know* that my stomach was *empty* gave me such a good feeling but now I can see that these are just the surface (.) uhrr surface uhr decorations of it that I used to be in something (.) socially acceptable so that I could live in that misery (.) and I wouldn't see it as a just a way of avoiding thought. It had to be, it had to convey some (.) messages or, (.) how to say, I mean I had to convince myself that it was good. (.) So I think my mind has worked in that way so that I could be happy in that (.) shit.

ZOE: I think I would say it's just not worth it. And I think if people saw it like the lot of insecurity, like I really think it comes from being insecure [. . .] and I think also it's, that also tends to be a way where like: Wow! everyone expects so much of me. I don't know if I can do all this. At least this one way I can succeed and be successful.

DENISE: I'd definitely like to point out the different strands and that there isn't one anorexic. I've learned that definitely from being here, that even with people who (.) sort of more fit the more classic sort of stereotypes, still they're, everyone, each one is is different. And there's a slightly different I mean some people it's (.) purely body weight. Other people it's that they were denying themselves cos they felt they didn't deserve things. You know there's, there are just so many different strands.

SIMONE: I'd want to say that a lot of psychiatrists don't know what they're talking about (laughter). They should get off our cases. Um I'd want to say (.) that it shouldn't be looked at on the surface. It shouldn't be looked at as an eating, just an eating problem.

CATHY: I've been writing about the experiences of isolation. Now I think that I *have* to say for (.) *most* people, I think when I say this I *do* represent most people, is that you feel so alone. I don't think there is any vocabulary to really express *just* how alone you feel. Um (.) nobody in the world understands you. Nobody cares um. You feel as if (.) um you're in a bubble and nobody can get in and you can't get out. [. . .] you want people to desperately comfort you and at the same time you *don't* want them near you because they *might* touch you. They might feel your *fat*.

NICKI: I think most people do' don't realize what it actually is. [. . .] It's such it's such a deep thing and it's all to do with a person's control, how they feel about themselves and how they're coping. [. . .] It's very sad and it and it numbs you completely. If I wrote a book I'd write one on how to get over it as it were.

symptoms of anorexia nervosa (APA, 1987; WHO, 1992). In short, the characterization and classification of eating disorders has varied somewhat over the hundred or so years that 'disordered' eating has been constituted as a category of medical or psychiatric discourse.

The lack of standardization in formal and informal diagnostic criteria has caused some problems in determining the prevalence of anorexia (Brumberg, 1986). However, there is a general consensus that diagnoses of this formerly rare condition (Bruch, 1978) have increased dramatically since the 1960s and it has been claimed that anorexia is reaching epidemic proportions (Bruch, 1978) at least in Europe and North America. (Epidemiological research has found a much lower prevalence of eating disorders in non-Western countries [Wardle et al., 1993].) However, the proportions of this Western 'epidemic' remain unclear (Brumberg, 1986). What is clear, though, is that diagnoses of eating disorders are particularly prevalent amongst young women and girls.

Approximately 90–95 per cent of those diagnosed as anorexic are female (Hsu, 1989). Estimates of its prevalence amongst young women rise to 1 per cent (Hughes, 1991; APA, 1987) and are higher in particular groups. Garner et al. (1987), for example, estimated that as many as 25.7 per cent of female ballet students may be 'anorexic', and other occupations such as modelling and beauty therapy (Garner and Garfinkel, 1980; Wolff et al., 1990) and women's athletics (Weight and Noakes, 1987) have also been associated with a particularly high prevalence of anorexia. High prevalence rates such as 4.2 per cent and 1 per cent (Pope et al., 1984) and 5.7 per cent (Mintz and Betz, 1988) have also been found in different female college populations. It has also been reported that anorexia is more common amongst girls attending private or grant-aided schools than those attending state schools (Crisp et al., 1976) and that eating disorders are more common in the professional or middle and upper social classes (Hughes, 1991; Wolff et al., 1990) and amongst white rather than black and Asian women in Europe and North America (Wardle et al., 1993). However, studies of the ethnic distribution of anorexia have produced conflicting results, with some authors finding that ethnicity was not predictive of eating disorders (Gross and Rosen, 1988) or that 'abnormal' eating attitudes occurred in women of all ethnic backgrounds (Dolan et al., 1990). Several studies have also suggested that eating disorders, including anorexia nervosa, have spread to all social classes (Pumariega et al., 1984) and that their incidence is now similar across all socio-economic levels (Edwards-Hewitt and Gray, 1993).

In short, it is difficult to determine the prevalence and demographic distribution of anorexia nervosa because of variations in formal and informal diagnostic criteria, because of conflicting results from different epidemiological studies, because of differences in referral practices for different sections of the population (Wardle et al., 1993) and because eating disorders may pass unrecognized when health-care workers believe, for example, that eating disorders do not occur in minority groups (Dolan, 1991). And if we are going to problematize the concept of 'anorexia nervosa' as individual pathology, if we are going to

4

Unfortunately I do not feel able to write a book about how to get over it. Neither have I aimed to write the books that these women might have done. As another thin woman I have my own agendas here, my own tale to tell. I hope, however, that in writing this account of *The Thin Woman* I will provide some new insights into the stories that these women have shared with me, the stories that they and we live by, the distress that many girls and women in contemporary Western society experience around eating and not eating, losing and gaining weight, being fat or thin, and around being a woman.

A ROUGH GUIDE TO ANOREXIA NERVOSA

'Anorexia nervosa' has existed as a distinct clinical entity since the early 1870s, when it first emerged in the medical literature as a nervous disorder associated with young women (Gull, 1874; Lasegue, 1873a). Now described as a mental and behavioural disorder or syndrome (WHO, 1992), or as a psychosomatic disorder (Wolff *et al.*, 1990), anorexia is currently defined as

1   a refusal to maintain a 'normal' body weight with body weight at least 15 per cent below that expected (either because of weight loss or lack of expected weight gain);
2   an intense fear of gaining weight or becoming fat despite being underweight;
3   body image distortion, 'feeling fat' and overvaluation of thinness;
4   a reduction of food intake, avoidance of 'fattening foods', often with extensive exercise, self-induced vomiting, laxative or diuretic abuse so as to achieve the weight loss and maintain a low body weight.

(APA, 1987; WHO, 1992)

Other symptoms, including amenorrhea, hypothermia, bradycardia, hypotension, edema, lanugo and a variety of metabolic changes, may also occur because of weight loss (APA, 1987; Hughes, 1991).

It is important to note, however, that diagnostic criteria have varied (Russell, 1984, 1985). Feighner *et al.* (1972), for example, included an age of onset prior to 25 as a diagnostic criterion and Russell (1970) included endocrinal disorder, as well as behaviour leading to weight loss and a morbid fear of becoming fat. There are also variations in the percentage weight loss considered necessary for diagnosis. Whereas *ICD-10* (WHO, 1992) and *DSM-III-R* (APA, 1987) state that weight loss (or lack of expected weight gain) should be at least 15 per cent, *DSM-III* (APA, 1980) states 25 per cent and others (e.g. Merskey, 1980) state 20 per cent. Precisely how much weight a woman has to lose before she is pathologized seems to vary, and to some extent the decision is arbitrary.

In addition, the now central symptoms of 'weight-phobia' and a drive towards thinness only emerged in the 1960s as a common characteristic of anorexia (Habermas, 1989), and the symptoms of self-induced vomiting and laxative abuse, rarely mentioned before the 1930s (Casper, 1983), have become central features of the now separate syndrome, bulimia nervosa, as well as being question the medical distinction between women's 'pathological' and 'normal' experiences, then determining the prevalence and demographic distribution of 'anorexia nervosa' or eating distress becomes even more complicated.

It is, nevertheless, widely accepted that diagnoses of 'anorexia' predominantly occur in young Western women and that such diagnoses have become increasingly common in the latter part of this century at a time when research also suggests that increasing numbers of girls and women in the general population are similarly experiencing some degree of distress around eating and not eating, losing and gaining weight, being fat or thin.

CULTURE AND GENDER IN ANOREXIA NERVOSA

This gender-bias in the distribution of diagnoses of anorexia nervosa strongly suggests that it is still as much a feminine disorder as it was in the nineteenth century. And it is probable that 'anorexia' and anorexia-like problems are also more widespread amongst women than prevalence studies might suggest: first, because it seems that women who elect not to participate in surveys on eating disorders often experience higher degrees of disordered eating than those who participate (Beglin and Fairburn, 1992), and second, studies of diagnostic trends may not include 'sub-clinical' eating disorders: body-dissatisfaction, a desire to lose weight, preoccupations with body weight, shape and food, dieting and also bingeing and vomiting are disturbingly common in Western women and even young girls (Wardle and Marsland, 1990; Hill and Robinson, 1991). Indeed, it has been suggested that dieting and an attendant 'diet mentality' are both descriptively and prescriptively normative (Polivy and Herman, 1987).

Notwithstanding the arguments of Bruch (1985) and Crisp (1980) that dieting and eating disorders are distinctly different, there is clearly some relationship between the cultural idealization of female thinness and the prevalence of dieting and the recent increases in eating disorders (Hsu, 1989; see Malson and Ussher, 1996b, 1997). The effects of the diet and fashion industries on many women's lives (and deaths) cannot be underestimated. The fairly specific distribution in diagnoses of anorexia nervosa as well as its apparent increase also strongly suggest a cultural influence (Garner et al., 1983b). And, indeed, its apparent spread to non-white, non-middle-class women has been interpreted by some as due to increased acculturation to Western values (Pumariega, 1986) and increased dissemination of cultural ideals of female beauty as thinness (Edwards-Hewitt and Gray, 1993).

In addition, the high profile of 'anorexia nervosa' in both the popular and academic press suggests a cultural fascination with eating disorders. It indicates that anorexia is not simply an individual pathology but is also of wider cultural relevance. Indeed, anorexia is increasingly recognized as a 'culture-bound syndrome' (Swartz, 1985a) which may be expressive of public concerns as well as personal predicaments (Littlewood and Lipsedge, 1987). Anorexia nervosa, like some other illnesses[2] can be viewed as a metaphor for, and a manifestation of, a *multiplicity* of socio-cultural concerns of the late twentieth century (Turner, 1992); concerns about femininity and feminism, about the body, about individual control and consumption within consumer society. Indeed, as the following quote from *Elle* illustrates, eating disorders have been taken as a metaphor for the very fashion industry with which they are associated (see Malson and Ussher, 1996b): 'The fashion industry is tirelessly voracious – frighteningly so for the girls who work at the sharp end. It's an industry that eats up trends and spits them out faster than a superbulimic' (Smither, 1994: 20).

The anorexic body, like other bodies, I shall argue, is then always-already caught up in systems of meanings, symbolic representations and power relations. 'Anorexia' is saying something about what it means to be a woman in late twentieth-century Western culture.

TOWARDS A REFORMULATION OF 'ANOREXIA'

Viewing eating disorders in this context illustrates the need to theorize and research 'anorexia' within a framework that acknowledges the complexities of its socio-cultural locations and that does not conceptualize 'anorexia' simply as an individual pathology, as a problem that originates in some way from the individual woman. It also indicates the necessity of placing gender issues at the centre of analysis. We need a perspective that transgresses the individual–society dichotomy of 'mainstream' non-feminist psychology so that we can engage more thoroughly in the socio-political complexities of women's experiences of 'anorexia'. What I shall be arguing throughout this book is, therefore, that it is necessary to theorize and research anorexia within a framework that acknowledges the *complexities* of its *multiple* socio-cultural and gender-specific locations; a framework that enables us to explore its multiple discursively constituted meanings. My aim, then, is to unravel some of those discourses and discursive practices that converge on the female body and on the anorexic body, constituting and regulating the body in various, often conflicting, socio-historically specific ways (see Foucault, 1972, 1977b).

In Part I of this book, therefore, I have set out a feminist post-structuralist perspective that I shall argue enables us to rethink our understandings of gender, subjectivity and embodiment and that thereby enables us to engage with the problem of 'anorexia' in its socio-cultural and gender-specific locations. Briefly, this perspective builds upon the work of Saussure (1960) and the work of French structuralism. Rather than taking the view that language is a transparent medium through which we can view the world, I am viewing language as constructive of reality (see Potter and Wetherell, 1987). To paraphrase Foucault (1972: 49), discourses systematically constitute the objects, the individuals, the bodies, the experiences of which they speak. That is, from a post-structuralist perspective, discourses do not simply reflect some reality existing elsewhere: they actively and systematically construct particular versions of the world, of objects, events, experiences and identities. And, in constructing 'reality' in one particular way rather than another, discourses also construct particular power relations, particular regimes of Truth by which we live (Foucault, 1979; Walkerdine, 1986; see also Chapter 1). In short, a post-structuralist perspective provides a framework within which to understand how power is always implicated in social practices and in the (discursive) production of different forms of knowledge.

Hence, analysing academic or clinical texts about anorexia or analysing interviews with women diagnosed as anorexic involves treating the accounts not as more or less objective but as versions which actively construct certain realities or representations of the world. It means moving from a view of people using language to express themselves, to a view of people struggling with one another and with themselves 'in talk and text over the nature of events and experiences' (Wetherell and White, 1992). A post-structuralist discourse analysis involves exploring the ways in which these subjectivities, events and experiences are constituted in language.

After having discussed in more detail this theoretical and methodological framework offered by psychoanalytic and post-structuralist theory, I shall, in the second and third parts of the book explore how this micro-physics of power operates on the female body and on the 'anorexic' body. In Part II I shall discuss a 'genealogy' of anorexia, exploring how anorexia has been discursively constructed as a clinical entity, first examining how it initially emerged as an object of medical discourse in the late nineteenth century and then how 'anorexia' has subsequently been multiply constructed by the medical and psychological discourses that produce different knowledges, different truths of 'anorexia nervosa'. In Part III I shall turn to popular discourse, to the discourses which daily constitute and regulate women's experiences of themselves, of eating and not eating, of losing and gaining weight, of being fat or thin. In these chapters I shall analyse the transcripts of interviews that I conducted with women diagnosed or self-diagnosed as 'anorexic', exploring those discourses and discursive practices that converge upon the female body, the thin body, the 'anorexic' body, those (ideological) and profoundly troubling discourses that conspire to produce women's bodies as 'anorexic' bodies, to produce 'anorexic' lives (and deaths).

Part I

TOWARDS A FEMINIST POST-STRUCTURALIST PERSPECTIVE

1

THEORIZING WOMEN

Discoursing gender, subjectivity and embodiment

I have argued that if we are to understand the problem of 'anorexia' better we need to engage more thoroughly with its socio-cultural and gender-specific dimensions. We must question the medical model of anorexia and the empiricist or positivistic assumptions concerning the nature and status of 'anorexia' that underlie many current perspectives and work instead from a perspective which situates anorexia within its socio-cultural context and which provides a more thorough theorization of gender. In this chapter I aim to provide such a perspective by drawing on psychoanalytic and post-structuralist theory. However, my aim is not to provide an exposition of psychoanalytic and post-structuralist theories in their entirety; such a project lies well beyond the scope of this book. I intend, rather, to discuss those aspects of psychoanalytic and post-structuralist theory which I think are particularly useful and inspirational in attempting to understand the experiences of the social subject and, more specifically, the distress that many girls and women in this society experience around eating and not eating, around losing and gaining weight, being fat or thin, around being a woman and around being 'anorexic'.

My discussion will focus particularly on Lacanian, feminist psychoanalytic theory and on the work of Foucault, setting out a theoretical framework for this book in which the category of gender is theorized rather than assumed, an individual–society dichotomy is transgressed and the nature and status of knowledges (about 'femininity' and 'anorexia') is problematized and politicized. Inevitably in this and the following chapter I have had to assume that the reader has some prior familiarity with psychoanalytic and post-structuralist theory and with the discourse analytic approaches as they have been developed in psychology by people such as Valerie Walkerdine, Wendy Hollway, Jonathon Potter and Margaret Wetherell, amongst others. I have, however, sought to render my discussion of these often complex issues as accessible as possible and where appropriate the reader is directed to texts which provide more detailed explanations of the various issues and concepts that have been used. Many of the theoretical themes discussed here will also be returned to and discussed further in subsequent chapters.

In this chapter I will first discuss Freud's psychoanalytic theorization of subjectivity as fundamentally gendered, and of gender as the effect of interpretation of the body rather than as a 'natural' effect of biology (see Sayers, 1982). I will then discuss Lacan's rereading of Freud in which the role of interpretation or signification is emphasized (see Grosz, 1990). This discussion will also draw on feminist appropriations and critiques of Lacanian theory and will then discuss Foucault's post-structuralist theorization of discourse, power subjectivity and the body.

PSYCHOANALYTIC THEORY

Freud's theory of psychosexual development

Many feminists have viewed Freud as an enemy (Mitchell, 1974; Ussher, 1991), claiming that psychoanalysis is patriarchalist and phallocentric (see Sayers, 1990)[1] and that it is a justification of the patriarchal status quo, regarding women as biologically inferior and 'true femininity' as subordination (see Mitchell, 1974). Feminists, including de Beauvoir (1953), have often criticized Freudian theory as a biological determinist account of gender (Sayers, 1982). Other feminists, however, have actively engaged with psychoanalytic theory in one form or another as a useful analysis of (rather than prescription of) patriarchal power relations (Grosz, 1990). The relationship 'between feminism and psychoanalysis' has long been both intense and ambivalent (Bowlby, 1989)[2] and the breadth of Freud's work, its theoretical developments and paradigmatic shifts (Loevinger, 1978), clearly enables a diversity of readings. Yet psychoanalytic theory is useful to feminism because

> if we actually look at Freud's account of the development of psychological sex differences we find that he did not subscribe to a biologically determinist account of female psychology. Instead he regarded the development of the characteristically female (and male) personality as the effect of the way the child construes her (or his) biology.

> (Sayers, 1982: 127)

That is, femininity and masculinity are not mechanistically determined by biology but are effects of society's *ideas* about biology (Mitchell, 1974). Psychoanalysis conceptualizes gender, not as a natural given, but as the possible and probable consequence of unconscious *interpretations* of genital sex differences (Sayers, 1982). It is not our female (or male) bodies that make us feminine (or masculine) but the way in which we interpret our bodies, the social and psychological meanings or significations that we attribute to our bodies. Psychoanalytic theory can therefore be read as an anti-essentialist theory of sexuality. Indeed, Freud (1935, quoted by Mitchell, 1982: 1) objected to those who attempted to 'establish a neat parallelism' between the biological and the psychic. And because psychoanalysis thus deconstructs our 'phallic illusions'[3] about gender and identity; because 'psychoanalysis is not a recommendation *for* patriarchal

12

society, but an analysis *of* one' (Mitchell, 1974: xv), it may be useful in under-standing feminine identity, and therefore 'anorexia', within the context of 'patriarchal' society. /

Freud argued that feminine and masculine sexuality (gender and identity) are not innate propensities. Masculinity and femininity are not natural categories, nor are they the natural or even inevitable consequence of physical sexual differ-ence. They are not reducible to the female or male body. Instead, Freud argued that the early infantile sexuality of boys and girls was similar (Sayers, 1982). Neither initially differentiates self from other (Laplanche and Pontalis, 1973); the newborn infant does not initially have a sense of itself as a unified, bounded and coherent whole. In psychoanalytic terms: there is at first no unified ego distinct from the external world for either sex (Laplanche and Pontalis, 1973); there is no distinction between ego-libido and object-libido (Freud, 1914). Rather, the baby is born in a 'primary narcissistic' state characterized by a total absence of rela-tionship to the outside (Laplanche and Pontalis, 1973). And it is only through the mother's absences that the infant recognizes her as a separate object and thus comes to experience itself as a discrete entity (Mitchell, 1974). Hence the fort-da game (where a baby repeatedly throws and retrieves a cotton reel on a string) in which the infant attempts to master this experience of loss, central to the devel-opment of the ego (Freud, 1920).

For Freud, then, the infant is not born with a differentiated and integrated sense of self (Laplanche and Pontalis, 1973), nor with a ready-made or complete sexuality (Mitchell, 1974). Rather, it is 'polymorphously perverse', bisexual[4] and initially auto-erotic.[5] Freud's theory provides, then, an explanation of how the infant develops from this initially undifferentiated and ungendered state towards a state that we would recognize as masculine or feminine sexual identity. He proposed a series of developmental stages (oral, anal, phallic) through which the child must progress (more or less 'successfully') towards this 'normality'. Hence, 'normality' is only precariously, if ever, achieved after a long and tortuous process of psychosexual development (Mitchell, 1974).

Freud proposed, then, that feminine (and masculine) sexuality is not a starting point but a (probable but always imperfectly achieved and precarious) end point to psychosexual development. Feminine and masculine sexualities cannot, there-fore, be seen as explanation for male and female psychosexual development. They cannot be understood as different starting points from which male and female infants develop since, as we have seen, both male and female infants are born in the same undifferentiated ungendered state. Both boys and girls also take the mother as primary love-object and both show active and passive aims during the oral and anal phases of psychosexual development.[6] And it is not until 'the phallic phase' of development that the two sexes begin to diverge psychologically (Sayers, 1982).

During this stage the penis or clitoris becomes the principal erogenous zone, and physical differences thus become significant (Sayers, 1982). For the boy, phallic eroticism leads to phallic desires for the mother so that the father becomes an Oedipal rival.[7] Fearing castration by the father in retaliation for these desires, he renounces the mother as love-object, forming instead an identification with the father, thus taking up a masculine position (Freud, 1924a). That is, the Oedipal father is fantasized (by both sexes) as a powerful figure who would punish the child with castration for realizing its Oedipal desire for the mother (Freud, 1923, in Sayers, 1990). Genital sexual difference is construed as signifying this paternal authority and the boy's renunciation of his mother is a recognition not only of the father's power but also that he will eventually accede to it (Sayers, 1990). The boy's belief in castration is, Freud argues, substantiated by:

> the sight of the female genitals. Sooner or later the child, who is so proud of his possession of a penis, has a view of the genital region of a little girl, and cannot help being convinced of the absence of a penis in a creature who is so like himself. With this the loss of his own penis becomes imaginable, and the threat of castration takes its deferred effect.
>
> (Freud 1924a: 318)

For girls, however, 'castration' is not a feared possibility but an accomplished fact (Freud, 1924a: 321).

> They notice the penis of a brother or playmate, strikingly visible and of large proportions, at once recognise it as the superior counterpart of their own inconspicuous organ, and from that time fall a victim to envy for the penis.
>
> (Freud, 1925: 335)

Freud argues that during the phallic phase the girl's clitoris has been her 'true substitute for the penis' (Freud, 1905: 114) and that the penis is always preferred to the clitoris (Sayers, 1982). Hence, her realization that she does not have a penis results in her sense of inferiority: 'She acknowledges the fact of her castration, and with it, too, the superiority of the male and her own inferiority' (Freud, 1931: 376). Freud argued that mothers are often blamed for their daughters' being 'so insufficiently equipped' (Freud, 1925, quoted by Sayers, 1982: 128). And when the girl discovers that all women lack a penis her mother also appears similarly devalued. In consequence the girl abandons her mother, taking instead her father as primary love-object (Sayers, 1982). And by replacing her wish for a penis with a wish for a baby she adopts a 'normal' feminine position (Freud, 1924a). Alternatively, she may avoid this unfavourable comparison with male genitals by giving up 'her sexuality in general' or she may continue in her wish for a penis and develop a 'masculinity complex' (Freud, 1931, 1925). In short, Freud argued 'that female psychology is based on envy of the greater size and visibility of the penis' (Sayers, 1982: 133) and on 'recognition' that it is only the penis that signifies (paternal/patriarchal) power.

For Freud, then, the female body is negatively defined by what it is not, and femininity begins with an acknowledgement of lack. However, as we have seen,

this 'femininity' is not conceived as a natural category nor as a *simple* consequence of female anatomy.

> It is essential to understand clearly that the concepts of 'masculine' and
> 'feminine', whose meaning seems so unambiguous . . . are among the most
> confused that occur in science . . . 'Masculine' and 'feminine' are used
> sometimes in the sense of *activity* and *passivity*, sometimes in a *biological*, and
> sometimes, again, in a *sociological* sense . . . The third, or sociological,
> meaning receives its connotation from the observation of actually existing
> masculine and feminine individuals. Such observation shows that in
> human beings pure masculinity or femininity is not to be found either in a
> psychological or a biological sense. Every individual on the contrary
> displays a mixture of the character-traits belonging to his own and to the
> opposite sex; and he shows a combination of activity and passivity whether
> or not these last character-traits tally with his biological ones.
>
> (Freud, 1905: 141–142, footnote added in 1915)

In short, Freud provides a theory of sexuality in which 'femininity' is conceptualized as a negative term but in which masculinity and femininity are also
problematized. They are not natural categories, nor are they the natural,
inevitable or certain consequences of genital sexual difference. Rather, feminine
and masculine sexualities are conceived of as the possible and probable (but
always precarious and imperfectly achieved) consequences of a long and
tortuous process of psychosexual development premised on an *interpretation* of the
body, not on the body *per se*.

In problematizing gender and (gender) identity, Freud's work can be read as
prefiguring post-modern understandings of subjectivity because he denaturalizes
and destabilizes both identity and gender (Grosz, 1990). In asserting that the
self/other distinction is predicated on a loss or absence (of the mother) and in
emphasizing the centrality of the unconscious in psychosexual development,
Freud 'deconstructs' our 'phallic illusions' about the individual (see Sayers, 1990,
1994). His theorization of the unconscious subverts the fantasy of the unitary,
rational, self-knowing 'man' because the conscious subject can no longer know
her (or his) unconscious thoughts (Grosz, 1990): 'The ego is no longer master of
its own house' (Freud, 1917: 141–143). That is, Freud posits a subject radically
split in itself and therefore 'radically *incapable* of knowing itself' (Grosz, 1990:
13). And psychoanalysis similarly deconstructs the notion of gender as a natural
given. Gender identity is achieved only after a complex process of psychosexual
development and is a result of *interpretation* of physical sexual differences. It is not
until the Oedipus complex that active or passive aims can be described as either
masculine or feminine, since it is only then that they are placed within the social
structure of sexual differentiation (Nagera, 1969). Gender and, therefore, human
subjectivity are constituted by the unconsciously acquired ideas and patriarchal
laws of human society (Mitchell, 1974; Coward *et al.*, 1976).

15

A Lacanian rereading of psychoanalysis

For Freud, then, 'the ego is first and foremost a body-ego' but 'it is not merely a surface entity, but is itself the projection of a surface' (1923: 703). Lacan's rereading of Freud emphasizes the importance for psychosexual development of this projection or interpretation of the body.

Like Freud, Lacan (1949) posits an initially undifferentiated and ungendered infant who achieves gendered identity only through a process of psychosexual development (see Mitchell and Rose, 1982). And, like Freud, Lacan 'deconstructs' our 'phallic illusion' (see Sayers, 1994, 1995) of the unitary, rational and self-knowing 'man'. It is Lacan's rereading of Freud through the French structuralist works of Saussure, Althusser and Lévi-Strauss that further emphasizes that it is the *Symbolic* rather than the *Real* of the body that structures this process of psychosexual development. Lacanian theory emphasizes that masculinity and femininity do not arise from the real of the body but from the way in which male and female bodies are *signified* within a Symbolic order.

This concept of the Symbolic order, central to Lacan's thought, moves psychoanalytic theory further in the direction of the social because the Symbolic order is primarily a linguistic (and therefore social) order (see Saussure, 1960). And it is within this Symbolic order that sexual difference acquires meaning and that (gender) identity is produced. For Lacan the unconscious is 'the site of interaction between the body, history and psychic representation' (Coward *et al.*, 1976: 8) so that

> In each man's [*sic*] unconscious lies all mankind's 'ideas' of his history; a history that can not start afresh with each individual but must be acquired and contributed to over time. Understanding the laws of the unconscious thus amounts to a start in understanding how ideology functions, how we acquire and live the ideas and laws within which we must exist. A primary aspect of the law is that we live according to our sexed identity, our ever imperfect 'masculinity' and 'femininity'.
>
> (Mitchell, 1974: 403)

Lacan's account of the unconscious simultaneously refers, then, both to what is 'within' the subject and also to what is beyond her. It transgresses the individual–society dichotomy. More specifically, Lacan argues that the unconscious is constructed precisely in the acquisition of language (Coward *et al.*, 1976) which always precedes the individual and comes to her (or him) from outside of herself (Mitchell, 1982). Hence, there is 'no subject independent of language' (Sarup, 1988: 12).

> Human beings become social with the appropriation of language; and it is language that constitutes us as a subject. Thus we should not dichotomise the individual and society. Society inhabits each individual.
>
> (Sarup, 1988: 7)

16

Lacan's emphasis on language makes it possible to interpret his work as a non-humanist (Mitchell, 1982), decentring (MacCannell, 1986) account of subjectivity; as a sociological account (Squire, 1983), or more specifically as an account which refuses any individual–society dichotomy. That is, for Lacan the ego is always constituted in a misrecognition (*méconnaissance*) of something outside of itself as itself. First, during 'the mirror stage'[8] the initially undifferentiated infant, whose body-image is fragmentary, identifies with its integrated 'whole' mirror-image. It misconstrues itself as its 'specular image' (Lacan, 1949). In terms of this mirror metaphor, the infant identifies herself not with herself but with her reflected (specular) image, an image which by definition is precisely something other than herself. It is therefore a misidentification in which:

> This jubilant assumption of his specular image by the child . . . would seem to exhibit in an exemplary situation the symbolic matrix in which the *I* is precipitated in a primordial form, before it is objectified in the dialectic of the identification with the other, and before language restores to it, in the universal, its function as subject . . . this form situates the agency of the ego before its social determination, in a fictional direction.
>
> (Lacan, 1949: 2)

This 'specular I' thus prefigures the infant's alienating destination in the 'social I' (Lacan, 1949). It prefigures the moment at which the subject is constituted in language or the Symbolic order (Rose, 1982), in an alienating misidentification of itself in the pre-existing linguistic position of 'I'.[9]

Lacan thus 'deconstructs' the subject, showing it to be social, decentred and fictional: "identity" and "wholeness" remain precisely at the level of fantasy' (Rose, 1982: 32) because subjectivity does not arise from within the individual, from the Real, but from without, created by and within language or the Symbolic order.[10] It is 'created in the fissure of a radical split' (Mitchell, 1982: 5) in which subjectivity is constituted as an effect of the Symbolic (Sheridan, 1977).

For Lacan the phallus stands for this moment of division in which subjectivity is constituted (Rose, 1982): 'it is to this signifier (the phallus) that it is given to designate as a whole the effect of there being a signified, in as much as it conditions any such effect by its presence as signifier' (Lacan, 1982d: 80). That is, the phallus has 'the privileged function of . . . representing human identity' (Benvenuto and Kennedy, 1986: 187). It signifies the effect of the signifier, of language or the Symbolic order in creating subjectivity (Lacan, 1958a). And, being constituted only in relation to the phallus, identity is also profoundly gendered. Sexual difference

> must exist because no human being can become a subject outside the division into two sexes. One must take up a position as either a man or a woman. Such a position is by no means identical with one's biological sexual characteristics.
>
> (Mitchell, 1982: 6)

17

And, because it is the phallus that represents human identity, sexual difference is always constructed in language (Coward *et al.*, 1976) such that masculinity is positively signified as 'I' whilst femininity is negatively signified as the 'not-I': 'Sexual difference is inscribed in language only in relation to the phallus; the other sex is such, only because it does not have the phallus' (Benvenuto and Kennedy, 1986: 189).

The phallus defines identity, the 'I', as masculine. As that which represents the effect of the Symbolic order, it designates the masculine as the position of 'Oneness', of knowing and of being, and the feminine as the negatively defined 'other of being', not-I, not-all, not-One (Benvenuto and Kennedy, 1986: 186). 'Woman' enters the Symbolic negatively, 'guarantee[ing] that unity [of identity] on the side of the man' (Rose, 1982: 47). Thus, like Freud, Lacan defines femininity negatively in terms of a lack.

Feminine subjectivity: 'woman' as ideology

As we have seen, Lacan's work can be read as a non-humanist and decentring theory of subjectivity in which (gender) identity cannot be reduced to biological difference or to the individual because it is fictionally constituted within the Symbolic order: 'It [sexuality] cannot be solved by any reduction to biological factors, as the mere necessity of the myth underlying the Oedipus complex makes sufficiently clear' (Lacan, 1982d: 75).

Lacan's rereading of Freud thus emphasizes that gender identity is an effect of signification (or interpretation). The definition of the feminine as a lack is *symbolic*. There can be nothing missing in the real because 'something can only be seen to be missing according to a pre-existing hierarchy of values' (Rose, 1982: 42). The negativity of the feminine is a consequence not of a 'real' lack but of the phallic nature of signification. And, drawing on structuralist linguistics, Lacan demonstrates the illusory and precarious nature of this Symbolic identity.

Following Saussure (1974), Lacan holds that, not only are language systems social and external to the individual; they are also 'systems of values maintained by social convention' (Lyons, 1981: 221).[11] That is, the relationship between the signified and signifier, which together make up the linguistic sign, is *arbitrary*. Language is conceptualized here not as a transparent nomenclature. Rather words are meaningful only within the structure of a language system and meaning is the product of the semantic relations between words (Lyons, 1981). It exists not in the word itself but in the divisions and differences produced within language. And, for Lacan, the phallus is *the* 'privileged signifier', signifying sexual difference:

> In Freudian doctrine the phallus is not a fantasy, if what is understood by that is an imaginary effect. Nor is it as such an object (part, internal, good, bad, etc. . . .) in so far as this term tends to accentuate the reality involved

in a relationship. It is even less the organ, penis or clitoris which it symbol-
ises . . . the phallus is a signifier whose function in the intrasubjective
economy of analysis might lift the veil which it served in the mysteries.

(Lacan, 1982d: 79)[12]

For Lacan, then, the phallus, which signifies the effect of the Symbolic in constituting (gendered) subjectivity, cannot be simply equated with the penis.
Moreover, whilst Lacanian theory has been accused of phallocentrism this
theory is also an exposure of the 'fraudulent' status of the phallus (Rose, 1982).
Whilst language fixes meaning and constitutes identity, meaning is also
constantly slipping along metaphoric and metonymic axes. The signified can
always become a signifier. Because meaning is produced only in the relations
between words, '[we] are forced . . . to accept the notion of an incessant sliding
of the signified under the signifier' (Lacan, 1977: 154): 'From which we can say
that it is in the chain of the signifier that meaning "insists" but that none of its
elements "consists" in the signification of which it is at the moment capable'
(Lacan, 1977: 153).

The meanings of words are uncertain, unfixed because they are always
'deferred' along chains of signifiers (because it is only in the relations between
words that meaning is produced). And because the signifier 'stands in' for the
object, signification also indicates loss: 'language speaks the loss which lay behind
that first moment of symbolisation' (Rose, 1982: 32). Because the phallus signifies the effect of the Symbolic, its presence also signifies an absence (Benvenuto
and Kennedy, 1986). The phallus represents 'One-ness' (Benvenuto and
Kennedy, 1986: 190); it represents identity and certainty. But, as we have seen,
Lacan also deconstructs this 'omnipotent fantasy of the self as whole and undi-
vided, showing it instead to be founded in the illusory elision of division – of
inner and outer – at its very inception' (Sayers, 1990: 200).

Hence, the phallus also signifies that 'lack in being', the splitting in which
subjectivity is constituted outside of itself. It signifies both subjectivity and desire
which arises precisely because of the lack or gap in the Symbolic (see Rose,
1982).[13] Thus, the 'idealization of separation and the idealization of the phallus
go together' (Benjamin, 1985: 4), so that in signifying the certainty of identity the
phallus is a fraud (Rose, 1982): 'the very ideology of oneness and completion'
that it signifies 'closes off the gap of human desire' also signified by the phallus
(Rose, 1982: 46). And, as Irigaray argues,

> from the moment that a pole of difference pretends to decree the
> Universal, it says that its discourse is not sexualized. However, there are
> indications of sexual difference in this discourse that has *pretensions* to the
> universal.
>
> (Irigaray 1988: 161)

The concept of the phallus in Lacanian theory indicates, then, not so much an
assertion of unproblematic male privilege as the problematic, complex and

conflictual nature of human subjectivity and sexuality (Rose, 1982). In short, Lacan decentres subjectivity, conceptualizing it as an identification with the pre-existing position of 'I' within the Symbolic order. Drawing on structural linguistics, he shows how profoundly precarious, problematic and fictional that subjectivity and sexuality are. And, because Lacanian theory thus questions the Symbolic as a 'register of absolute fixity', it thereby questions and deconstructs the category of woman (Rose, in Sayers, 1986: 92)

Lacan emphasizes that femininity is not a natural category but a symbolic position. And this rereading of femininity also elucidates the particularly prob-lematic nature of this fictional, Symbolic 'feminine' identity. As we have seen 'femininity' is conceptualized as a socially, symbolically constructed (im)position that is negatively signified in relation to the phallus. It is the not-I, the not-One (Benvenuto and Kennedy, 1986), the Other of identity. But it is not that 'the woman' is outside of the Symbolic order; rather 'she' is excluded within it: 'Her being not all in the phallic function does not mean that she is not in it at all. She is in it not not at all. She is right in it' (Lacan, 1982b: 145). And, as Lacan argues, there is therefore 'something unacceptable' for 'woman' 'in the fact of being placed as an object in a Symbolic order to which, at the same time, she is subjected just as much as the man' (Lacan, in Rose, 1982: 45). The category of femininity is thus theorized as unacceptable at least for women. But it is also 'fundamentally conflictual' because 'woman' is (impossibly) contained within an exclusion. 'She' stands as an impossible contradiction – a subject position as the other-of-identity: 'That the woman should be inscribed in an order of exchange of which she is the object, is what makes for the fundamen-tally conflictual, and, I would say, insoluble, character of her position . . . ' (Lacan in Rose, 1982: 45).

Whereas for Riviere (1929) 'masquerade . . . indicated a failed femininity', for Lacan 'masquerade is the very definition of "femininity"' because 'woman' is defined in terms of that which 'she' is not (Rose, 1982: 43). Hence, 'The woman does not exist' (Lacan, quoted in Rose, 1982: 48). 'Femininity' thus indicates 'the fundamental duplicity' of the Symbolic (Rose, 1982: 42) because it points to the lack in the Symbolic, to 'something more', 'to a *jouissance* proper to her, to this "her" which does not exist' (see Lacan, 1982b: 145). Hence Lacan's theorization of feminine sexuality is

> an exposure of the terms of its definition, the very opposite of a demand as to what that sexuality should be . . . it involves precisely a collapse of the phallus . . . giving the lie, we could say, to the whole problem outlined.
>
> (Rose, 1982: 44)

Lacanian psychoanalytic theory thus elucidates the profoundly problematic, 'unacceptable' and perhaps subversive nature of 'femininity' as the negatively signified Other within the Symbolic order. As Sayers (1986: 94) argues, feminist Lacanians have deconstructed the category of woman. Problematically, however, it is not clear what relationship actual women might have to this category of 'woman' nor from what (symbolic) position women might resist this unacceptable (im)position.

Other femininities (for feminism?)

Freud argued that femininity and hysteria are linked both historically and psychologically: '"the feminine" (being a woman in a psychological sense) was in part a hysterical formation' (Mitchell, 1974: 48). The profoundly problematic and conflictual nature of 'femininity' as theorized by Freud and Lacan clearly indicates the difficulties of female psychosexual development. And the elucidation of the impossibility and unacceptability of 'femininity' must surely further our understanding of 'female maladies' such as hysteria (see Showalter, 1985) and more contemporarily anorexia (Malson, 1992). As Mitchell argues,

> Hysteria was, and is – whatever the age and generational status of the man or woman who expresses it – the daughter's disease. To 'her' 'femininity' really seems to equal the gap indicated by castration or, in Joan Riviere's words, it is enacted as 'a masquerade' to cover it.
>
> (Mitchell, 1984: 308)

And, as noted above, for Lacan 'masquerade' is the very definition of femininity in that it is defined in terms of a male sign (Rose, 1982). This is not to argue, however, that women are somehow 'naturally' hysterical or that all (or most) women come to be hysterical (Malson, 1992). Rather it is to suggest that 'the hysterical woman' or 'the anorexic woman' *parodies* the deeply embedded gender ideologies that devalue women, insisting that we inhabit a dependent and restricted social role (Selig, 1988).

Several psychoanalytic feminists have similarly argued that 'the hysteric' can be understood as a quasi-feminist refusal of patriarchal heterosexuality (see Ramas, 1985), that 'she' makes 'permanent war' with the phallocentrism and patriarchy of the Symbolic order (see Cixous, in Gallop, 1985: 203). Cixous, for example, describes Freud's Dora as 'a radiant example of feminine revolt' (Moi, 1985: 192). Whilst not denying the rejecting/protesting aspect of hysteria or anorexia, the location of feminist protest in such self-destruction is also inevitably problematic (see Swartz, 1985b). Moreover, hysteria may be not so much a feminist political resistance to patriarchy as a dissenting but co-opted defeat. As Clément argues, it

> introduces dissension, but it in no way makes anything burst; that does not *disperse* the bourgeois family, which only exists through her dissension, which only holds together in the possibility or the reality of its own disturbance, always re-closable, always re-closed.
>
> (Cixous and Clément, 1975: 287)

That is, whilst 'the hysteric' can be understood as (not) voicing 'her' dissent in 'her' symptoms, 'she' is always assimilable within the phallocentric order 'she' contests. The hysteric (and also 'the anorexic') 'both refuses and is totally entrapped within femininity' (Mitchell, 1984: 290). And, indeed, this paradoxical entrapment-rejection might in itself be seen as bound up with the problematic nature of femininity discussed above.

A related response to the problem of 'the feminine'/feminist is proposed by Kristeva. She shifts Lacan's focus on symbolic abstraction to include the semiotics – the 'texture', gestures and rhythms of speech (see Sayers, 1995). She argues that women speak and write as 'hysterics', as 'outsiders' of phallocentric discourse (Jones, 1985). Her project of 'semanalysis' thus attends to marginal and resistant meanings. 'A feminist practice' she argues 'can only be . . . at odds with what already exists so that we may say "that's not it" and "that's still not it"' (Kristeva, 1974, in Jones, 1985: 88). For Kristeva, then, 'woman's' function (which can also include men) can only be negative, challenging, subverting and reclaiming (masculine) language as our own.

In contrast with Kristeva, Irigaray argues that women have their own specificity distinct from men. For her, a feminist resistance to phallocentrism must focus on formulating the specificity of the female body and of the mother–daughter relationship. In this latter respect her work converges with that of many non-Lacanian feminists who, objecting to the phallocentric, father-centredness of Freud's work, have shifted their focus from the father to the mother (see Sayers, 1988, 1991). Following on from Klein and later Winnicott, feminists like Chodorow (1978), Benjamin (1990) and Orbach (1993) have increasingly focused on the pre-Oedipal mother–child relationship and (following Winnicott) on the effects of its individual material realities rather than fantasies.[14] And, given 'the value Winnicott, unlike Freud, attaches to the work of women as mothers . . .' it is little surprise that feminists have found his theories particularly sympathetic' (Sayers, 1995: 126). Yet it is also paradoxical that this feminist analysis focuses on individual issues about the mother to the neglect of issues about the father, because feminism has 'repeatedly insisted on the necessity of going beyond the individual-centredness of psychoanalysis to take account of the social and patriarchal factors conditioning women's ills and discontents' (Sayers, 1988: 368–369).

In focusing on the specificity of the female body, Irigaray's work also converges in part with the much earlier work of Horney (1926), who argued that 'feminine' psychology does not simply result from penis envy but is rather 'rooted in women's "specific biological nature"' (Horney, 1926: 17, in Sayers, 1982: 130). Yet, whilst Horney's attempt to counter Freud's 'male-bias' is appealing, it has also been described as essentialist because it posits a 'primary' natural femininity (see Sayers, 1982). Lacan (1982a: 127) has also asserted that her disputing 'the anatomical priority' of the penis (or clitoris) 'in no sense detracts from Freud's basic thesis on the phallic conditioning of narcissism in the subject irrespective of its sex'.

Like Horney, Irigaray argues for a female psychology specific to the female rather than the male body. As a post-Lacanian, she asserts that because women are caught up in a phallocentric Symbolic order they 'have had no way of knowing or representing themselves' (Jones, 1985: 88). Thus, she argues, the mother has no identity as a woman to give to her daughter:

> If the mother is the alienator it is because she has no identity as a woman. And this effectively plunges the mother and the little girl into the same nothingness. But the problem is neither to accuse the mother nor to say that it is the father who comes to liberate the little girl. The mother has to find her identity as a woman and from that point, she would be able to give an identity to her daughter. But this is the key point to which our system is most blind.
>
> (Irigaray, 1988: 157)

Irigaray (1988: 156) argues that society is built not just on the Oedipal myth of patricide but primarily on matricide: 'when fathers took the power they had already annihilated the mother'. What is required, she claims, if women are to find their identity as women, is a return to the specificity of the female body, to the 'two lips' of the vulva and to a specific female desire of multiple libidinal energies (Jones, 1985).

Clearly Irigaray's project can be read as essentialist, as an argument that feminists should fight patriarchy so that we could express a 'femininity' that is 'essentially constituted in biology' (Sayers, 1982: 131–132). Her 'solution' is bound up with the very system it claims to undermine (Jones, 1985) for 'the female body hardly seems the best site to launch an attack on the forces that have alienated us from what our sexuality might become' (Jones, 1985: 93). Whilst Cixous' description of femininity as flowing from her body or Irigaray's celebration of female sexuality as diverse and diffused, of woman as 'infinitely other in herself', as 'temperamental, incomprehensible, perturbed, capricious', 'a little crazy' and incoherent (Irigaray, 1977, in Jones, 1985), is certainly opposed to phallic identity, it seems to oppose from that very position in which patriarchal order placed it.

Irigaray's work can, however, be read quite differently. It can be seen as non-essentialist because it can be reread at the level of the Symbolic rather than at the level of the 'real' body (Whitford, 1989). Whitford (1989), for example, argues that Irigaray's project is the formulation of a female Symbolic that would allow the mother to be mother *and* woman, that would not reduce women to a maternal *function* and that would give women a (feminine rather than phallocentric) identity as women. In this reading, Irigaray is arguing that women have been left in a state of 'dereliction', not because of women's 'nature' but because they cannot successfully emerge as subjects within an order that only signifies the feminine as a negative (Whitford, 1989). Because the mother–daughter relationship and the female body remain as yet unsymbolized in their own specificity, women are hindered from having a (symbolic) identity. The 'problem for women lies', therefore, 'in the *non-symbolization* of the relation to the mother and to the mother's body' (Whitford, 1989: 114). Irigaray thus criticizes the partiality of the

Symbolic and argues for the formulation of a feminine imaginary and Symbolic based on the constantly touching lips of the vulva and on a diffused multiplicity of 'female desire':

> The symbolic that you (Messieurs les psychanalystes) impose as universal, free of all empirical or historical contingency, is *your* imaginary transformed into an order, a social order.
>
> (Irigaray, 1985: 311–313, in Whitford, 1989: 118)

> To turn the 'body without organs' into a 'cause' of sexual pleasure, isn't it necessary to have had a relation to language and to sex – to the organs – that women have never had.
>
> (Irigaray, 1977, in Whitford, 1989: 113)

Hence Irigaray's description (1977) of 'femininity', Whitford (1989) argues, is not so much a demand for a return to the 'real' of the female body as an attempt to formulate a 'female imaginary' which could be transformed into a 'female symbolic' based on the female body.

Whether Irigaray is talking about the literal physicality of the female body or is using 'the two lips' as an alternative symbolic term is unclear – at least it is to me. However (and setting aside the question of whether or not a 'female symbolic' is possible), Irigaray's work still remains problematic because, like Lacan's, it posits an homogenized category of '*the* woman'. And it seems implausible to suggest that any *one* 'feminine' libidinal voice, however non-phallocentrically defined, could speak for *all* women in our diverse socio-cultural and economic situations (Jones, 1985). Both Lacan and Irigaray seem problematically to theorize only one 'woman' (however 'she' is defined). Black, white, working-class and middle-class, feminist and non-feminist, Western and non-Western women surely cannot all be adequately accounted for by any single 'monolithic myth' of femininity (see Jones, 1985). A single concept of femininity seems to 'flatten out the lived differences among women' (Jones, 1985: 95) because 'woman' is a sliding signifier, a plural collectivity of mother, daughter, lover, prostitute, Black and so on (Sayers, 1986). Lacanian and post-Lacanian theories often lose sight 'of the social realities that go to make up the category "woman"' and outside of actual social relations the concept of '"woman" becomes an abstraction' (Eisenstein, in Sayers, 1986: 93). It is therefore necessary, I would argue, to retheorize 'woman' as a multiplicity of these various and often contradictory 'femininities' as they are constituted within actual socio-cultural, historically varying discursive practices:[15]

> 'woman' is a volatile collectivity in which female persons can be very differently positioned, so that the apparent continuity of the subject of 'woman' is not to be relied on; 'woman' is both synchronically and diachronically erratic as a collectivity.
>
> (Riley, 1988: 1–2)

In short, the category of 'woman' fluctuates both culturally and historically, encompassing a multiplicity of socio-historically specific 'femininities'. Whilst 'the phallic mode of identity' (Benjamin, 1985) and the negative definition of femininity as Other may be ubiquitous, 'the ways in which it is defined, imposed, accepted, subverted and defied will vary' (Malson, 1992: 83). Moreover the relationship of actual women to this category of 'woman' is also uncertain because, as

> Freud argues,[16] there is no libido other than masculine. Meaning what? other than that a whole field, which is hardly negligible is thereby ignored. This is the field of all those beings who take on the status of the woman – *if, indeed, this being takes on anything whatsoever of her fate.*
>
> (Lacan, 1972–73, in Rose, 1982: 27; my emphasis)

Denise Riley (1988: 6) similarly questions 'how far any woman can take on the identity of being a woman in a thoroughgoing manner'. How, she asks, 'could someone "be a woman" through and through, make a final home in that classification without suffering claustrophobia?'. Perhaps, then, as women we have a fluctuating shifting relationship with the already fluctuating category of 'woman'. Women's subjectivities might then be best theorized in terms of 'plural collectivities' of often contradictory subject positions constituted in and by various socio-historically specific discourses of which the Symbolic is an abstraction. And whilst gendered subject positions lean on the corpo-reality of the body, on genital difference, women take up and are taken up by a multiplicity of different subject positions with 'different densities of sexed being' (Riley, 1988: 6).

FROM THE SYMBOLIC TOWARDS DISCOURSE

Lacan's rereading of Freud emphasizes the central function of interpretation, of language or the Symbolic order in constituting (gendered) subjectivity. And, as I have argued, this emphasis on language makes it possible to read his work as a non-humanist, decentring account of subjectivity that refuses a dichotomization of individual and society. First, because he theorizes subjectivity as constituted outside of itself as a symbolic position in language and, second, because he thereby shows (gender) identity to be fictional. Adopting Saussurean linguistics as an epistemological framework he demonstrates the precarious, uncertain, problematic and fictional nature of subjectivity and of femininity. He questions 'the register of the absolute fixity . . . of the category of woman' (Rose, in Sayers, 1986: 92). However, in focusing on the abstract concept of the Symbolic order (cf. Saussure's *langue*), Lacan's and some post-Lacanian theories tend to neglect the actualities of speech (cf. Saussure's *parole*), the discourses and discursive practices in which language and therefore (gendered) subjectivities are 're-produced' (Henriques *et al.*, 1984). As Saussure himself argued, language systems are social and material (Lyons, 1981). Language, like any other social institution, must be put into a social setting so that it can be understood as 'something used daily by all' and as 'constantly . . . influenced by all' even though it cannot be changed by any one individual (Saussure, 1960: 73–74). Language or discourse cannot exist independently of its daily re-production and it is therefore changeable (Hollway, 1992). Hence, language can be understood both as an established system that pre-exists the individual and as an historically evolving system that changes because of its continual use:[17]

> In a certain sense . . . we can speak of both the immutability and the muta-bility of the sign . . . the sign is exposed to alteration because it perpetuates itself. What predominates in all change is the persistence of the old substance; disregard for the past is only relative. That is why the principle of change is based on the principle of continuity . . . Regardless of what the forces of change are . . . they always result in *a shift in the relationship between the signified and the signifier.*
>
> (Saussure, 1960: 74–75)

By locating language within its social context, Saussure thus shows it to be socio-historically mutable. Moreover, attention to the social indicates the necessity of moving from Lacan's and Saussure's structuralist concept of language or the Symbolic order as universal totalities (see Walkerdine, 1988) towards a post-structuralist concept of discourses characterized by diversity and power struggle.

I have argued in this chapter that psychoanalytic theory, particularly Lacanian and post-Lacanian theory, is useful precisely because it 'deconstructs' our notions of gender and identity. (Gender) identity is shown to be not a natural state but the problematic and precarious effect of a process of psychosexual development which is predicated on the *interpretation* or Symbolic meaning and value of the body. Psychoanalytic theory is useful, therefore, because it shows (gender) identity to be problematic and precarious and also to be socially (rather than naturally) constructed. From a feminist perspective, however, we need to go further still. I would argue that we need to 'deconstruct' Lacan's abstracted concept of the Symbolic order; to ground this order in the actualities of the Social so that we can explore the specificities of the social-political contexts within which our experiences of gender, identity and embodiment are consti-tuted. And post-structuralism, I shall argue, may provide a more adequate theoretical framework within which to understand subjectivity and femininity (and therefore anorexia) as socio-historically located, multiple and shifting subject positions constituted in discourses and discursive practices.

DISCOURSE, POWER/KNOWLEDGE, SUBJECTIVITY AND GENDER

Many critiques of structuralism have stressed that 'the social "totality" is not a well-fitting and founded structure' and that it may be better understood as 'a contradictory nexus of social practices' (Hirst and Woolley, 1982). Hence, structuralist conceptions of language or the Symbolic order as universal totalities might be better reformulated in terms of a post-structuralist Foucauldian theory of discourses and discursive practices. In the remainder of this chapter I will therefore discuss how post-structuralist theory can contribute to our understandings of subjectivity, gender, power and knowledge and consequently to an understanding of anorexia.[18]

For Foucault (1972) language is not a unitary, trans-historical totality but rather consists of a variety of different historically specific discourses; for example, economic, medical, psychiatric and psychological discourses. Foucault defines these discourses as regulated systems of statements. However, what unites a system of statements, what constitutes the unity of a discourse, is always provisional. Whilst discourses are realized in texts and speech, this realization is always fragmentary; we only ever find pieces of discourse (Parker, 1990b). The unity of a discourse cannot be found in the document or the *oeuvre* because the 'frontiers of a book are never clear-cut: . . . it is always caught up in a system of references to other books, other texts, other sentences: it is a node within a network' (Foucault, 1972: 23). A document only provides 'a weak, accessory unity in relation to the discursive unity of which it is the support' (Foucault, 1972: 23). Hence, for Foucault, a discourse is a dispersed system whose hypothesized unity is always provisional: 'we must conceive of discourse as a series of discontinuous segments whose tactical function is neither uniform nor stable' (Foucault, 1979: 100). The division of language into discourses 'cannot be regarded either as definite or as absolutely valid; it is no more than an initial approximation that must allow relations to appear that may erase the limits of this initial outline' (Foucault, 1972: 30). Hence, to identify a discourse 'is not to close it upon itself; it is to leave oneself free to describe the interplay of relations within and outside it' (Foucault, 1972: 29).

Moreover, the unity of a discourse cannot be based simply upon the existence of its objects – on, for example, the economy, the mind, madness, sickness or the body – because, discourses are social 'practices that systematically form the objects of which they speak' (Foucault, 1972: 49). For Foucault and the post-structuralist and discourse-oriented researchers and theorists that have followed him, discourse is not a transparent medium which simply describes or reflects some underlying reality.[19] Rather, discourses (and discursive practices) are constitutive of their objects (Foucault, 1972, 1979).

This view of language is very different from the notion of language as reflective because it implies that language does not simply transmit an already-existing meaning. Rather, it involves 'the more active labour of *making things mean*' (Hall, 1982: 64). Objects do not exist beyond or 'anterior' to discourse, 'waiting' to be discovered and more or less accurately, objectively described (Foucault, 1977a). A discourse 'finds a way of limiting its domain, of defining what it is talking about, of giving it the status of an object – and therefore of making it manifest, nameable, and describable' (Foucault, 1972: 41). Objects of social reality

27

are not 'things' set apart from and independent of discourse but are real-ized only in and through the discursive elements which surround the objects in question. Things then are made visible and palpable through the existence of discursive practices, and so [objects, events and experiences] are not referents about which there are discourses but objects constructed by discourse.

(Prior, 1989: 3)

Similarly, discourses produce 'identities', subject positions, 'institutional sites' from which a person can speak or be addressed (Foucault, 1972: 51; see Henriques *et al.*, 1984). Discourses do not simply describe individuals; they offer up a variety of subject positions (see Walkerdine, 1986). Subjectivity does not come from within but is constituted and reconstituted in texts and talk (Wetherell and White, 1992). Hence 'identity' can be reconceptualized as a multiplicity of different, shifting, often contradictory subject positions (Walkerdine, 1993). Femininity, for example, can be understood not so much as a collection of char-acteristics found within the individual or as a consistent unitary identity than as an empty category that takes on a variety of historically contingent shapes within different discourses (Wetherell, 1986; Poovey, 1988).

From a post-structuralist perspective, then, subjectivity is not only decentred as *a* subject position in discourse (cf. Lacan); it is also multiple and dispersed:

I do not refer the various enunciative modalities[20] to the unity of the subject . . . instead of referring back to *the* synthesis or *the* unifying function of *a* subject, the various enunciative modalities manifest his [*sic*] disper-sion. To the various statuses, the various sites, the various positions that he can occupy or be given when making a discourse. To the discontinuity of the planes from which he speaks. And if these planes are linked by a system of relations, this system is not established by the synthetic activity of a consciousness identical with itself, dumb and anterior to all speech, but by the specificity of a discursive practice . . . discourse is not the majesti-cally unfolding manifestation of a thinking, knowing speaking subject, but, on the contrary, a totality in which dispersion of the subject and his discontinuity with himself may be determined.

(Foucault, 1972: 54–55)

Moreover, a discourse is not simply a set of linguistic practices. The concept of discourse includes discursive practices; it consists of a whole assemblage of concepts, objects, events and activities (Prior, 1989). A discourse is a social prac-tice and discursive relations are neither simply 'internal to discourse' nor 'exterior to discourse . . . they are in a sense, at the limit of discourse' (Foucault, 1972: 46). 'Of course, discourses are composed of signs; but what they do is more than use these signs to designate things. It is this *more* that renders them irreducible to the language (*langue*) and to speech' (Foucault, 1972: 49). That is, discourses as social practice have powerful, 'real' effects (Walkerdine, 1986).

They regulate and normalize human behaviours and activities, defining what is normal and abnormal in various social settings and for various groups of people (Walkerdine, 1986).

Similarly, as practices, discourses are not simply conditioned by linguistic rules. The coming into existence of, for example, 'madness' as an object of discourse was 'ruled' by 'the conditions of possibility' (Woodiwiss, 1990: 63) of a discourse on madness. Such conditions included its 'surface of emergence' – the social conditions such as the rise of the bourgeois family and of the medical profession which as an authoritative, institutionalized body of knowledge and practice 'delimited, designated, named, and established madness as an object' (Foucault, 1972: 41–42). Clearly, then, discourses as social practices have 'real' effects, legitimating particular practices, particular forms of authority, constituting particular 'truths' about 'reality' and positioning and constituting people as, for example, sane or insane. Yet at the same time as acknowledging these powerful real effects we must also acknowledge that these 'truths' are not absolute but are 'historically produced within certain specific conditions of possibility' (Walkerdine, 1986: 64), so that

> the possibility exists for fiction to function in truth, for fictional discourse to induce effects of truth, and for bringing it about that a true discourse engenders or 'manufactures' something that does not as yet exist, that is, 'fictions' it.
>
> (Foucault, 1980: 193)

For Foucault, then, discourses are about power. In constituting a field of knowledge, a discourse rules out other truths. In not saying everything it represses what it does not say (Foucault, 1972). Power and knowledge are inextricably linked, in that

> power produces knowledge (and not simply by encouraging it because it serves power or by applying it because it is useful); that power and knowledge directly imply one another; that there is no power relation without the correlative constitution of a field of knowledge, nor any knowledge that does not presuppose and constitute at the same time power relations.
>
> (Foucault, 1977b: 27)

Power functions in and through discourse (and discursive practices). But this post-structuralist concept of power is not a sovereign power, a fixed possession of particular individuals. Instead Foucault (1977b: 139) reconceptualizes power in terms of a 'micro-physics of power', as an aspect of the regulative function of knowledge itself (Walkerdine, 1986: 65). Discourses regulate and discipline by constituting fields of knowledge, instituting truths, constituting subjectivities in particular ways, positioning people within discourses and subjecting them to normalizing judgements (Foucault, 1977b, 1979), so that power relations, although unevenly distributed, are everywhere (Foucault, 1979: 95).

However, as Foucault (1977b: 170) argues, this infinitesimal control is not simply a repression. Power/knowledge is productive as well as repressive: it 'makes' individuals.

> The individual is no doubt the fictive atom of an 'ideological' representation of society, but he [sic] is also a reality fabricated by this specific technology of power that I have called 'discipline'. We must cease once and for all to describe the effects of power in negative terms: it 'excludes', it 'represses', it 'censors', it 'abstracts', it 'masks', it 'conceals'. In fact, power produces; it produces reality, it produces domains of objects and rituals of truth. The individual and the knowledge that may be gained of him belong to this production.
>
> (Foucault, 1977b: 194)

Power/knowledge does not simply repress but rather produces 'the individual' and other objects in particular ways. And, as Foucault (1979: 96) argues, discourses also produce their own 'plurality of resistances' to power. Nineteenth-century medical discourse on sexuality, for example, produced 'the homosexual' as perverse but it thereby produced a subject position from which such pathologization could be resisted (Foucault, 1979). Hence, there 'is not, on the one side, a discourse of power, and opposite it, another discourse that runs counter to it. Discourses are tactical elements or blocks in the field of force relations' (Foucault, 1979: 101–102). In short, Foucault (1979: 102) conceptualizes power in terms of a 'multiple and mobile field of force relations' functioning in discourses and discursive practices 'wherein far-reaching, but never completely stable, effects of domination are produced'.

The idea of the body is also central to Foucault's theorization of discourse and power/knowledge (McNay, 1992). He argues that discourses 'discipline' the body through 'a multiplicity of minor processes of domination' (Foucault, 1977b: 138). Discourses construct the body in particular ways, 'exercising upon it a subtle co-ercion, . . . obtaining holds upon it at the level of the mechanism itself – movements, gestures, attitudes, rapidity: an infinitesimal power over the active body' (Foucault, 1977b: 137). He insists, therefore, that the body is an historically and culturally specific entity, shaped and reshaped in different discourses and discursive practices (McNay, 1992):

> The body is the inscribed surface of events (traced by language and dissolved by ideas), the locus of a dissociated self (adopting the illusion of a substantial unity), and a volume in perpetual disintegration. Genealogy, as an analysis of descent, is thus situated within the articulation of the body and history. Its task is to expose a body totally imprinted by history and the process of history's destruction of the body.
>
> (Foucault, 1977a: 148)

Despite its corpo-reality the body is not an originating point (Riley, 1988). The body that we know is a result or effect of discourse because it is 'always already' produced within discourse and discursive practices (McNay, 1992). It is not possible to know it outside of discourse, before it is 'inscribed' within social practices and power relations (McNay, 1992). Discourses do not, however, simply produce docile useful bodies, since, as noted above, discourses produce their own 'plurality of resistances' (Foucault, 1979). Bodies can never be totally once and for all subjected to any one inscription: they articulate and sustain a multiplicity of often conflicting meanings. Foucault thus provides a radically anti-essentialist account of the body in which, at the same time, the materiality of the body is not denied (McNay, 1992). The physical body is 'always already' multiply produced in socio-historically specific discourses which constitute, 'penetrate' and regulate it in particular ways, but which also produce resistances to their 'infinitesimal controls'.

In short, post-structuralist theory offers an account of subjectivity and the body, as produced in and regulated by discourses, which constitutes a useful framework for feminist analyses of 'anorexia' as well of many other aspects of women's (or men's) experiences and of social reality more generally.

First, the theorization of subjectivity as decentred, as constituted in and regulated by socio-historically specific discourses, enables an analysis of 'femininity' as a 'plural collectivity' (Riley, 1988) of historically and culturally varying subject positions rather than as an eternal, asocial category. In contrast with psychoanalytic theory, which often lacks historical specificity (McNay, 1992), post-structuralism offers a more grounded theory of subjectivity as it is variously constituted, regulated and resisted.

Second, Foucault's theorization of the body is radically anti-essentialist: the body is 'always already' constituted in and regulated by discourses and discursive practices. Foucault (1977a) attacks the search for origins, whether in body or in history, as 'an epistemologically problematic quest' for ahistorical, asocial essences (McNay, 1992). He conceptualizes the body as a locus in which power relations are manifest most concretely (Foucault, 1977b). His project thus coincides with that of feminism in its analysis of the body as a material site of power struggle. For Foucault, the body and sex are constructs of discourses and discursive practices which regulate and normalize activities, subjectivities and sexualities (Foucault, 1979; Walkerdine, 1986). And, as I have argued, it is through discourses that power/knowledge functions (Foucault, 1977b, 1980). Furthermore, because knowledge is always bound up with historically specific regimes of power, Foucauldian theory rejects any categorical distinction between ideology and science, between fact and fiction. The notion of an empirically verifiable, objective or absolute Truth becomes untenable because societies produce their own specific, normalizing, regulating truths (Foucault, 1979). Post-structuralist theory thus enables a feminist questioning of those scientific 'truths' which have constituted women as (biologically) inferior and defective or as otherwise lacking (see Ussher, 1992a). And at the same time it provides a theoretical framework within which to analyse the 'real' effects of these truths that 'fiction' women in a multiplicity of socio-historically specific ways.

CONCLUSIONS

In this chapter I have aimed to draw out some of the theoretical insights provided by psychoanalytic and post-structuralist theories. I have not set out to offer an exhaustive account of these theories but rather to discuss those aspects of psychoanalytic and post-structuralist theory that may be both useful and inspirational in our understanding of issues of gender, subjectivity and embodiment and, more specifically, in our attempts to understand the problem of 'anorexia'.

Specifically, I have argued that Lacan's rereading of Freud offers a particularly useful theory of subjectivity and gender as constituted outside of itself within the Symbolic order. However, as we have seen, Lacanian and some post-Lacanian theory tends to lack the socio-historical specificity that Foucauldian theory offers. Foucault's post-structuralist concept of discourse not only allows for a more socially grounded analysis of subjectivity and gender; it also enables a conception of 'woman' as an unstable collectivity of *multiple*, often contradictory subject positions in discourse. In addition, Foucault's concept of the body as discursively constituted and regulated is not only anti-essentialist but also acknowledges and theorizes the corpo-reality of the body. And because power and knowledge are seen as bound together, functioning in discourse (Foucault, 1979), Foucauldian theory provides an account of the body as a site of power struggle as well as a critique of scientific truths of the female body as inferior and defective.

Feminists have, however, been critical of Foucault's lack of attention to the gendering of discursive positionings and regulations (McNay, 1992). Whilst he provides a detailed theorization of the discursive production of sex and sexuality and of technologies of sex (Foucault, 1979), he often fails to attend to how women and men are differently positioned, disciplined and regulated (McNay, 1992). It is important, therefore, to retain the psychoanalytic, Lacanian insights into the phallic nature of signification (Frosh, 1994) and the problematic nature of 'woman' as the negatively signified Other. Moreover, a theorization of subjectivity as a 'sum total of positions in discourse' leaves an important area of desire and investment largely unexplored (Walkerdine, 1986). Lacan theorizes the signifier that by its presence also signifies an absence (Benvenuto and Kennedy, 1986). Hence, desire is conceptualized as an effect of the fundamental loss and splitting of signification (Rose, 1982): 'it is as a derivation of the signifying chain that the channel of desire flows' (Lacan, 1958b: 259). Desire, then, is intimately bound up with subjectivity, since both are effects of signification so that 'Insofar as a cultural phenomenon succeeds in interpellating subjects – that is, in summoning them to assume a certain subjective (dis)position – it does so by evoking some form of desire or by promising satisfaction of some desire' (Bracher, 1993: 19).

The psychoanalytic insights into desire, into the irrational and unconscious nature of identification and into the phallic nature of signification are therefore important in understanding the ways in which women (and men) are interpellated

(Althusser, 1977) or taken up by and positioned in discourses, and in under-standing our 'investments' in particular subject positions (Hollway, 1992). Sayers (1994), for example, has illustrated how those unconscious defences, theorized by psychoanalysis, are imbricated in maintaining our 'phallic illusions' in identity. And, as Walkerdine (1990) argues, 'woman is fiction, lived as fact, and imbued with fantasy'.

In this discussion of post-structuralist and psychoanalytic theory I have sought to demonstrate how the theoretical perspective outlined above will enable us to theorize and research 'anorexia nervosa' as a multiply produced object of discourse and as a category that is particularly relevant to women, to the (discur-sive) constitution and regulation of femininities, subjectivities and the *female* body. Importantly, therefore, whilst drawing on Lacanian as well as post-structuralist theory, my analyses of 'anorexia' 'shall remain, or try to remain, at the level of discourse itself' (Foucault, 1972: 48). It is the texts about 'anorexia' rather than any putative reality 'behind' these texts that will be the object of my analysis. In Part II of this book I shall explore the genealogy of 'anorexia' – its historical emergence as an object of medical discourse – and the subsequent development and proliferation of this discursive object as increasing numbers of different clin-ical and academic discourses appropriate and re-produce it as their own – in terms of physiological dysfunction, genetic propensity, cognitive biases or psychodynamic or familial dysfunction, or within socio-cultural feminist discourse as an effect of cultural ideals of female thinness and women's oppres-sion in patriarchal capitalist society. In Part III of the book I shall be turning to the discourses deployed by women diagnosed or self-diagnosed as anorexic to explore how a variety of culturally sanctioned discourses converge on the body – in this case, the female body, the (very) thin body, the 'anorexic' body – to consti-tute and regulate the body, subjectivity and femininity in multiple, often contradictory ways.

2

DISCOURSE, FEMINISM, RESEARCH AND THE PRODUCTION OF TRUTH

In Chapter 1 I discussed psychoanalytic and post-structuralist theories and explored how these theories undermine our commonsense and mainstream psychological notions of gender, identity and embodiment. In providing a radically anti-essentialist account of subjectivity, gender and embodiment, I argued that a feminist post-structuralist perspective, informed by Lacanian theory, provides a useful and inspirational theoretical space within which to question critically the status of our current knowledges of 'anorexia' and in which we can re-examine the problem of 'anorexia' in its socio-historically specific and gender-specific discursive contexts. A feminist post-structuralist perspective, I have argued, enables us to transgress the individual–society dichotomy and to engage more thoroughly with a concept of 'anorexia' as a socio-culturally constituted phenomenon, manifested in individual women. It enables us to locate women's and girls' experiences and distress around food and eating and around gender, subjectivity and embodiment within those discourses that constitute and regulate our lives in late twentieth-century Western society. It also enables us to explore the gendered dimensions of these discourses, allowing us to engage with the socio-political dimensions of our own and/or others' subjectivities. By unravelling some of those discourses that converge upon the female body and on the 'anorexic' body we can explore how the 'micro-physics of power' that functions in discourse operates upon the anorexic body.

This feminist post-structuralist perspective has radical implications not only for how we conceptualize the social world but also for how we can investigate that world and the status we give to our resulting knowledges of that world. Feminist post-structuralism has radical implications for the way we view mainstream psychological approaches to research and how we can then conduct our own research. For, as I argued in Chapter 1, objects of social reality

> are not 'things' set apart from and independent of discourse but are realised only in and through the discursive elements which surround the objects in question. Things then are made visible and palpable through the existence of discursive practices.
>
> (Prior, 1989: 3)

34

And 'it is in discourse that power and knowledge are joined together' (Foucault, 1979: 100). What, then, of psychological theory and research? How, from a post-structuralist perspective, should we view the discourses of psychology and the processes in which we engage to produce 'scientific' knowledges about social reality, about individuals and about gender and pathology? In this chapter I shall discuss some of the methodological implications of feminist post-structuralism for psychological research. I shall begin with a brief review of the critiques of 'mainstream' positivist methodologies made by feminist and 'new paradigm' psychologists. I will then discuss how post-structuralist theory has further undermined the epistemological and methodological assumptions that underlie positivist research.

These critiques have also been accompanied by the development of new, often qualitative approaches to social and psychological enquiry (Henwood and Pidgeon, 1992). Amongst these approaches are the discourse analytic methodologies promoted in psychology by, for example, Potter and Wetherell (1987), Burman and Parker (1993), Hollway (1989) and Walkerdine (1986, 1988). It will be argued that discourse analysis is, or can be, epistemologically compatible with the theoretical perspective developed in Chapter 1. And it is this methodology that has been applied to the problem of 'anorexia' in Parts II and III of this book.

CRITIQUES OF POSITIVISM

Since at least the 1930s the hypothetico-deductive or positivist methodology has been presented as the dominant paradigm in psychology (Kitzinger, 1987). This approach might be characterized by its idealization of experimental control and manipulation of variables and by its concern with the minutiae of research procedures, with quantification, measurement and statistical analysis.[1] The philosophy of science underpinning this approach is that of logical positivism, formulated by the Vienna Circle in the early 1920s. It assumes an objective knowable reality and is based on the empiricist epistemology that 'true' knowledge must be grounded in experience and observation (Harre and Secord, 1972). The 'objective truth' of research findings are seen here to be guaranteed by the researcher's rigorous adherence to particular research procedures. Objective knowledge, it is argued, is attainable only by scientific experimentation and observation which could verify (or falsify) the truth of logical prepositions (Bechtel, 1988): 'By reducing complex concepts to simple logical functions of simple concepts, related to unambiguous experimental operations, science, it was thought, could be built upon a solid foundation of indisputable facts' (Harre and Secord, 1972: 33).

The critiques of logical positivism by, for example, Popper, Kuhn, and Quine, and the works of Lakatos, Lauden, Feyerabend and others, have also led to the emergence of post-positivist philosophies of science (Bechtel, 1988; Outhwaite, 1987). Broadly speaking, however, the positivist view of scientific research as progressively accumulating objective, universally applicable knowledge, determined by the actual nature of the world, persists (see Woolgar, 1988) and it remains the dominant paradigm within psychology. Nevertheless, it has received much criticism both within and outside of psychology (Henwood and Pidgeon, 1992; Parker, 1989).

Much of this criticism has come from 'new paradigm' psychologists such as Harre (1979) and Shotter (1975, 1984). Harre and Secord (1972: 28), for example, argued that the positivist methodology does not automatically produce reliable, scientific knowledge; that behaviourism, the epitome of positivist psychology, has yielded only an illusion of objectivity and that the results of animal and laboratory experiments, so favoured by positivist psychologists, could not be generalized to humans in their social contexts. Positivist social psychology, they argued, was inadequate because it took no account of the meanings or contexts of human behaviour nor of human agency or experience. Consequently 'new paradigm' psychologists adopted ideas and methodologies, such as ethnomethodology (Garfinkel, 1967), role-play analysis, interviewing and speech act theory (Austin, 1962) from other disciplines in an attempt to produce a more person-centred and context-oriented psychology (Harre and Secord, 1972; see also Parker, 1990a).

Feminism has also provided a number of valuable critiques of the positivist quest for scientific objectivity. There are, however, 'virtually as many different theories and arguments in the feminist debate as there are feminists' (Ussher, 1991: 187). Given the myriad feminist perspectives it would be naive to talk of 'the feminist position' (Ussher, 1991) or *the* feminist critique of positivism. Rather, there is a diversity of different feminist critiques and feminist agendas for research.

Many feminists have argued that, whilst science claims to be objective, value-free and apolitical, it is in fact masculine and androcentric.[2] First, the positivist 'scientific' epistemology is based on a liberal ideology which posits 'rational *man*' producing objective knowledge of the natural world through scientific endeavour (Fee, 1981). This ideology entails the often unstated assumption that the characteristics of 'rational man' are actually the characteristics of males (Fee, 1981). Thus, whether intentionally or unintentionally, science has systematically excluded the possibility that women could be the 'agents of knowledge' (Harding, 1987: 3). Whereas 'man' is associated with culture, rationality, knowledge and science, 'woman', as the Other of man (see Chapter 1), is associated with nature, superstition and emotion (Jordanova, 1989). Associated with nature, 'woman' could only be the object, not the subject, of scientific knowledge (Fee, 1981; Jordanova, 1989; Bleier, 1984).

Second, feminists have shown how, within the social sciences, people are often assumed to be male (Harding, 1987). 'Mainstream' research has thus been termed by some feminists as 'the academic male-stream' (Siltanen and Stanworth, 1984) and as 'men's studies' (Spender, 1980). This androcentrism has not only excluded many aspects of women's lives from 'legitimate' research (Harding, 1987); it has also resulted in a 'male-as-norm' principle (Griffin, 1986) which inevitably marginalizes and pathologizes women. Women are either rendered invisible or are construed as inferior deviations of men (see Jordanova, 1989). And the feminist critique of this 'male-as-norm' principle is not simply a demand for a more 'balanced' focus in research, since 'if you take women seriously, if you make women's experience the central feature of what you're doing, then you *can't* leave the rest undisturbed' (Stanley and Wise, 1983: 3).

It is not an adequate solution simply to add women into a scientific research programme that is already deeply embedded within patriarchal ideology (Griffin, 1986; Harding, 1987). For what status should we accord to the positivist concepts of 'objectivity' and 'validity' premised as they are on a notion of science as an apolitical endeavour? And how should we interpret the 'objectivity' of research programmes that preclude engagement with the socio-political dimensions of our experiences?

Many feminists have also shown how science has been used in the interests of (white, bourgeois) men by, for example, constructing masculinity and femininity in particular ways and by naturalizing these notions. Hence, gender, the sexual division of labour and the sexual status quo have been constituted as putatively natural facts rather than as socio-political constructions and practices. That is, science has played a part in the construction and regulation of gender and oppressive gender relations (Walkerdine, 1986; Foucault, 1979; Ussher, 1991). An allegedly value-free science has produced supposedly objective evidence that women are naturally suited (only) to domesticity and mothering (Jordanova, 1989); that women are less intelligent than men (see Sayers, 1982; Bleier, 1984), less capable at mathematics (see Walkerdine, 1986, 1988) and more prone to sickness (see Ehrenreich and English, 1974) and mental instability (Ussher, 1991). For many years, feminists have challenged these scientific definitions of woman and have sought in a number of ways to produce different, more positive knowledges of women (Walkerdine and Lucey, 1989).

In short, feminists have challenged 'science' by elucidating the 'masculinity' of its alleged objectivity, by highlighting its androcentric foci and by demonstrating how science has often functioned in support of a patriarchal status quo. Using a variety of epistemologies (Ussher, 1991) and methodologies (Harding, 1987), feminist researchers have sought to falsify and undermine scientific knowledges of women's alleged inferiority; to reclaim women's experiences (Stanley and Wise, 1983) and women's voices (Gilligan, 1982) and to deconstruct scientific accounts of gender (Gavey, 1989; Bleier, 1984); to show that 'the line between scientific accounts and science-fictional narratives may be a lot finer than is usually thought' (Walkerdine and Lucey, 1989: 31). Feminist researchers are increasingly rejecting 'traditional' positivist methodology for ethical, epistemological and emancipatory reasons (Henwood and Pidgeon, 1992). As feminist standpoint theorists argue (see Griffin and Phoenix, 1994), feminist research should not only be 'woman-centred' but should also aim to be reflexive and to be critical of accepted epistemologies and methodologies. Feminist research should adopt epistemological and methodological perspectives that are appropriate both to its research questions and to its emancipatory aims.

37

POST-STRUCTURALIST THEORY AND RESEARCH

Post-structuralist critiques of science have much in common with some aspects of the feminist critiques discussed above (Gavey, 1989). Indeed, some feminists explicitly locate feminism within post-structuralism or post-modernism (e.g. Flax, 1987) or argue that post-structuralism simply reiterates feminism (e.g. Burman, 1990). Like some feminist critiques, post-structuralist theory undermines science's claims to objectivity and asserts that power is inevitably imbricated in knowledge (see Chapter 1).

The post-structuralist critique of science proceeds from post-Saussurean linguistic theory, which problematizes the relationship between signifier and signified, between language and reality. Language is understood not as a transparent medium through which we can view the world. It does not simply describe reality more or less objectively. Rather, it is constructive of reality (Parker, 1990b). Discourses are social practices that 'systematically form the objects of which they speak' (Foucault, 1972: 49). They actively construct certain realities in particular ways (Wetherell and White, 1992), and thereby constitute certain power relations and normalize certain forms of social regulation (Foucault, 1979; see also Chapter 1).

Post-structuralist theory, therefore, radically undermines the claims that scientific discourses objectively describe and explain a reality existing anterior to and independently of discourse. It recasts empirical 'facts' as theory- and language-dependent contentions (Lawson, 1985), and 'scientific methodology' not as a means of revealing reality but as a technique of constructing particular realities and truths (Tseelon, 1991). So from a post-structuralist perspective there is no simple correspondence between ontology and epistemology (Parker, 1990b), between extra-discursive reality and our knowledges of the world. Hence, the notion that 'propositions of scientific theory are true or false by virtue of the way the world is, cannot fruitfully be used to characterise a defensible realism' (Harre, 1992: 153). This is not to argue, à la Derrida (1976: 158), that 'there is nothing outside of the text', that there is no material reality outside of discourse. Rather, post-structuralist theory demonstrates the implausibility of 'brute empiricist' claims that the extra-discursive physical reality of things can be directly known (Parker, 1990a). That is, post-structuralist theory disputes the 'philosophical concept of Truth which can provide the ultimate seal for a particular account' (Outhwaite, 1987). It denies the possibility of objectively knowing a reality outside of discourse. It does not, however, necessitate denying the existence of an extra-discursive reality, existing 'independently of the perceptions, actions or whatever of human subjects' (Woodiwiss, 1990: 25). As Bhaskar (1978: 250) argues, there are things which 'exist and act independently of our descriptions, but we can only know them under particular descriptions':

> the relations between the 'real material' object and the practices of its production are complex: there is never a moment of 'reality' which is

comprehensible or possible outside a framework of discursive practices which render it possible and transformable.

(Walkerdine, 1984: 163)

In exploring the problem of 'anorexia' I shall be taking up this 'critical realist' post-structuralist stance, assuming the existence of a material, extra-discursive reality whilst maintaining that our knowledges of 'the real' are always socio-historically contingent rather than objective or absolute; and that knowledge is always ideological, not because it is biased or distorted but because it can only ever offer a partial view (Hall, 1982).

Post-structuralist theory thus coincides with feminism in disputing science's claims to objectivity and in asserting that power is imbricated in knowledge. It demonstrates again that 'scientific' attempts to eliminate the subjective, to guard against bias and other sources of 'error' do not guarantee a value-free objectivity (Tseelon, 1991). Indeed, the very possibility of *absolute* truth is rejected as fantasy (Walkerdine and Lucey, 1989). And, in rejecting the possibility of absolute universal truth, post-structuralist theory allows for a plurality of 'truths', including feminist truths (Gavey, 1989: 462).

However, post-structuralism also problematizes certain feminist perspectives such as the 'privileged standpoint' (see Flax, 1987) and essentialist feminism (see Sawicki, 1991). In particular, it problematizes a feminist (or non-feminist) notion of an authentic feminine or female experience, identity or desire, repressed by patriarchy (Sawicki, 1991). The feminist research focus on women's experience (see Harding, 1987; Stanley and Wise, 1983) and the call for women-centred research (see Nicolson, 1986) has clearly addressed many of the problems of 'male-oriented' positivist research discussed above. But post-structuralist theory necessitates a re-evaluation of the ways in which 'women' and 'women's experience[s]' are conceptualized: first, because it problematizes or deconstructs the category of 'woman' and, second, because it posits a decentred subject whose experience is discursively constituted outside of itself. Post-structuralist theory indicates that there can be no quasi-natural feminine/female experience outside of patriarchy or essentially different from male experience. Rather, women's (or men's) subjectivities, experiences and desires are 'always already' constituted in and regulated by discourses and discursive practices (Walkerdine, 1986; see Chapter 1). Feminist post-structuralist research is therefore concerned not with an exploration or reclamation of an authentic female experience but with analysing the ways in which women's subjectivities, experiences and desires are discursively constituted and regulated and with elucidating the socio-historical specificities of gender power/knowledges (see Gavey, 1989).

DISCOURSE ANALYSIS AND POST-STRUCTURALISM

These various critiques of positivism have been accompanied by the development of new, often qualitative approaches to research (Henwood and Pidgeon,

1992). And amongst these methodologies are the discourse analytic approaches promoted in psychology by, for example, Potter and Wetherell (1987), Burman and Parker (1993), Hollway (1989) and Walkerdine (1986).

There are a number of different trends covered by the term 'discourse analysis' (Potter *et al.*, 1990) and 'discourse' itself is often conceptualized in different ways (Walkerdine, 1986). Broadly speaking, however, the discourse analytic approach to research can be understood as part of a 'turn to language' within the social sciences (Parker, 1990a).

Social psychology has traditionally taken the view 'that language acts as a neutral, transparent medium between the social actor and the world' (Wetherell and Potter, 1988: 168); that people's ordinary discourse *reflects* real and often stable phenomena and processes such as attitudes, personalities or cognitions that exist within the individual, independently of language. Researchers have, therefore, aimed to reveal (objectively) these phenomena as if they were transparently reflected in the language through which they are studied. Yet developments in linguistics, literary theory, philosophy and sociology have shown this view of language to be implausible (Wetherell and Potter, 1988). Discourse analytic psychologists have therefore drawn on ideas in ethnomethodology (Garfinkel, 1967), speech act theory (Austin, 1962), post-structuralism, linguistics, conversation analysis and literary criticism to develop alternative conceptualizations of language and discourse (Wetherell, 1986; Walkerdine, 1986). Within discourse analysis discourse is viewed as action-oriented and as constructive of reality (Potter and Wetherell, 1987, 1991); that is, discourse is understood as socio-historically located social practice (Parker, 1990a): 'People perform actions of different kinds through their talk and their writing' (Potter and Wetherell, 1991: 3). They construct particular versions of reality using particular socially available discursive resources. Discourses construct particular truths, particular realities and subjectivities and thereby re-produce power relations. 'Particular regimes of truth, bodies of knowledge, make possible both *what can be said* and *what can be done*' (Walkerdine, 1984: 154–155). They thereby constitute our subjectivities, interpellating the speaking (or listening) subject in particular ways (Hollway, 1992; Parker, 1990a). Discourse analytic research is concerned therefore not with revealing any objectively knowable reality outside of discourse but with analysing discourses themselves as they are manifest in texts and talk.

There are, however, a number of different approaches encompassed within 'discourse analysis'. Indeed, 'it is very difficult to speak of "discourse" or even "discourse analysis" as a single unitary entity, since this would blur together approaches subscribing to specific and different philosophical frameworks' (Burman and Parker, 1993: 3). These various approaches have been differentiated in a number of different ways and have been discussed in detail elsewhere.[3] Potter and Wetherell (1991), for example, identify at least four different types of work commonly described as discourse analysis.

The first of these has been strongly influenced by speech act theory and is primarily concerned with analysis of conversational exchange in particular

40

institutional settings. Sinclair and Coulthard (1975), for example, analysed class-room discourse in terms of verbal 'acts', similar to grammatical clauses, which could be combined to form moves such as 'focusing' and 'framing' of classroom activity. A second form of 'discourse analysis' is characterized by the work of van Dijk, who conceives of discourse analysis as 'part of a more embracing cognitive and social theory about the rules and strategies that underlie the production and under-standing of (media) discourse' (van Dijk, 1983: 27). Here, 'discourse analysis' is concerned with the effects of 'discourse' on cognitive processes such as under-standing and recall. His analysis of newspaper articles, for example, was used to develop a cognitive model of media production, comprehension and recall.

Beyond a concern with language, these forms of 'discourse analysis' share little with the approach that will be adopted here. They are not opposed to the conceptualization of language as a transparent medium through which we can access 'the real world'. Neither are they epistemologically compatible with post-structuralist theory. Such approaches to 'discourse analysis' might be viewed as methodological developments *within* empiricist psychology rather than as radical alternatives to that paradigm. Indeed, the latter approach quite explicitly conceptualizes the analysis of 'discourse' as a means of revealing underlying cognitive processes.

A third type of discourse analysis is that developed within the sociology of science. This body of research (e.g. Gilbert and Mulkay, 1984; Woolgar, 1988) is concerned with analysing scientists' talk and texts so as to elucidate the ways in which they produce their actions as rational and their findings as factual, whilst conversely others' 'scientific' activities are produced as flawed. This approach to discourse analysis is closer to a post-structuralist approach in that it eschews the notion of an objectively knowable Truth existing anterior to discourse and is, rather, concerned with an analysis of the ways in which discourses constitute their objects in particular ways. However, there are also important differences between this approach and the approach that I have adopted in this book.

A further approach that might be distinguished within 'discourse analysis' is primarily concerned with analysing rhetoric, with examining the ways in which particular discursive resources are deployed in talk and text to produce particular effects. Rhetorical analysis is not therefore concerned with questions of 'accuracy', of how an account relates to some putative reality (Potter and Wetherell, 1991). Rather, its aim is to elucidate how an account is constructed to compete successfully with other versions of 'reality' (Billig, 1991). Potter *et al.* (1991), for example, have examined the quantification rhetoric used in a recent TV documentary on cancer and by British cancer charities. They showed how particular forms of calculation (for example, of incidence rates, frequencies of different types of cancer and success rates of treatments) and particular presentation practices were successfully deployed by different groups to produce conflicting accounts of the degree of success (or otherwise) of medical research in treating cancers. Similarly, Widdicombe (1993) has examined 'the rhetorical processes of negotiation and argument' involved in talking about changes in identity. By

41

analysing interviews with 'punks' and 'goths' she identifies some of the ways in which speakers orientate to, and negotiate, the problem of appearing to be authentic members of a subculture rather than as simply copying others.

In short, this approach to discourse analysis is concerned with explicating the discursive resources deployed in constructing particular accounts of reality, in, for example, warranting particular accounts as factual whilst undermining alternative versions. As such, these studies emphasize the constructive nature of discourse; the way in which discourses and discursive resources do not simply reflect some reality that exists anterior to discourse but rather constitute their objects or events in particular ways. And by focusing on the argumentative aspects of talk and text they also begin to elucidate the ways in which power is imbricated in discourse. This approach thus shares some of the theoretical and methodological concerns of post-structuralism. It opposes itself to the empiricist project of objectively revealing a (putative) reality existing anterior to discourse and is concerned rather with an explication of the ways in which discourses and discursive resources constitute their objects within particular socio-cultural contexts (Potter and Wetherell, 1987). However, there are also significant differences between this approach and a post-structuralist approach to discourse analysis.

This post-structuralist approach is characterized by the works of, for example, Henriques *et al.* (1984), Hollway (1989), Walkerdine (1986, 1988) and Wetherell (1996). It is concerned with elucidating the ways in which discourses constitute and regulate particular (discursive) practices, experiences and subjectivities; the ways in which discourses constitute particular knowledges or Truths and thereby regulate our lives. Unlike those approaches described above, this form of discourse analysis draws on continental social philosophy and cultural analysis, most notably on the post-structuralist theory of Foucault. It can be distinguished from those other approaches by its more explicitly theorized concern with epistemology and with the development of a post-structuralist theoretical framework for research (see Parker, 1990a, 1990b). Valerie Walkerdine (1986), for example, has examined 'everyday social practices' in the family and the school to show how particular discourses have defined 'childhood', 'good' teaching and 'good' mothering, and how these definitions constitute 'part of a variety of "regimes of truth" which have positive and powerful effects in regulating the modern order'. Her study was

> concerned with understanding how assumptions about 'good mothers', 'sensitive teachers' and the 'nature of the child' operate and have effects in those domestic and pedagogic practices which make up the daily lives of many women and children. [It was] concerned primarily with the relationship between conceptions of truth, power and the construction of the subject . . . [with exploring] the way in which post-structuralism may help us to understand the positioning of girls and women in these practices.
>
> (Walkerdine, 1986: 57)

In short, this approach is distinguished by its explicit concern with post-structuralism; with the ways in which discourses constitute and regulate knowledges, objects, practices, subjectivities and experiences; and with eluci-dating the socio-historical specificities of these power/knowledges. The differentiation of these different forms of discourse analysis is, I think, useful in locating 'discourse analytic' studies within their particular methodological and theoretical frameworks. This categorization is, however, provisional in that many studies draw on more than one of these approaches. For instance, Widdicombe's study of the rhetorical resources used in autobiographical accounts of 'becoming a goth' exhibits a concern with the discursive production of the subject that is more often associated with a post-structuralist than with a rhetoric-oriented approach. The distinction between the different forms of discourse analysis described above is therefore often blurred with studies drawing on more than one approach. Indeed, I would argue that the methodology adopted by, for example, Potter and Wetherell (1987), Gilbert and Mulkay (1984) and rhetoric-oriented 'discourse psychologists' is not incompatible with the theoretical framework of post-structuralism. Both approaches are premised on a conception of discourses as 'action-oriented' and as constitutive of reality. Both share 'a concern with the ways language produces and constrains meaning, where meaning does not reside within individuals' heads, and where social conditions give rise to the forms of talk available' (Burman and Parker, 1993: 3). Yet, as I have argued, there are also important differences between these approaches. First, the post-structuralist approach might be characterized by its tendency to be concerned with 'global' analysis, with *broadly* explicating discourses and discur-sive resources and analysing the ways in which they constitute and regulate their objects. In contrast, the rhetoric-oriented approach may be characterized as 'fine-grained', in that it focuses on the more *detailed* discursive procedures (such as rhetorical devices) that are deployed in the production of particular accounts (Wetherell and White, 1992).

Second, and more important, these approaches differ in terms of their theo-retical framework. Whilst the methodology deployed in 'fine-grained' analyses is not incompatible with post-structuralism, neither is it explicitly post-structuralist. It is not, for example, committed to the use of a Foucauldian conceptualization of 'discourse'. As the debate between Parker (1990a, 1990b) and Potter *et al.* (1990) illustrates, the use of the term 'interpretive repertoires' rather than 'discourse' indicates subtle but important distinctions between the two approaches in terms of the way in which 'discourse' is conceptualized and in the way in which post-structuralist theory does or does not inform analysis.

A FEMINIST POST-STRUCTURALIST APPROACH TO DISCOURSE ANALYSIS

The term 'discourse analysis', then, covers a wide range of approaches to research, some of which have little in common with the post-structuralist methodology adopted in this book. In analysing the discourses surrounding 'anorexia nervosa' I shall be concerned primarily with a 'global', rather than 'fine-grained', analysis of the discourses and discursive resources deployed in the production and regulation of 'anorexia', subjectivity and gender.

The approach that I have adopted and developed can therefore be broadly located within those approaches which eschew any notion of an objectively knowable reality existing anterior to discourse, and are concerned with an analysis of the ways in which discourses and discursive resources are constructive, rather than reflective, of their objects. I shall be concerned with analysing the ways in which discourses as social practices construct particular truths, particular realities and subjectivities and thereby re-produce particular (gendered) power relations. In exploring the problem of 'anorexia' I shall, then, be drawing on Foucauldian theory, particularly on Foucault's theoretical discussions of discourse and knowledge (1972), power and regulation (1977b, 1980) and genealogy (1977a). But I shall also be drawing on Lacanian theory of subjectivity and gender and its feminist appropriations (see Chapter 1), in its focus on the ways in which *women's* bodies, subjectivities, desires and experiences are discursively constituted and regulated within a *patriarchal* discursive context.

This form of discourse analytic research is concerned, therefore, not with revealing any objectively knowable reality about 'anorexia' outside of discourse, but with analysing discourses themselves as they are manifest in texts, talk, practices and institutions (see Henriques *et al.*, 1984). It is concerned with elucidating the inseparability of discourses from their conditions of emergence and from the institutions and practices of which they are a part (see Walkerdine, 1984). It seeks to demonstrate how objects, practices, subjectivities and desires are constituted in and regulated by discourses and discursive practices and how the discursive production of truths can be understood in terms of a 'micro-physics of power' (Foucault, 1977b: 139) that operates upon the female body and upon the 'anorexic' body.

This is, I think, an approach which enables a critical questioning of the 'mainstream' conceptions of 'anorexia nervosa' and which facilitates a mode of enquiry that more fully locates 'anorexia' within its socio-cultural discursive contexts. It enables an exploration of the discourses in which anorexia, femininity, subjectivity and the body are discursively constituted and regulated. It enables an exploration of the ways in which the micro-physics of power that functions in discourse operates upon the female and the anorexic body.

Part II

INSTITUTING THE THIN WOMAN

The discursive productions of 'anorexia nervosa'

3

A GENEALOGY OF 'ANOREXIA NERVOSA'

> while the name of the symbolic female disorder may change from one historical
> period to the next, the gender asymmetry of the representational tradition remains
> constant.
>
> (Showalter, 1985: 4)

In late twentieth-century Europe the concept of 'anorexia nervosa' has taken up
a prominent place in the pathologization of certain aspects of women's experiences. 'Anorexia nervosa' has become the name of, and an 'explanation' for, the
extreme distress that some girls and women experience in relation to food and
body weight and for the seriously self-destructive behaviours that accompany this
distress. And if we are to understand better how 'anorexia' has come to function
as an explanation for women's 'disordered' eating and not eating; if we are to
understand better its high cultural, clinical and academic profile; and if we are
to understand better the relationships between 'anorexia nervosa', 'woman' and
women, then it is necessary to take a genealogical perspective and 'trace the
descent' of anorexia. One must explore how 'anorexia' has emerged and developed as an object of medical and psychological discourses and examine the part
that discursive constructions of femininity have played in this historical process.
For, as feminist authors have repeatedly demonstrated, an affinity between
deviance, 'insanity', sickness and the category of 'woman' has existed in a variety
of different socio-historical contexts.[1] How might 'anorexia nervosa' fit into this
history of female and feminized pathology?

This relationship between 'woman' and 'pathology' has been apparent both
in the gender-bias of various clinical diagnoses and in cultural representations of
insanity and sickness as feminine. For example, more women than men have
been diagnosed and treated for 'mental illness' in the twentieth century (Ussher,
1991; Chesler, 1972) and in the eighteenth and nineteenth centuries (Showalter,
1985; Ehrenreich and English, 1974).[2] And, as the Other of 'rational man',
'woman' has often been 'fictioned' as sick, intellectually impaired and as irrational and mad (Ussher, 1991). For, as the Other of rational 'man' (see Chapter
1) 'women and madness share the same territory', positioned in relation to a
fundamentally male norm (Martin, 1987: 42).

47

This equation of femininity with sickness and insanity was certainly apparent in the nineteenth century, during the period in which 'anorexia nervosa' first emerged as an object of medical discourse. And, whilst medical and cultural discourses about gender have certainly changed significantly since the nineteenth century, femininity is still associated with sickness and insanity. In their classic study of clinicians' concepts of mental health, Broverman *et al.* (1970), for example, found that clinicians' concepts of a healthy adult corresponded with their concepts of a healthy man, but not of a healthy woman. Women, they found, were much less likely than men to be attributed with 'healthy adult' characteristics. This disjuncture between 'woman' and (mental) health is amply illustrated by a recent journal article in which the symptom list of a screening test for 'somatization disorder' was organized in such a way that the following mnemonic could be used: 'somatization disorder besets ladies and vexes physicians' (Othmer and DeSouza, 1985: 1148). It seems that medical misogyny did not die with the Victorians: the category of 'woman' continues to be constituted as a category of otherness, of deviance and pathology.

Woman's association with pathology has been interpreted as the result of patriarchy, either because patriarchal oppression makes us sick and/or because patriarchal society seeks to portray us as 'naturally' inferior (see Ussher, 1991). Either way, the discourses and discursive practices surrounding 'anorexia nervosa' can be seen as part of a plethora of patriarchal discursive strategies by which 'woman' has historically been constituted as other, as deviant, pathological and inferior. Hence, if we are to better understand this contemporarily prominent category of 'female pathology', then it is important to take a genealogical perspective, examining the socio-historical discursive contexts within which (European) women's self-starvation has been constituted and regulated. Thus, after briefly discussing pre-medical and early medical accounts of women's self-starvation, I shall consider those aspects of eighteenth- and nineteenth-century medicine which, I shall argue, converged to produce 'anorexia nervosa' as an object of medical discourse.

In this chapter I shall not, therefore, be concerned with assessing the 'accuracy' of historical accounts of self-starvation or with retrospectively establishing diagnoses. Nor shall I attempt to 'restore an unbroken continuity' (Foucault, 1977a: 146) between past and present, between those women diagnosed as anorexic in the twentieth century and historical accounts of medieval, Georgian or Victorian women who starved themselves. Nor shall I be demonstrating that 'anorexia nervosa' has always existed (independently of its socio-historical discursive contexts), since 'Genealogy . . . rejects the metahistorical deployment of ideal significations and indefinite teleologies. It opposes itself to the search for "origins"' (Foucault, 1977a: 140).

This chapter is not, therefore, about 'the discovery' of 'anorexia nervosa' since, as Foucault argues,

the object does not await in limbo the order that will free it and enable it to become embodied in a visible and prolix objectivity; it does not pre-exist itself, held back by some obstacle at the first edge of light. It exists under the positive conditions of a complex group of relations.

(Foucault, 1972: 45)

The object 'anorexia nervosa' did not exist independently of medical discourse, 'waiting' to be revealed by scientific progress. Rather, 'anorexia nervosa' was constituted through the medical discourses and discursive practices that defined and treated it:

In these fields of initial differentiation, in the distances, the discontinuities, and the thresholds that appear within it, psychiatric discourse finds a way of limiting its domain, of defining what it is talking about, of giving it the status of object – and therefore making it manifest, nameable, and describable.

(Foucault, 1972: 41)

We cannot, therefore, look to the female 'anorexic' body for the meanings or origins of anorexia. Rather, we must look to the discourses and discursive practices in which it emerged and is constituted. Because the body is not, for all its corpo-reality, a natural, transhistorical object (Riley, 1988). It is always-already constituted in and regulated by socio-historically specific discourses. As Foucault (1977a: 147) argues, history or 'descent' 'attaches itself to the body'. Discourses and discursive practices are 'inscribed' in the body and the aim of this genealogy is therefore to 'expose a body totally imprinted by history and the process of history's destruction of the body' (Foucault, 1977a: 148).

In producing this genealogy my aim is to demonstrate the discursive nature of 'anorexia nervosa'; to analyse those discourses and discursive practices that, first, made possible and, second, constituted anorexia as a category of medical discourse. The late nineteenth-century medical discourse in which 'anorexia nervosa' emerged did not, I shall argue, simply describe a 'reality' that existed independently beyond it. Rather, medical discourse in dialogue with the wider culture was 'inscribed' on the (female) body that could be diagnosed as anorexic. The body is historically mutable; it is 'always already' inside culture (Riley, 1988). The diagnosed body cannot be easily distinguished from the discourses that speak of it.

The emergence of 'anorexia nervosa' was, then, a discursive event made possible by the gaps *in* and the relationships *between* discourses (see Foucault, 1977a). As we shall see, anorexia emerged at the interface of medical and cultural discourses on hypochondria, hysteria and femininity. It was constituted as a feminine nervous disorder at a time when 'the nervous woman' was a significant cultural figure (see Ehrenreich and English, 1974), and when explanations of female nervous debility were shifting (see Rousseau, 1991). Anorexia thus figured as a political forum, as much as a medical one, in which to debate and therefore constitute and reconstitute feminine nervousness.

PRE-MEDICAL CASES OF FEMALE SELF-STARVATION

There have been numerous documented cases of religiously inspired female self-starvation in medieval Europe, the most famous being that of Catherine of Siena (1347–1380).[3] Other such cases include 'Joan the Meatless' and 'Christina the Astonishing', 'who gave up food because she had nothing else to give up for Christ'. The sainted Princess Margaret of Hungary similarly fasted until she died in 1271, aged 26 (Halmi, 1983: 2), whilst Liduine of Schiedam (c. 1500) was said to have existed on nothing but 'a little piece of apple the size of a holy wafer' (Strober, 1986: 231).

Several historians of anorexia have asserted that many such cases can be retrospectively diagnosed as anorexia. Halmi (1983: 1), for example, argues that anorexia nervosa 'did, in fact, exist as early as the 13th century' and that Margaret of Hungary 'had a typical anorectic premorbid personality'. Palazzoli (1974: 3–4) similarly claims that it is 'quite possible that cases of anorexia nervosa have been known since time immemorial' and that 'the disease was not uncommon in the Middle Ages'. Whilst others (e.g. Habermas, 1989; Tolstrup, 1990) are more cautious in their retrospective diagnoses it is clear that many historians of anorexia assume that it is legitimate to apply the twentieth-century concept of 'anorexia nervosa' more or less categorically to a variety of historical cases of women's self-starvation. These histories thereby privilege modern medical and psychological knowledges of anorexia as objective, transhistorical truths. They assume 'anorexia' to be a transhistorical medical entity, existing independently of the discourses in which it is currently constituted and the cultural milieu in which it is now experienced. As Brumberg (1988: 42) notes, 'some medical writers and historians . . . would have us believe that Karen Carpenter and Catherine of Siena suffered from the same disease'.

Yet such retrospective diagnoses are highly problematic (Dinicola, 1990). Historical analyses of self-starvation demonstrate that medieval European meanings of food and fasting were very different from those that are available today (see Bynum, 1987). Famines were still present in Europe and ascetic practices, including fasting, were common religious practice. Fasting, a thirteenth-century commentator claimed, was 'useful for expelling demons, excluding evil thoughts, remitting sins, mortifying vices, giving certain hope of future good and a foretaste of celestial joys' (cited in Bynum, 1987: 2–3).

Food, particularly the Eucharist, was located within a religious framework. God and Jesus were frequently represented as both feeders and food. The Eucharist symbolized union with God through eating, and many of the female fasters ate nothing but the host (Bynum, 1987). Within medieval Europe fasting was understood not as an individual pathology but as an instrument of spirituality (Brumberg, 1986).

There are inevitably similarities between medieval descriptions of fasting women and twentieth-century descriptions of anorexia nervosa in terms of the physical effects of starvation (Brumberg, 1988). Beyond this, however, the differences are so great as to make an argument of equivalence between the two phenomena almost meaningless. The differences between medieval and contemporary culture indicate that fasting resulted in very different social consequences and had very different meanings from contemporary 'anorexia'. The subject positions, and hence the experiences, of religious female faster and twentieth-century 'anorexic' are very different. Thus, symptomatic continuities between self-starvation in medieval and twentieth-century Europe are not evidence of a continuity of personal experiences or of social meanings (Brumberg, 1986). Nor do they indicate some transhistorical 'natural' feminine propensity to eating disorders. Contemporary records construe Catherine of Siena's fast as an admirable and holy expression of piety. Her death was not presented as a regrettable or tragic culmination of a disease or disorder.

SELF-STARVATION IN EARLY MEDICAL DISCOURSE

With the Protestant Reformation, traditional Catholic practices, including harsh asceticism and the worship of saints, were disavowed. Female fasters thus came under greater scrutiny and suspicion (Brumberg, 1988). However, cases of female fasting continued to be recorded into the nineteenth century. Examples include Martha Taylor (c. 1669) the 'Famed Young Derbyshire Damsel', Ann Moore (c. 1807) the 'Fasting Woman of Tutbury' and, most famously, Sarah Jacobs (c. 1873), the 'Welsh Fasting Girl', who died whilst her fast was being monitored (Morgan, 1977).

These records of 'miraculous maids' and 'fasting girls' represent an important transition in the history of women's self-starvation. Whilst they were often recorded within a religious framework they were also increasingly being appropriated into the domain of the emerging medical profession. During the sixteenth and seventeenth centuries 'anorexia mirabilis' became a subject of heated debate amongst doctors and civil authorities as well as clergy. Physicians and magistrates began to be considered as suitable investigators of claims of miraculous fasting (Brumberg, 1988). The term 'anorexia mirabilis', coined by François Boisser de Sauvages de la Croix in the late eighteenth century (Brumberg, 1988), itself indicates this transitional point from theological to medical explanations of fasting.

This transition from religious to medical formulations of self-starvation did not occur instantaneously. Yet the juncture nevertheless marks the beginning of a 'radical discontinuity' in discursive constructions of self-starvation as 'scientific' theories began to displace theological interpretations. With the ascendency of the medical profession, the 'flesh was brought down to the level of the organism' (Foucault, 1979: 117) so that by the end of the eighteenth century a new *medical* technology had emerged which 'escaped ecclesiastical institutions without being truly independent of the thematics of sin' (Foucault, 1979: 116). And as medical interpretations of self-starvation became detached from previous religious formulations, constructions of fasting as miraculous or divine were increasingly viewed as ideological. Hence the scepticism with which doctors often wrote of 'fasting girls' (see Smith-Rosenberg and Rosenberg, 1973/1974). Hammond (1879, cited in Strober, 1986), for example, criticized the religiosity of many early descriptions of 'fasting girls' as unscientific, claiming that they were probably cases of deception, fraud or organic disease.

This juncture in which self-starvation became a more medical than religious concern is also often taken as 'the beginning' of the history of anorexia. A number of late seventeenth-century accounts of 'wasting' through lack of appetite have been presented as early medical descriptions of anorexia nervosa. One such retrospectively diagnosed case (see Strober, 1986) is a description by the physician Fabricius in 1611 of a 13-year-old girl said to have lived without food or drink for three years:

> She was of a sad and melancholy countenance; her body was sufficiently fleshy except only her belly which was compressed so as that it seemed to cleave to her back-bone . . . As for excrements she voided none; and did so abhor all kinds of food. That when one, who came to see her privately, put a little sugar in her mouth she immediately swooned away.
>
> (cited by Strober, 1986: 232)

Although many other contemporaneous cases of self-starvation were still interpreted religiously this account is recognizably medical. That Fabricius was a physician and that he documents the girl's physical condition also guarantees its medical status. This is clearly an example of early medical discourse. Yet, contrary to assertions that 'the clinical resemblance to true anorexia nervosa is self-evident' (Strober, 1986: 232), it is not so clearly a description of anorexia nervosa as it is presented in late twentieth-century medical and psychological literature. Although the girl's belly was described as very 'compressed' her body, whatever its weight, was construed as otherwise 'sufficiently fleshy'. As with earlier religious accounts of fasting, and in contrast with modern descriptions of anorexia, there is an emphasis on apparently continued health despite self-starvation: 'what was most wonderful was, that this maid walked up and down, played with other girls, danced and did all other things that were done by girls of her age' (cited by Strober, 1986: 232).

Similarly, 'to swoon away' when 'a little sugar' is put in the mouth is not characteristic of current descriptions of anorexia and there is no mention in the text of the now central characteristics of fear of fatness or body-image distortion.

Other seventeenth- and eighteenth-century reports that have also been presented as early medical descriptions of anorexia nervosa include Hobbes' *Medical lectures and clinical aphorisms* (1668), Reynolds' (1669) *A discourse on prodigious abstinence* (see Bliss 1982) and Whytt's (1767) discussion of 'nervous atrophy' (see Dowse, 1881). Most commonly, however, it is Richard Morton's *Phthisiologica: or, a treatise of consumption* (1689/1694) that is credited as the earliest report of anorexia in the medical literature (Bruch, 1974). Many historians of anorexia (e.g. Tolstrup, 1990; Waltos, 1986) describe this as the first detailed, comprehensive and easily recognizable description of anorexia nervosa. In *Phthisiologica*, Morton described the cases of several women and one man who were 'wasted' with 'nervous atrophy or consumption'. Mr Dukes' Daughter, he wrote,

> fell into a total suppression of her Monthly Courses from a multitude of Cares and Passions of her Mind . . . From which time her Appetite began to abate, and her Digestion to be bad; her flesh also began to be flaccid and loose, and her looks pale . . . I do not remember that I did ever in all my practice see one, that was conversant with the Living so much wasted with the greatest degree of a Consumption (like a Skeleton only clad with skin) yet there was no Fever, but on the contrary a coldness of the whole Body; no cough, or difficulty with breathing, not an appearance of any other distemper of the lungs, or any other entrails.
>
> (cited in Bliss and Branch, 1960: 10–11; Waltos, 1986: 1–2)

Morton categorizes this 'nervous atrophy' as a form of 'consumption' or 'phthisis', that is, as a 'wasting' disease, characterized by a lack of appetite, amenorrhea, extreme emaciation and an absence of fever, cough or other 'distemper'. However, it does not follow from this, as some historians of anorexia have argued, that Morton had identified a disease in the modern medical sense or that the 'distemper' he describes is 'anorexia nervosa'.

> A Nervous Atrophy or Consumption is a wasting of Body without any remarkable Fever, Cough, or Shortness of Breath; but it is attended with a want of Appetite, and a bad digestion, upon which there follows a Languishing Weakness of Nature, and a falling away of the Flesh every day more and more . . . The Causes which dispose the Patient to this Disease, I have for the most part observed to be violent Passions of the Mind, the intemperate drinking of Spirituous Liquors, and an unwholesome Air, by which it is no wonder if the Tone of the Nerves, and the Temper of the Spirits are destroy'd.
>
> (cited by Bliss and Branch, 1960: 9–10)

Georgian conceptualizations of disease were clearly rather different from modern medical and psychological theories. As L.P. Hartley (1953: 1) noted, 'The past is a foreign country; they do things differently there.'

Pre-modern medicine lacked a systematic nosological system and theory of disease. Diagnosis depended on patients' accounts of illness, thus creating an ongoing dialogue between lay folklore and the 'scientific' theories of the emerging medical profession (Porter and Porter, 1988). A multiplicity of explanatory models existed. Among these, the theory of 'humours', a preoccupation with 'nerves' and 'nervousness', the effects of the imagination on the body, the dangers of the environment, and an holistic concern with 'constitution' predominated (Rousseau, 1991). Traditional humoral theory, for example, posited that temperament, physique and health were 'all determined by the same fluctuating equilibrium of internal fluids, spirits, appetites and "souls"' (Porter and Porter,

1988: 201). Diseases were not understood as 'generic fixed entities' but were frequently explained in terms of temporary concentrations of humours. Hence one disease could mutate into another (Porter and Porter, 1988). Any illness could be caused by humours, by the imagination or by nervousness (Stainbrook, 1965). Sickness was often seen as the sign of a 'vitiated constitution'. It was deep-seated and, however trivial, could involve the whole body and the whole person (Porter and Porter, 1988).

Morton's medical discourse thus differs significantly from modern medical discourse. In the eighteenth century 'consumption' or 'phthisis' denoted a state rather than a thing (Porter and Porter, 1988). For Morton it was the state of 'wasting' that constituted the disease. His distinction between 'nervous' and other consumptions is not equivalent, therefore, to a modern differentiation of TB from 'anorexia nervosa'. Moreover, consumption indicated a 'broken constitution' (Porter and Porter, 1988). Nerves or imagination could play a part in 'organic' as well as 'nervous' consumption (Stainbrook, 1965). Morton attributes the cause of 'nervous atrophy' to 'Violent Passions of the Mind' (as well as alcohol and 'unwholesome Air') which destroy 'the Tone of the Nerves', 'the Temper' and 'the Spirits'. He thus produces a typically Georgian holistic explanation of disease to which the modern distinction between psychological and somatic causation are not applicable. Even until the end of the nineteenth century, 'nervous disorders' referred as much to physically diseased or inflamed nerve fibres as to psychopathology (Rousseau, 1991). Dowse (1881: 96), for example, wrote of 'inflamed, irritated, or softened ... pneumogastric nerves' causing a lack of hunger. To describe Morton's account as heralding contemporary psychosomatic thought is, therefore, anachronistic, since the discourses within which Georgian physicians construed the relationship between mind and body differed significantly from those that prevail today. For them 'self and soma [were] at least synergistically united, if not the same. Their mutual interplay, through experience, result[ed] in their mutual transformation' (Porter and Porter, 1988: 201).

In short, the early medical texts of Fabricius (1611/1646), Morton (1689/1694), Whytt (1767), Naudeau (1789) or Willan (1790), so often presented as more or less definite descriptions of anorexia nervosa, are more appropriately understood as early medical explanations of fasting (see Dinicola, 1990; Brumberg, 1988). Attempts at retrospective diagnosis inevitably deny the differing cultural significances of self-starvation as well as the considerable differences and discontinuities in medical 'knowledge'. They also gloss over the substantive differences in descriptions. Attributing differences in presented symptomatology to faulty observation and lack of medical expertise of earlier physicians problematically privileges current medical and psychological knowledge as transhistorical truth, and presumes (rather than demonstrates) that 'anorexia nervosa' has always existed as a 'disease entity' independently of medical knowledge or cultural context.

THE SURFACES OF EMERGENCE OF ANOREXIA NERVOSA

Hypochondria and nervousness in the eighteenth and nineteenth centuries

Medical accounts of 'wasting', fasting or lack of appetite continued to appear throughout the eighteenth and nineteenth centuries with various explanations. Whytt (1767), for example, a famous 'nerve doctor', attributed food aversion to disturbances in the gastric nerves (Dowse, 1881). Marce (1860) wrote of a 'form of hypochondriacal delirium occurring consecutive to dyspepsia and characterized by refusal of food', which he claimed was very common in 'young girls . . . at the period of puberty'. Mesmer and Naudeau similarly discussed food aversion as a nervous complaint (Strober, 1986). In fact, from the mid-seventeenth century, and through the nineteenth, medics paid great attention to the stomach and its disorders (Porter and Porter, 1988). Numerous disorders were attributed to the stomach, which was often regarded as 'the crucible of the metabolism', the body being regarded as 'a through-put machine, requiring efficient digestion and speedy waste disposal' (ibid.:144). Hence, Thomas Trotter, considered the stomach to be

> endued by nature, with the most complex properties of any of the body, and forming a centre of sympathy between our corporal and mental parts, of more exquisite qualifications than even the brain itself.
> (Trotter, 1807: 203, cited in Porter and Porter, 1988: 144)

Georgian society described itself as plagued by various gastro-intestinal disorders such as colic, hysteric colic, biliousness, 'gouty wind', gastralgia and vomiting (Porter and Porter, 1988). And these 'horrors of digestion' were construed not as local disorders but as disorders of the whole constitution. Cases of food aversion or of wasting through want of appetite thus occurred in a context in which disorders of the stomach evidently had particular historically specific cultural significance. Indeed, 'hypochondria' – defined until the turn of the eighteenth century as a somatic abdominal disorder accompanied by multiple symptoms moving around the body – was a deeply enculturated illness (Rousseau, 1991; Porter and Porter, 1988).

During the Georgian era traditional humoral theory began to be replaced by a Lockian empiricist theory of the person 'which restated the synthesis of body and consciousness via the notions of sensations and the nervous system' (Porter and Porter, 1988: 201; Stainbrook, 1965). Increasing importance was accorded to 'sensibility' and a capacity for 'exquisite feeling', including suffering, was often viewed as the hallmark of superior people (Scull, 1983). In addition, Lockians accorded considerable importance to the role of the imagination in health. The physician John Moore, for instance, wrote of epidemics of 'imaginary complaints' (Hunter and Macalpine, 1963). Nervous delicacy, hypersensitivity and pain constituted a particular socio-cultural identity (Porter and Porter, 1988;

Rousseau, 1991). This nervous delicacy, especially common in women but also existing in men, was epitomized in the figure of 'the hypochondriac' (Scull, 1983). Hypochondria, or the grand 'English malady' (Scull, 1983) became increasingly defined by the multiple secondary symptoms of the body rather than somatic abdominal disorder. It became a protean *'malade imaginaire'* (Jackson, 1986) and a fashionable disease (Adaire, 1790; Rousseau, 1976).

This rise of the hypochondriac as 'a cultural type' was a socially significant process; first, because it was associated with a 'medical consumerism' and thus illustrates how the development of medicine was a part of the wider development of 'market society', and, second, the figure of 'the hypochondriac' was profoundly associated with the rise of individualism in bourgeois capitalist society. Suffering facilitated and legitimated the assertion of one's 'individuality', providing a form of social bargaining power (Porter and Porter, 1988). That is, hypochondria, and more generally 'nerves', formed an integral part of Georgian society – economically, politically, culturally and medically. Hence, it was not so much that scientific progress produced a cultural concern with nerves but rather that 'a cultural myth engulfed medical theory *itself*, privileging the nerves and exalting them as never before' (Rousseau, 1991: 42). Nervousness produced an enormous economy in terms of 'quack' and 'medical' treatments, spa town industries and doctors' fees (Rousseau, 1991). Nerves, as the mark of superior people (Scull, 1983), segregated social ranks anew and constituted an integral part of the development of bourgeois individualism. The concept of nerves was so deeply enculturated in Georgian society that it was 'metaphorized' to describe the social body, and social commentators like Samuel Johnson sought to define a 'nervous style' of literature (Rousseau, 1991). Henry Mackenzie's claim that 'this is an Age of Sensibility' (quoted in Rousseau, 1991: 40) and Jane Austen's depiction of *Sense and Sensibility* (1811) both illustrate the deeply enculturated nature of 'nerves'.

This is not to argue that there was a universal sympathy for hypochondriacs. There is evidence of stigmatizing and ridicule as well as romanticizing sympathy and individualizing connotations (Porter and Porter, 1988). What is important, however, in terms of a genealogy of 'anorexia', is that 'nervous disorder', epitomized by 'hypochondria', was a profoundly significant cultural concept.

Inevitably theories of nerves did not remain static through the eighteenth and nineteenth centuries. However, medical concern with hypochondria, already institutionally fixed throughout Europe by the eighteenth century, continued to grow throughout the nineteenth century (Rousseau, 1991). As late as 1893 Sir William Gull is attributed with describing the stomach as 'a mad organ' (Robinson, 1893: 1381), and reports of 'hysterical vomiting' were quite common.[4]

'Nervousness' and particularly 'hypochondria' – historically associated with gastric disorder and increasingly viewed as 'nervous' – were highly significant concepts of the surface of emergence (see Foucault, 1972) or cultural and discursive context in which 'anorexia nervosa' would emerge as a distinct disease entity.

Gendered nerves and hysteria in the eighteenth and nineteenth centuries

A second facet of eighteenth- and nineteenth-century medical culture that is relevant to a genealogy of anorexia is the way in which nerves were gendered so that nervousness was increasingly feminized (see Rousseau, 1991). The medical and cultural milieu in which anorexia nervosa was to emerge was one in which the socio-historical affinity between 'woman' and pathology was particularly apparent. This relationship was evident in the cult of 'female invalidism'; in the concepts of hysteria, neurasthenia, chlorosis and in the pathologization of the female body.[5] Puberty, menstruation, pregnancy, childbirth and menopause were considered to be both causes of illness and pathological in themselves (Smith-Rosenberg and Rosenberg, 1973/1974). The female reproductive system was thus alleged to render woman 'a natural invalid' and, moreover, to determine feminine nature in general (Ehrenreich and English, 1974: 25). It was to the ovaries that woman owed her 'artfulness and dissimulation', but also her 'physical perfection . . . all that is great, noble and beautiful, all that is voluptuous, tender and endearing' (Bliss, cited by Ehrenreich and English, 1974: 30). 'Feminine nature' was thus considered to be determined by the female reproductive system and was thereby inextricably linked with sickness and mental instability. Hence, S.W. Mitchell (1888) claimed that 'the man who does not know sick women does not know women' (quoted by Veith, 1965: 220). In nineteenth-century scientific medical discourse, woman's 'natural biology' was discursively (ideologically) constructed in such a way as to render women apparently incapable of surviving the sexual equality demanded by the suffrage movements (Sayers, 1982). This theoretical divergence of the sexes that rendered 'woman' increasingly sickly functioned as a convenient strategy for resisting women's demands for equal employment, education and suffrage and for dismissing such demands as manifestations of female pathology in themselves (see Sayers, 1982).

It was the concept of hysteria that epitomized this increasingly prominent notion of 'feminine nervousness' (Showalter, 1985). And, like 'hypochondria', 'hysteria' constituted an integral part of the fashionable language of 'nervous disease' of the eighteenth and nineteenth centuries (Rousseau, 1976; Scull, 1983). Since Egyptian (Strong, 1989) and Greek antiquity (Shafter, 1989), hysteria had been defined as an authentic somatic disease of women in which the 'wandering womb' rose up, affecting various parts of the body and finally constricting the throat in 'globus hystericus' (Veith, 1965; Micale, 1990). Hysteria was thus constituted as a *fundamentally* gendered disorder (Showalter, 1985). By the eighteenth century, however, the term was breaking from its etymological origins and increasingly denoted 'the volatile physical symptoms associated with hypersensitivity' (Porter and Porter, 1988: 209). Morton Prince (1895, quoted by Stainbrook, 1965: 13), for example, concurring with French psychiatry, argued that 'it is evident that we must look for the origins of hysteria in the brain or mind itself and not in irritations from distant parts'.

One consequence of this development was that men as well as women might be diagnosed hysterical (e.g. Cavafy, 1874). Nevertheless, 'hysteria' continued to be viewed as a 'quintessentially female malady' (Showalter, 1985). This was partly because, as late nineteenth-century medical debate demonstrates, the dissociation of 'hysteria' from 'uterine irritation' was not entirely decisive. Many medics continued to attribute all manner of illness in women to 'disease of the womb'. Dr M.E. Dirix for example, asserted in 1869 that

> women are treated for diseases of the stomach, liver, kidney, heart, lung etc., yet in most instances, these diseases will be found, on due investigation, to be no disease at all, but merely the symptoms of one disease, namely, a disease of the womb.
>
> (cited by Ehrenreich and English, 1974: 29–30)

Thus, de Berdt Hovell, campaigning against the continued use of the term 'hysteria', berated other medics for their adherence to the 'heresy of uterine irritation in connection with the hysteric hypothesis' (1888b: 597) and questioned the grounds on which 'examining the patient with the speculum' was still 'gravely advocated in all cases of hysteria' (1873: 873). The historical connection between hysteria and the womb thus continued to have some influence on medical conceptualizations of women. And, even as this influence diminished, hysteria remained a 'female malady', since women were assumed to have more delicate and sensitive nerves than men and therefore to be more prone to nervous disorder (e.g. Wilks, 1888). Women's 'nerves' were 'smaller and of a more delicate structure. They are endowed with greater sensibility, and, of course, are liable to more frequent and stronger impressions from external agents or mental influences' (Tracy, 1860: xv, cited in Smith-Rosenberg and Rosenberg, 1973/1974: 334).

Paradoxically, this theory which disputed the etymologically determined exclusive femininity of hysteria succeeded in increasing the hysterization of 'woman'. Woman's entire nervous system, rather than one organ, became pathologized. The new medical 'technologies' that began to emerge in the eighteenth century hysterized the female body so that it was '*thoroughly saturated with sexuality*; whereby it was integrated into the sphere of medical practices, by reason of a pathology intrinsic to it; whereby finally, it was placed in organic communication with the social body' (Foucault, 1979: 104, my emphasis). It was now not only woman's womb but her entire nervous system that was hysterized.

In addition, during the nineteenth century mental and 'moral' factors began to be viewed as causes of hysteria and nervous disorder (Rousseau, 1991; Stainbrook, 1965). It had been theorized that hysteria resulted from bodily conditions such as 'taut' or disordered nerves, and this concept of 'taut nerves' was then metaphorized to signify a pathologized mentality. Hence, nineteenth-century medics increasingly explained hysteria as a consequence of mental weakness, of suppressed feelings, especially of sexual desire, as evidenced in psychoanalytic theories of hysteria (e.g. Freud and Breuer, 1895). Yet, whether because 'she' was dominated by her reproductive organs, because 'her' nervous system was so delicate, or because 'she' suppressed her feelings and was mentally weak, 'woman' was construed as especially prone to nervous disorders, particularly hysteria (Showalter, 1985).

The nervous or hysterical woman was not, however, the only conceptualization of 'woman'. Indeed working-class and immigrant women were frequently excluded from 'nervous femininity'. Whereas upper- and middle-class women were allegedly invalids, working-class and immigrant women were considered capable of enduring severe deprivation and continual hard work without ill effects (Veith, 1965). In addition, social reformers such as Mary Wollstonecraft or J.S. Mill presented alternative, more positive images of women (Showalter, 1985). And women physicians like Mary Livermore (cited by Ehrenreich and English, 1974: 25) argued against 'the monstrous assumption that woman is a natural invalid' as others disputed the reality of nervousness more generally (Porter and Porter, 1988).

Nevertheless 'the hysteric' was a deeply enculturated figure, particularly during the late nineteenth century, 'the golden age of hysteria' (Showalter, 1985: 129). The concept of hysteria was thoroughly imbricated in the theoretical divergence of the sexes over the eighteenth and nineteenth centuries and in the Victorian preoccupation with, and regulation of, sex and sexuality (Foucault, 1979). 'Hysteria' and 'gendered nerves' played a central part in women's oppression. Along with neurasthenia, chlorosis and other female nervous disorders, hysteria was constituted as a cultural bar to education and suffrage for women (Sayers, 1982; Smith-Rosenberg and Rosenberg, 1973/1974). 'Grant suffrage to women', one Massachusetts legislator claimed, 'and you will have to build insane asylums in every county, and establish divorce courts in every town. Women are too nervous and hysterical to enter politics' (cited in Ehrenreich and English, 1974: 22).

The establishment of the first colleges for women similarly precipitated numerous warnings of the injurious effects education would supposedly have on the female reproductive system (Ehrenreich and English, 1974). Herbert Spencer (1896), for example, declared that 'the deficiency of reproductive power [of upper class women] may be reasonably attributed to the overtaxing of their brains – an overtaxing which produces serious reactions on the physique', including 'absolute sterility', an 'earlier cessation of childbearing' and an inability to breastfeed (cited by Sayers, 1982: 8).

Medical discourse on hysteria, in continual dialogue with popular culture, thus played a very considerable part in the regulation of gender, in the 'cult of female invalidism' and the fashionability of female debility (Douglas-Wood, 1973), in determining women's 'proper' social role (Sayers, 1982) and indeed in constituting the category of 'woman' (Foucault, 1979). The discursive production of hysteria as a 'quintessentially female malady' was therefore inextricable from the gender politics of the times (see Sayers, 1982).

In short, the cultural and medical milieu in which 'anorexia nervosa' was to emerge in the late nineteenth century was one that was preoccupied with sickness and especially with nervous disorders. Hypochondria and hysteria were dominant concepts, 'institutionally fixed' and culturally entrenched. In the prevailing 'nervous mythology', hypochondria provided an historical and etymological relationship between nervous and gastric disorders whilst hysteria epitomized the gendering of nerves and the cultural patriarchal construction of 'woman' as pathologically nervous and inferior.

A CONVERGENCE OF THE MEDICAL DISCOURSES ON HYSTERIA AND HYPOCHONDRIA

As both 'hysteria' and 'hypochondria' became progressively detached from their etymological roots, the two concepts appeared to converge. Both concepts increasingly denoted general and protean nervous disorder associated with hypersensitivity. And nervous disorders became increasingly feminized to the extent that some physicians claimed they were entirely limited to women (e.g. Raulin, 1758; see Rousseau, 1991). In addition, gastric disorders, including lack of appetite, constituted common symptoms of nervousness and nervous disorder (e.g. Gull, 1874; Marce, 1860) in both medical and cultural discourses. Jane Austen's portrayal of Marianne in *Sense and Sensibility* (1811) illustrates both the cultural entrenchment of feminine nervousness and the intimate relationship between nervousness and the stomach.

> Elinor . . . returned to Marianne, whom she reached just in time to prevent her from falling on the floor, faint and giddy from a long want of proper rest and food; for it was many days since she had had any appetite, and many nights since she had really slept; and now . . . the consequence of all this was felt in an aching head, a weakened stomach, and a general nervous faintness.
>
> (Austen, 1811: 154)

As Austen comments 'her sensibility was potent enough!' (ibid.: 69), evidenced both by her 'weakened stomach' and her 'nervous faintness'.

The extent of this convergence of hypochondria and hysteria was also evident in the interchangeability of the two terms and in constructions of gastric symptoms, such as vomiting, gastralgia, constipation and diarrhoea, as hysterical.[6] For instance, Louis-Victor Marce's account of 'a form of hypochondriacal delirium occurring consecutive to dyspepsia, and characterized by refusal of food' (see Silverman, 1989), evidences a discursive convergence of mental weakness, 'nervous femininity', 'hysteria', 'hypochondria' and gastric disorder.

Marce presented 'inappetency' as a common nervous symptom: 'the majority of hysterical and nervous sufferers make themselves remarkable for the slenderness of their diet, by their liking for indigestible food, and their antipathy for bread, meat, and strengthening dishes' (Marce, 1860, quoted in Silverman, 1989: 834). He described two 'very common' varieties of hypochondriacal dyspepsia – 'inappetency' and painful digestion – which occurred even though 'The stomach digests perfectly what is committed to it' (ibid.: 833) and 'was perfectly uninjured' (ibid.: 834): 'Deeply impressed, whether by the absence of appetite or by the uneasiness caused by digestion, these patients arrive at a delirious conviction that they cannot or ought not to eat. In one word, the gastric nervous disorder becomes cerebro-nervous' (ibid.: 833).

This hypochondriacal disorder thus encompasses both nervous dyspepsia and a more mental nervous disorder. The sufferers, presented as 'young girls . . . at the period of puberty' (ibid.: 833) are described as mentally weak throughout his paper. 'They' are 'predisposed to insanity from hereditary antecedents and [are] rendered still more impressionable by that profound nervous disturbance which accompanies the establishment of the menstrual functions' (ibid.: 833). 'They' are in 'a state of partial delirium' and their 'intellectual energy' and 'affective sentiments' are debilitated (ibid.: 833). Without relinquishing the classical connection between female reproductive functions and hysteria/nervousness, Marce consolidates the femininity of this nervous disorder by constructing an emotionally and mentally weak woman as the sufferer. And, like other physicians of the nineteenth century (see Ehrenreich and English, 1974), in constructing a mentally weak female patient Marce simultaneously produces the 'necessity' of patriarchal 'moral ascendency' over 'her' (Silverman, 1989: 834).

THE DISCURSIVE CONSTRUCTION OF 'HYSTERICAL ANOREXIA'

By the nineteenth century the culturally embedded medical concepts of hypochondria and hysteria were converging and the nervous gastric symptoms of 'inappetency' and gastralgia had become distinctly feminized. The discursive construction of 'hypochondria' discussed above, for example, was remarkably similar to the constructions of 'hysterical anorexia' and 'anorexia nervosa' presented only a few years later by Lasegue (1873a) and Gull (1874).

The medical texts in which 'anorexia nervosa' was first constituted began with an article, 'De l'anorexie hystérique', by the French professor of medicine, Charles Lasegue (1873a) in a French journal *Archives générales de médicine*. The *Lancet*'s summary of this paper (anon, 1873c) gave it the title 'Hysteric anorexia', again denoting that 'the malady' was hysterical: ' . . . Dr. Lassegue [*sic*], in concluding, insists on the important part played in certain forms of hysteria by the mental disposition of the patient, and on the intimate relation between hysteria and hypochondria' (anon, 1873c: 49).

'Hysteric anorexia' was thus presented as a form of hysteria in which 'the mental disposition of the patient' played an important part. That 'the disease' was hysterical immediately signified that it was a 'feminine' disorder, whilst the reference to patients' 'mental disposition' was typical of the increasing concern with the role of mental or 'moral' factors in nervous disorders. Significantly, 'hysteric anorexia' was also construed as intimately related to hypochondria, thus suggesting again a convergence of these two culturally entrenched concepts in this newly emerging disorder.

This convergence of hysteria and hypochondria, of feminine nervousness and nervous gastric disorder, was again apparent in the abridged translation of Lasegue's article which appeared in the *Medical Times and Gazette* two months later (Lasegue, 1873b). Here 'hysterical anorexia' was presented as a form of 'hysteria of the gastric centre' and was located amongst the numerous 'disturbances of the digestive organs which supervene during the course of hysteria' (ibid.: 265). Such disturbances included 'incoercible vomiting, . . . gastric pains, . . . constipations or diarrhoea', along with 'curious perversions of appetite', particularly food aversion (ibid.: 265). 'Hysterical anorexia' was itself described as a peculiar 'dyspepsia' (ibid.: 368) involving 'sensations, which in more than one particular resemble the impressions of hypochondriacs' (ibid.: 367). The text thus suggests a convergence of hypochondriacal and hysterical symptoms such that the two disorders were presented as intimately related and nervous gastric symptoms were construed here as symptoms of hysteria. However, whilst the link with hypochondria was explicit, the predominant emphasis throughout the article was on the hysterical nature of 'hysterical anorexia'. The paper opens by justifying itself, presenting it as part of a wider project to understand hysteria.

> In my opinion we shall never succeed in composing the hysterical affections but by the separate study of each symptomatic group. After this preliminary analytic labour, we may collect the fragments, and from them reproduce the whole disease . . . The object of this memoir is to make known one of the forms of hysteria of the gastric centre which is of sufficient frequency for its description not to be, as too readily happens, the artificial generalization of a particular case.
>
> (Lasegue, 1873b: 265)

'Hysterical anorexia' was construed as worthy of attention not so much because it was itself important, but more because it was a 'symptomatic group' of 'sufficient frequency' to warrant its description as part of an attempt to understand hysteria as a whole. And throughout the article the 'hysterical' nature of the condition was repeatedly asserted. It was, for instance, attributed to 'the reflex impression of a perversion of the central nervous system' associated with 'certain cerebral conditions' (ibid.: 266); a construction typical of medical discourse on hysteria. And, typically also of this time, Lasegue's account evidences the break with traditional theory on hysteria, locating the cause in the nervous system and 'nervous' emotions rather than the womb.

Many other aspects of this illness are similarly construed as hysterical. For example, Lasegue reports that 'The repugnance for food continues slowly progressive', but that for 'weeks or months' the patient's health does not appear to suffer. 'There is no emaciation' (ibid.: 266) despite the lack of food, and this is explained as typically hysterical:

The power of resistance of the general health in the hysterical is too well known for astonishment being excited at seeing them support without injury a systematic inanition to which robust women could not be exposed with impunity.

(Lasegue, 1873b: 266)

What had once been construed as a miraculous ability to exist without food was now explained as typical of 'the hysteric's' resilient constitution. The formulation also suggests that, whilst 'the hysteric' was by definition ill, she was also more healthy than other women. 'Hysterical anorexia' is thus constructed, as hypochondria also was (Porter and Porter, 1988), as a *maladie imaginaire*. However, it is not only the patient's resilience but also her eventual 'inanition' that is presented as hysterical: 'In the end the tolerance of the economy, marvellous as it is, becomes exhausted, and the disease enters upon its third stage' (Lasegue, 1873b: 368). This 'stage' is characterized by a variety of new symptoms, including 'emaciation', 'inanition' or 'cachexia', 'obstinate constipation', 'anaemic cardio-vascular souffle' and 'neuralgias' (ibid.: 368). However, the first mentioned of these symptoms is amenorrhea. Menstrual irregularities, a preoccupation of nineteenth-century medics (Porter and Porter, 1988) and a standard symptom of hysteria (Ussher, 1991; Showalter, 1985), again confirmed the 'hysterical nature' of this 'morbid condition'.

Similarly, the patient's resistance to her family's attempts – 'entreaties and menaces' – to make her eat was also presented as hysterical. The 'excess' of her family's 'insistence begets an excess of resistance' on her part. And this 'obstinacy of the hysterical' is extended to cover the entire family:

The anorexia gradually becomes the sole subject of preoccupation and conversation. The patient thus gets surrounded by a kind of atmosphere from which there is no escape during the entire day . . . Now there is another most positive law that hysteria is subject to the influence of the surrounding medium, and that the disease becomes developed and condensed so much the more as the circle within which revolve the ideas and sentiments of the patient becomes more narrowed.

(Lasegue, 1873b: 367)

This passage articulates a particular concern with the relationship between the emerging bourgeois family and hysteria. Its medicalization of the family can be seen as part of a wider strategy in which 'an entire medico-sexual regime took hold of the family milieu' (Foucault, 1979: 42). As bourgeois family relationships intensified, so the family became 'an agency for control' and was itself subject to medical regulation (Foucault, 1979: 120). This strategy included the medicalization and attempted eradication of childhood masturbation, the psychiatrization of 'peripheral' (i.e. non-reproductive) sexuality, the pathologization of birth control, the medical interventions in determining women's 'proper' role and the hysterization of women's bodies (Foucault, 1979; Sayers, 1982). Thus, it was in the 'bourgeois' family that the sexuality of children and adolescents was first problematized and feminine sexuality medicalized; it was the first to be alerted to the potential pathology of sex, the urgent need to keep it under close watch and to devise a rational technology of correction . . . It is worth remembering that the first figure to be invested by the deployment of sexuality, one of the first to be 'sexualized', was the 'idle' woman. She inhabited the outer edges of the 'world', in which she always had to appear as a value, and of the family, where she was assigned a new destiny charged with conjugal and parental obligations. Thus there emerged the 'nervous' woman, the woman afflicted with 'vapors'; in this figure, the hysterization of woman found its anchorage point.

(Foucault, 1979: 120–121)

By implicating the family in the patient's hysteria Lasegue simultaneously asserts the hysterical nature of 'hysterical anorexia', the 'moral element' of hysteria and the necessity for medical intervention in the family:

It must not cause surprise to find me always placing in parallel the morbid condition of the hysterical subject and the preoccupations of those who surround her . . . Whenever a moral element intervenes in a disease, as here it does without any doubt, the moral medium amidst which the patient lives exercises an influence which it would be equally regrettable to overlook or misunderstand.

(Lasegue, 1873b: 368)

'The bourgeois family' is thus constituted as potentially pathological and its intimacies are thoroughly medicalized. It is construed as a prime site for medical intervention, for regulating both the individual and the social body and it is profoundly imbricated in 'the hysterization of woman' (Foucault, 1979). In firmly locating 'the hysterical subject' within the family Lasegue thus asserts a medical authority over the family at the same time as consolidating the 'moral' nature of hysteria and the hysterical status of the patient.

In short, hysterical anorexia was discursively constructed as a form of gastric hysteria, intimately related to hypochondria. Its hysterical nature was, however, paramount. 'Hysterical anorexia' was constituted as a distinct 'symptomatic group' by its symptoms of hysterical gastralgia, a suppressed appetite, food aversion and eventually emaciation and inanition. 'On hysterical anorexia' was not so much the differentiation of a distinct disorder as a catalogue of the ways in which this 'symptomatic complexus' was in every respect hysterical.

CONSTRUCTING THE HYSTERICAL ANOREXIC SUBJECT

Lasegue's paper articulates contemporary medical truths about the nature of the body and hysteria. The body is essentially 'nervous' and the stomach is particularly prone to nervous disorders which themselves are caused by 'cerebro-spinal diseases' and 'mental perversions'. And as it constructs a 'nervous' body and an hysterical disorder so it also constructs a sexualized body and an hysterical female patient. As we have seen, nineteenth-century medical discourse construed nerves as gendered and this gendering was epitomized in hysteria, which was feminized either through the classical theory of 'uterine irritation' or more frequently in the nineteenth century through the theory that women's nerves were more delicate and therefore more prone to disorder than were men's.

Throughout 'On hysterical anorexia', the patient is consistently presented as female. Of the eight cases on which the paper was based, all were women (Lasegue, 1873b: 368), and in discursively constructing the patient gender is paramount. Indeed, Lasegue's paper goes far beyond a technical feminization of the patient. It evidences a dialogue between medical discourse and the wider culture to produce a 'densely' gendered patient (see Riley, 1988). The discursive construction of 'woman' is at once medical and social. The typical patient is presented as

> A young girl, between fifteen and twenty years of age, suffer[ing] from some emotion which she avows or conceals. Generally it relates to some real or imaginary marriage project, to a violence done to some sympathy, or to some more or less conscient desire.
>
> (Lasegue, 1873b: 265)

This passage draws on a particular cultural 'knowledge' of women to present young girls as emotional and at least potentially hysterical. Lasegue does not differentiate this typical patient from other young women. Rather, 'her' hysterical tendencies are 'explained' precisely by her gender. The passage can thus be read as a dialogue between medical and non-medical discourses, producing a particular but unremarkable construction of 'woman-as-pathological'. And, as we have seen, this pathologized 'woman' constituted a dominant cultural and medical figure.

Having thus pathologized this unremarkable 'woman' Lasegue elaborates to construe 'her' as childlike and mentally weak. Although aged between 15 and 20 (ibid.: 265) or 18 and 32 (ibid.: 368), the patients are presented as 'young girls' who resist all attempts to make them eat because 'A single concession would transfer them from the position of patient to that of capricious children; and to this concession, in part from instinct and in part from obstinacy, they will never consent' (ibid.: 266).

The patient is thus construed as 'in part' an obstinate 'capricious' child. But 'she' is also mentally and morally weak and therefore not responsible for her actions:

> The fault does not altogether lie in a pathological vitiation of disposition. Under the influence of sensations, which in more than one particular resemble the impressions of hypochondriacs and the delirious ideas of the

65

insane, the hysterical constantly find themselves unable to resist this domination [of illness and surroundings] by a voluntary effort.

(Lasegue, 1873b: 367)

The 'hysterical' woman is thus presented as so mentally weak as to be incapable of conscious, voluntary control of her symptoms. And this mental weakness or 'perversion' is central to her diagnosis. She develops 'that mental perversion, which by itself is almost characteristic, and which justifies the name which I have proposed for want of a better – hysterical anorexia' (ibid.: 266): 'in fact the whole disease is summed up in this intellectual perversion' (ibid.: 368).

In short, Lasegue's 'typical patient' is thoroughly gendered. 'She' is produced as a woman who is at once unremarkable *and* pathological, characterized as emotional, childishly capricious and mentally perverse. Like other works on hysteria, 'On hysterical anorexia' discursively produces a gendered disorder and a pathologized woman. And in producing 'woman' as the other of adult (masculine) rationality, the paper simultaneously produces the necessity of 'moral treatment' (ibid.: 266) and the assertion of a patriarchal medical authority over the patient. The discursive emergence of 'hysterical anorexia' formed part of the wider medical *and* cultural strategy which oppressively constituted 'woman' as Other, as deviant, defective and therefore as requiring patriarchal control.

THE NOSOLOGY OF 'ANOREXIA NERVOSA' AND THE POLITICS OF 'DISCOVERY'

Lasegue's article was shortly succeeded by a paper entitled 'Anorexia hysterica (apepsia hysterica)' by Sir William Gull which he read at the October meeting of the Clinical Society in 1873 (anon, 1873b) and published as 'Anorexia nervosa (apepsia hysterica, anorexia hysterica)' a year later (Gull, 1874). As the aliases of the titles indicate, there was a nosological contention which was both medical and political. In contrast with Lasegue, Gull did not construe his paper as an attempt to understand hysteria through understanding one of its 'symptomatic groups'. Rather, he presented this condition as 'a peculiar form of disease' (Gull, 1874: 22) which he claimed he was the first to describe. His rather spurious claim rests on a passing reference to 'hysteric apepsia' made in a wide-ranging 'Address in medicine' in 1868:[7]

In the diagnosis of abdominal disease, we want an increase in the number of our more cardinal facts; . . . At present our diagnosis is mostly one of inference, from our knowledge of the liability of the several organs to particular lesions; thus we avoid the error of supposing the presence of mesenteric disease in young women emaciated to the last degree through hysteric apepsia by our knowledge of the latter affection, and by the absence of tubercular disease elsewhere.

(Gull, 1868: 175)

In his 'Address' Gull mentioned 'hysteric apepsia' to illustrate a general point about the inferential nature of diagnosis. It is only in 1873 (see anon, 1873a) that the passage is reconstructed as a 'discovery' of 'apepsia hysterica/anorexia hysterica/anorexia nervosa' that preceded Lasegue's. Significantly, however, the passage suggests a common knowledge of 'young women emaciated to the last degree through hysteric apepsia'. 'Hysteric apepsia' is presented as already part of 'our knowledge' and, like Lasegue, Gull (1868) construes hysterical gastric disorder as a familiar occurrence.

Gull's reconstituting this passage (anon, 1873a; Gull, 1874) as a discovery is significant as a professional-political strategy. It indicates a prestige in the 'discovery'. In fact, Gull's 'Address' continues to be credited as a description of 'anorexia nervosa' (e.g. Tolstrup, 1990; Waltos, 1986), and he is frequently given priority over Lasegue, at least in the English literature (see Vandereycken and Van Deth, 1989). More immediately, however, medical publications functioned as commercial advertisements for physicians (Rousseau, 1991) and Gull's claim to discovery may therefore have been economically as well as professionally advantageous.

More importantly, the prestige of 'discovery' suggests a wider strategic importance in constituting 'anorexia nervosa' as an object of medical discourse. As Foucault argues, 'no one is responsible for an emergence; no one can glory in it, since it always occurs in the interstices' of discourse (1977a: 150). It is not that either Gull or Lasegue discovered 'anorexia nervosa' through individual scientific endeavour. Rather, its 'discovery' or emergence was a discursive event made possible by the gaps *in* and the relationships *between* discourses. Anorexia emerged at the interface of medical discourses on hysteria and on nervous gastric disorders. It was constituted as a feminine nervous disorder at a time when 'the nervous woman' was a significant cultural figure (Showalter, 1985), when explanations of female nervous debility were shifting (see Rousseau, 1991) and when women were challenging their social and economic subordination (see Sayers, 1982). Anorexia could thus figure as a forum in which to debate, and therefore constitute and reconstitute, feminine nervousness.

Gull's initial term 'hysteric apepsia' denoted an inability to digest food caused by a peripheral (stomach) disorder of hysterical origins. In 1873 'the word *anorexia* had been preferred to that of *apepsia*, as more fairly expressing the facts, since what food is taken, except in the extreme stages of the disease, is well digested' (anon, 1873a: 534). Like Lasegue, Gull construed 'anorexia hysterica' as a 'want of appetite . . . due to a morbid state' (anon, 1873a: 534). And like Lasegue he also categorized it as hysterical without implying uterine causation.

He [Gull] had not observed in the special cases in question any gastric disorder to which the want of appetite could be referred. He believed that the origin was central not peripheral . . . We might call the state hysterical without committing ourselves to the strict etymological value of the word, or maintaining that the subjects of anorexia hysterica had any of the common symptoms of hysteria proper.

(anon, 1873a: 534)

Anorexia hysterica was thus differentiated from 'hysteria proper' since its cause was attributed to the central nervous system rather than the uterus. As we have seen, this nineteenth-century shift in theories of hysteria meant that it was no longer considered that only women could suffer from hysteria. This shift is presented by Gull (1874) as the reason for renaming 'anorexia hysterica' as 'anorexia nervosa'. Yet, whilst the name of this 'disorder' was changed, the standard nineteenth-century causal explanation of hysteria provided by Lasegue (1873a) was maintained. This change both consolidated Gull's claims on the disorder but it also further emphasized that 'anorexia nervosa' was not 'hysterical' in the etymological sense; that it was not to be found exclusively in women. And yet it remained markedly feminine.

CONSOLIDATING 'THE NERVOUS WOMAN'

Like Lasegue, Gull (1874) asserted an absence of organic disease and the ineffectiveness of medical treatments except 'warmth and a steady supply of food and stimulants' (ibid.: 25). The patients' physical condition was presented as 'one of simple starvation' (ibid.: 22) caused by a 'nervous' (ibid.: 23) or 'morbid mental state' (ibid.: 25). 'Anorexia nervosa' was thus constructed as a nervous disorder. Whilst it was no longer presented as hysterical, both the disorder and the patient remained profoundly gendered. Like Lasegue, Gull consistently presented his patients – Misses A, B and C – as female. And, whilst 'the disease occurs in males as well as females' (ibid.: 25–26), the construction of this nervous pathology centred upon a construction of pathologized femininity that was cultural as well as medical: 'That mental states may destroy appetite is notorious, and it will be admitted that young women at the ages named are specially obnoxious to mental perversity' (ibid.: 25).

'Anorexia nervosa' was caused by 'mental perversity' which was simply a characteristic of young women. The passage feminizes this nervous disorder by deploying a discursive construction of 'woman' as 'specially obnoxious to mental perversity'. As in 'On hysterical anorexia', patients are not differentiated from other young women but are pathologized precisely by their gender. 'They' are pathologically nervous with 'peevish tempers' and feelings of jealousy (ibid.: 23), 'wilful patients . . . persons of unsound mind . . . Mind weakened. Temper obstinate' (ibid.: 26). Gull clearly had little respect or sympathy for his female patients, or for women in general.

Interestingly, Gull is often praised today for his understanding of 'the essential psychogenic element' of anorexia (Tolstrup, 1990: 2) and its 'emotional etiology' (Waltos, 1986: 3). Historians of anorexia have even discussed the above passage without commenting on its obnoxious portrayal of women. Strober (1986: 234), for example, commends Gull for noting the 'preponderance of females, and significant psychological component'. Clearly there is some continuity of this nineteenth-century construction of denigrated and pathologized femininity into the late twentieth century. How confident can we be, then, that the misogyny which so clearly suffused nineteenth-century texts does not also inform the more 'scientific' accounts of anorexia today?

In constructing a nervous female patient of weak mind and pathological obstinacy, Gull, like Lasegue, simultaneously produced the necessity of asserting a medical authority in this distinctly gendered doctor–patient relationship. Hence, 'The inclination of the patient must in no way be consulted' (Gull, 1874: 24) and the 'restless activity referred to is also to be controlled' (ibid.: 25):

> these wilful patients are often allowed to drift their own way into a state of extreme exhaustion, when it might have been prevented by placing them under different moral conditions. The treatment required is obviously that fitted for persons of unsound mind. The patients should be fed at regular intervals, and surrounded by persons who would have moral control over them.
>
> (Gull, 1874: 26)

As 'anorexia nervosa' emerged as a new object of medical discourse it brought with it further reinforcement of the supposed need for patriarchal control over women. 'Anorexia' functioned as a forum in which the pathological nature of women could be rearticulated. Whether 'hysterical' or 'nervous', the subject of 'anorexia hysterica/nervosa' was constituted as an archetypal nineteenth-century 'nervous woman'. Hence, the discourses articulated in the papers of both Lasegue and Gull can be read as part of the wider discursive context in which women were constructed and regulated as other, as inferior, as 'naturally' unable to participate in any form of equality with men.

THE ENSUING DEBATE: 1874–1900

Consolidating anorexia as an object of medical discourse

The debate that followed the publication of Lasegue's and Gull's seminal papers was significant in consolidating 'anorexia nervosa' as a legitimate object of medical discourse. In the discussion of Gull's presentation at the Clinical Society (reported in anon, 1873a), Drs Quain, Greenhow, Carter, Thompson, Smith and Edis all confirmed the reality of 'the form of disease described by Sir William Gull' (ibid.: 535). Seven years later, Dr Dowse's report of a case of 'anorexia nervosa' (Dowse, 1881; anon, 1881b), and his discussion of those cases reported by Drs Gull, Fenwick, Winslow, Wilks and Johnson further reified this newly emerged diagnostic entity in the contemporary medical discourse.[8] A further case of 'anorexia nervosa' published by Gull in 1888 prompted a flurry of debate in the medical press which again consolidated the legitimacy of 'anorexia nervosa' as an object of medical discourse. Between 17 March and 19 May 1888, three case reports, one note, six letters and one editorial on 'anorexia nervosa' appeared in the *Lancet*, and by the 1890s articles on 'anorexia nervosa' appeared fairly regularly in the medical press.[9]

This public debate reified 'anorexia nervosa' as a distinct disease entity, producing it as a familiar or even common disorder among women and thereby fixing it as a legitimate object of medical discourse. But the debate was also significant in shaping and consolidating the construction of its particular characteristics and causes, and in elucidating the nuances and ideological connotations of its construction.

Confirming femininity and symptomatology

One point of consensus in this sometimes vociferous debate was the femininity of 'anorexia nervosa'. With the exceptions of Fenwick's 'young man of 19 years' (see Dowse, 1881: 96), and Drummond's 'neurotic young man of 25' (anon, 1896: 7) all the reported cases were female. Although younger cases were reported (Collins, 1894; Marshall, 1895), the typical patients were young (often middle-class) women. And this gendering of 'anorexia nervosa' was repeatedly stressed:

> The patients are generally young girls from fourteen and upwards, though we have known a striking case at a much earlier age.
>
> (anon, 1888: 584)

> ... the subjects of this affection are mostly of the female sex, although it may occasionally be found in males, and Dr. Fenwick states that it is much more common among the wealthier classes.
>
> (Dowse, 1881: 96)[10]

There was also a general consensus on the symptomatology of 'anorexia nervosa'; that it was characterized by an aversion to food which was frequently attributed at least initially to stomach pains (rather than to any fear of fatness or pursuit of thinness) on the part of the patient.

> ... originally, on account of pain, she had been taking insufficient food until she had really starved herself into her present condition ... She stated that food, even in small quantity, caused her a feeling of fullness and pain in the stomach.
>
> (Mackenzie, 1888: 614)

The subsequent emaciation and other symptoms of starvation such as constipation and amenorrhea were construed as effects of starvation and it was repeatedly asserted that there was no organic disease to which the disorder could be attributed:

> Careful examination failed to reveal any signs of disease in the chest,

abdomen, and fundi.

(Mackenzie, 1888: 613)

On examination she was found to be extremely emaciated, but there were no signs of organic disease.

(Marshall, 1895: 149)

Both the absence of organic disease and the frequently reported 'restlessness' of the patients (e.g. anon, 1888; Edge, 1888; Playfair, 1888) were presented as indications of the 'nervous' nature of the anorexia. However, the nature of this 'nervousness' was a subject of contentious debate.

The politics of nerves: debating causes, classification and treatment

Both Lasegue and Gull had asserted that 'anorexia hysterica/nervosa' was in part caused by a 'perversion' of the central nervous system. And several authors developed this construction to produce anorexia as 'a distinct form of disease, having its seat in nerves of the stomach' (Myrtle, 1888: 899) or 'a functional neurosis' caused by 'a profound alteration of the nervous system' (Playfair, 1888: 817). Dowse (1881: 9; see also anon, 1888), for example, suggested 'that in many of these cases there is some functional derangement of the pneumogastric nerve, such in fact as may warrant the use of the term "pneumogastric neurose" [*sic*]'.

'Anorexia nervosa' was thus construed to be the result of diseased nerves. But it was also associated with 'mental perversion' and many texts (e.g. Dowse, 1881; de Berdt Hovell, 1873) emphasized psychological as well as physiological causation. Physiological and psychological explanations were not presented as mutually exclusive and were indeed often merged. Playfair (1888: 817–818), for example, attributed 'so-called anorexia nervosa' to 'this age of culture, overstrain and pressure' and 'moral causes', as well as to an altered nervous system, writing that he had

> seen many instances in young girls which have followed severe study for some higher examinations for women now so much in vogue. Other common causes of an analogous kind are domestic bereavement, money losses, disappointments in love, strain of over-athletic work . . .

(Playfair, 1888: 818)

His account is thus typical of the contemporary medical 'theorizing' about the consequences of allowing women an education (see Sayers, 1982). But it also illustrates a combination of a 'scientific', 'biomedical' discourse on nerves with more psychological and context-oriented discourses about the effects of the social and domestic environment upon 'mentality'. Authors argued over whether 'anorexia' was hysterical, neurasthenic or nervous. What varied, however, were not so much the explanations of physical causations as the constructions of the patient's mental and 'moral' state and consequently of the treatments that she supposedly required or deserved.

71

Many texts consolidated the initial construction of 'anorexia nervosa' as a 'mental perversion', presenting the patient as mentally weak, childish and obstinate:

> She was rather affected in her manner and at times almost childish in her conversation.
>
> (anon, 1895a: 31)

> She had a wild, hysterical appearance . . .
>
> (Marshall, 1895: 149)

> She would cry at the slightest opposition to her wishes, and often without any apparent reason. . . . in her sullen fits at this time she would never speak to her mother except in tones of the greatest insolence.
>
> (Dowse, 1881: 96–97)

The subject of 'anorexia nervosa' was thus produced as perverse, mentally weak, irrational, obstinate and childish; even as deceitful, selfish, vain and spoilt. 'She' was, as Marshall's comment indicates, still 'hysterical'. And, in construing the patient as the other of rational masculinity, these texts simultaneously constructed and consolidated a justification for asserting medical authority and force.

> . . . she became stupid, and everything had to be administered to her forcibly.
>
> (Edge, 1888: 818)

> The cure consists of three things – rest, warmth and the regular and frequent introduction of food, in utter disregard of the anorexia of the patient.
>
> (anon, 1888: 584)

> She was ordered milk and beef-tea, eggs, pudding, and brandy mixture at regular intervals, with instructions that if the food was not taken each time it was to be administered by the stomach-pump or enema.
>
> (Mackenzie, 1888: 614)

By constituting 'the patient' as other, as pathological, 'perverse' and childish, medical discourse thus provided its 'justification' for forcibly administering often appalling 'treatments' 'in utter disregard' of the woman's objections. And these texts not only advocated force-feeding and/or enemas as a cure for anorexia: medical authority also asserted the need for 'moral control' 'fitted for persons of unsound mind' (Gull, 1874: 26). Patients were often removed from their families (Garry, 1888) and hospitalized (Mackenzie, 1888; Edge, 1888) or 'isolated' (Playfair, 1888) to this end.

The treatment advocated for 'anorexics' (e.g. Playfair, 1888) was very similar to the 'moral treatment' of 'bed rest' frequently prescribed for many female nervous disorders such as neurasthenia and hysteria (Mitchell, 1877; Charcot,

1889; Ussher, 1991) and dramatically described by Charlotte Perkins Gilman (1892) in *The Yellow Wallpaper*. These 'treatments' can thus be seen as part of a wider range of misogynistic 'cures' including bleeding the genitals and breasts, clitoridectomies and ovariotomies commonly advocated for other female nervous disorders, for hysteria in particular.[11]

Nineteenth-century medical discourse thus constructed the 'anorexic' subject as 'hysterical'; as a mentally weak and childishly obstinate woman requiring 'moral' control and often forced feeding. Within this construction a clearly moralistic theme emerged in which the patient was construed as a 'hardened neurotic sinner' (Playfair, 1888: 818) and in which treatment therefore involved punishment. This punitive aspect becomes particularly apparent in arguments against isolation. Myrtle, for example, argued that, whilst

> for the 'hardened neurotic sinner' removal from the usual and, above all, unwholesome domestic surroundings is essential . . . the subject of nervous dyspepsia is more sinned against than sinning and can be cured without imprisonment.
>
> (Myrtle, 1888: 899)

This text makes explicit the punitive aspects of isolation. And at the same time it also reconstructs the patient as a victim rather than a perpetrator of sin.

De Berdt Hovell, in his campaign against 'the pernicious doctrines' on hysteria (1873), similarly emphasized the moralistic and punitive theme that prevailed in medical discourse on hysterical and nervous disorders including 'anorexia nervosa'. He described the practice of removing patients from their families to 'so-called hysterical home[s]' as ineffective and humiliating (1888a: 949), arguing that 'the doctor has become vindictive, and desired to punish the patient . . . our province is to heal and not to judge' (1873: 873).

The moralistic condemnation of the 'anorexic' was, however, an almost inevitable consequence of the way in which 'anorexia' was discursively constituted in the majority of medical texts. Like other nervous or hysterical disorders (see Strong, 1989; Showalter, 1985), 'anorexia nervosa' was constituted as simultaneously real and fictitious. There were neurological causes, but the patient was also construed as wilful, obstinate and mentally perverse, implying that 'she' had purposely made herself ill. Anorexia nervosa, like hysteria and hypochondria, was implicitly construed as a '*maladie imaginaire*':

> [One] main difference between the hypothesis of hysteria and that of neurosis is that the first is apt to regard complaints as unreal and fictitious, the result of wilfulness and obstinacy and the aforesaid moral obliquity in various forms; while the second deals with facts instead of imputing motives. The hysterical doctrine is positively mischievous; . . . it cannot possibly treat with judgement a disease which it considers to be unreal.
>
> (de Berdt Hovell, 1873: 873)

De Berdt Hovell presented his articles as attacks upon the 'really absurd and objectionable nomenclature' of 'hysterical anorexia' (1873: 874) and the 'illogical' theory of 'Uterine Irritation' (1873: 873). However, his construction of anorexia nervosa as the result of a perturbed nervous system (1888a: 949) coincided substantively with those of his opponents. The dispute over the cause (nervous or hysterical) of anorexia fronts a more fundamental dispute about the moral status of the patient. For the majority of texts combined *both* the 'hypothesis of neurosis' and the 'hysterical doctrine' to produce anorexia nervosa as simultaneously a real neurological disorder *and* a fictitious result of young women's obstinate irrationality. They produced a 'nervous woman' who was both scientifically pathologized and viewed as morally culpable for her own pathology.

In countering 'the hysterical hypothesis', de Berdt Hovell repeatedly asserted that it was the doctors' rather than the patients' egos that were perverted, arguing that 'it is not an unfair inference that "the perversion of *ego*," which Sir W. Gull attributed to the patient, may perhaps with greater force be applied to the profession' (de Berdt Hovell, 1888b: 597). The subjects of anorexia nervosa, he argued, were neither 'mentally perverse' nor intellectually impaired.[12] 'They' were not, he argued, merely wilful but were physically and emotionally or 'morally' weakened. 'The complaints of such patients', he asserted, were 'often better founded than they appear to be . . . "They speak truth who breathe their words in pain"' (de Berdt Hovell, 1873: 874). De Berdt Hovell thus presented an alternative construction of 'anorexia nervosa' and its subjects, which highlighted the tensions of those other texts with which he takes issue. If the 'disease' was real – the result of diseased nerves – then how could it also be the fictitious product of obstinate, irrational femininity?

De Berdt Hovell certainly produced a more sympathetic construction of 'the nervous woman', advocating encouragement and kindness rather than condemnation, force and isolation (1873: 873). Nevertheless, 'woman' remained the pathologized other of rational masculinity. 'She' did not deserve blame and punishment, but her 'loss of moral power' resulted in a 'loss of moral control or . . . temper' (1873: 874) and 'implies disability and more or less incapacity of action' (1888a: 949). And his texts produced much the same aetiology for anorexia as his opponents, combining as he did a 'neurological' explanation with a construction of 'woman' as inherently weak and pathological. The subject of anorexia nervosa remained distinctly 'feminine', and pathologized 'femininity' was precisely the explanation of the disorder. Throughout the ensuing debate, in which 'anorexia nervosa' became an established object of medical discourse, the figure of the morally and physically weak woman in need of patriarchal control and medical authority was never far away.

CONCLUSION

In this chapter I have examined the medical texts in which anorexia first emerged and was then consolidated as an object of medical discourse. I have aimed to explicate the medical and cultural discourses deployed in these texts and thereby to demonstrate that 'anorexia' was not so much discovered through scientific endeavour as discursively constituted in the gaps in, and the relationships between, pre-existing medical and cultural discourses (see Foucault, 1977a). Anorexia nervosa was constituted at a point of convergence between medical discourses on hysteria, hypochondria and nervous disorders. It was produced as an hysterical/nervous disorder characterized by loss of appetite due to gastric pain or aversion to food, resulting in emaciation and other symptoms of starvation.

In examining this initial discursive production of 'anorexia nervosa', I have also sought to show how the already culturally significant figure of 'the nervous woman' was deeply imbricated in the emergence and consolidation of 'anorexia' as an object of medical discourse. As a feminine nervous disorder 'anorexia' reproduced the 'nervous woman' as the 'natural' object of medical discourse and practice. The typical patient was consistently represented as female (although male and child cases were occasionally reported), and this gendering of 'anorexia' involved both the feminization of the patient and the pathologization of 'woman' in general. 'Femininity' figured as a causal explanation in and of itself. And, in combining neurological explanations with this pathologized femininity, many texts produced 'anorexia nervosa' as simultaneously a real and fictitious illness. The subject of anorexia nervosa had a disordered nervous system but, being feminine, 'she' was also irrationally, pathologically, obstinate and mentally perverse and therefore culpable for her own illness. Throughout the debate 'femininity' and 'pathology' were merged to produce a profoundly gendered subject whose intrinsic nature requires the existence of (masculine) medical authority.

In short, by producing this genealogy I have sought to illustrate the discursive nature and the socio-historical specificity of 'anorexia nervosa'; to elucidate some of the socio-political dimensions of the discourses within which 'anorexia nervosa' first emerged. Clearly the figure of 'woman as invalid', so deeply imbricated in nineteenth-century medical discourse, is a socio-historically specific construction. The medical and cultural discourses in which 'anorexia' emerged in the nineteenth century are very different from the discourses of the late twentieth century in which 'anorexia' is now constituted. However, whilst there are clear discontinuities, there are also continuities in these discourses, particularly in the discursive construction of 'woman' at the interface of medical and cultural discourses. In the following chapter it is these twentieth-century discourses surrounding 'anorexia' to which I shall turn.

4

DISCOURSING ANOREXIAS IN THE LATE TWENTIETH CENTURY

In Chapter 3 I examined how 'anorexia nervosa' first came to emerge as an object of nineteenth-century medical discourse, exploring how, with the rise of science over theology, women's self-starvation was gradually taken into the remit of medical rather than ecclesiastical authority (see also Brumberg, 1986). As the medical profession established itself as a source of secular authority, so it also developed an increasing array of knowledges and technologies by which it classified, explained, treated and regulated the population. And, with the concomitant rise of the bourgeois family, sexuality and gender featured as prominent targets of medical discipline (Foucault, 1979) such that 'woman', particularly white middle-class woman, was repeatedly constituted as a pathological category (Showalter, 1985). During the nineteenth century, explanations for women's supposed pathological nature were shifting, however, and 'anorexia nervosa' emerged as a distinct disease entity at precisely this juncture in time. The discourse on hysteria was detaching itself from its classical origins so that women's nerves replaced their wombs in accounts of female pathology. At the same time the equally culturally entrenched discourse on hypochondria was also changing. Whilst retaining its historical reference to the stomach as a nervous organ, hypochondria increasingly referred to general 'nervousness' and to 'malades imaginaires'. And 'anorexia', I argued, emerged at the interface of these two converging discourses. It was constituted as a disease entity in which 'hysteria' and 'hypochondria' became merged and in which pathologized femininity could be rearticulated as nervous rather than classically hysterical.

Medical, psychological and cultural discourses have clearly changed substantially since the nineteenth century. The categories of woman, pathology and anorexia are now produced quite differently. In this chapter, therefore, my intention is to take this genealogy of anorexia up to the present day, to continue my analysis of these changing and proliferating institutional discourses in which 'anorexia' has been and is constituted and regulated; to explore the multiplicity of twentieth-century knowledges and 'truths' of 'anorexia nervosa'.

ANOREXIA NERVOSA: FROM NINETEENTH- TO TWENTIETH-CENTURY TEXTS

By the close of the nineteenth century 'anorexia nervosa' had become an established object of medical discourse, and throughout the twentieth century it has become the object of an increasing variety of different discourses and different disciplines which have variously constituted it as a psychosomatic, psychological and/or organic disorder (see Brumberg, 1986). During the early part of the twentieth century the problem of 'anorexia nervosa' was taken up by psychoanalysts and was thereby reconstituted as an object of psychoanalytic discourse. Psychoanalytic discourse did not seek to explain 'anorexia' in terms of (female) physical pathology. Rather it was concerned with the unconscious psychological meanings of anorexic symptoms, emphasizing the symbolic and unconscious relationship between eating and sexuality (see Brumberg, 1986). And, in general, these psychoanalytic texts constituted anorexia nervosa as a neurotic defence against sexual trauma and as a manifestation of 'poor heterosexual adjustment' (Brumberg, 1986).

The early 1920s, however, saw the growing influence of the logical positivist approach to science, in which empirically verifiable 'objective fact' was posited as the only 'true' form of scientific knowledge (see Chapter 2). Clearly psychoanalytic accounts of anorexia did not meet these positivistic criteria for Truth, and by the 1920s and 1930s explanations of anorexia as an endocrinal dysfunction came to predominate (Bruch, 1974). Following the German endocrinologist, Simmonds, self-starvation was increasingly diagnosed as Simmonds' disease (Simmonds, 1914; Tolstrup, 1990). Self-starvation, emaciation and other symptoms of 'anorexia nervosa', such as hair loss, low blood pressure and amenorrhea were attributed to atrophy of the anterior lobe of the pituitary gland (Brumberg, 1986). Biomedical discourse thus reconstituted 'anorexia nervosa' as an organic endocrinal dysfunction, as a 'natural' disease category.

Whilst biomedical discourse has continued to hold sway over the clinical realm, its hegemony has not gone unchallenged. By the beginning of the 1940s there arose an international interest in 'psychosomatic disorders', and texts on 'anorexia' again became increasingly concerned with producing theories about psychological rather than physical aetiologies (see Tolstrup, 1990) so that 'anorexia' was again discursively constituted as psychologically meaningful. Hence, by the mid-twentieth century 'anorexia' had become the object of several competing discourses, each of which constituted their object in quite different and often conflicting ways. As with the earlier historical discourses around anorexia, it was not the case that one discourse simply replaced another in a linear progression. Rather, these discourses coexisted, exerting a degree of influence over each other even as they produced different knowledges of their object. Indeed, the medical construction of 'anorexia' as a disease entity continues to exert its influence over the many discourses which in the late twentieth century have produced a plethora of different power/knowledges, different truths of 'anorexia nervosa'. In taking this genealogy of 'anorexia' up to the present day it is to this multiplicity of knowledges that I shall now turn.[1]

ANOREXIA NERVOSA AS NATURAL DISEASE CATEGORY

As we have seen, researchers have speculated about the possible organic causes of anorexia nervosa since its emergence as a disease entity at the end of the nineteenth century. De Berdt Hovell (1888a: 949), for example, considered anorexia nervosa to be 'the result of intestinal rather than uterine irritation, coupled with a perturbed state of the nervous system', whilst Myrtle (1888: 899) claimed that anorexia had 'its seat in the nerves of the stomach'. More recently, biomedical researchers have investigated a wide range of physical variables including dermatological, cardiovascular, gastro-intestinal, endocrine, neuro-physiological, thermoregulatory and musculoskeletal abnormalities, often 'in the hope of identifying those that are not epiphenomena . . . but, instead reflect underlying biological pathogenic variables' (Kaplan and Woodside, 1987: 648). Biomedical discourse thus tends to constitute 'anorexia nervosa' as a consequence of some (as yet unidentified) 'biological pathogenic variable'; as an essentially 'natural' disease category.

Anorexia has, for example, been constituted as an effect of primary hypothalamic dysfunction (Russell, 1977), of female reproductive endocrinal disturbances (see Halmi, 1987) and of abnormalities in growth hormone (GH) and GH-releasing hormone (de Marinis *et al.*, 1991). And, indeed, there is now considerable evidence of abnormalities in the hypothalamic–pituitary–adrenal axis of at least some women diagnosed as anorexic (Weiner and Katz, 1983). Similarly, several studies have found that underweight women diagnosed as anorexic demonstrate 'immature patterns' of gonadotrophins and that these patterns sometimes persist after weight recovery (see Halmi, 1987). The fact that amenorrhea is an almost universal symptom of 'anorexia' has similarly been interpreted as evidence of hormonal disturbance. Such findings, however, do not in themselves justify constructions of 'anorexia' as a natural disease category. For the balance of evidence suggests not that 'anorexia' has some physical cause but that the amenorrhea and endocrinal abnormalities associated with 'anorexia' are best understood as the physical effects of girls' and women's 'anorexic' behaviours and consequent low body weight (Wakeling, 1985). Indeed, such biomedical constructions presuppose, rather than demonstrate, that 'anorexia' is a distinct category of 'natural' disease.

Contemporary biomedical discourse has also sought to constitute 'anorexia' in terms of neurological disturbances. Again the evidence is inconclusive, with some studies (e.g. Laessle *et al.*, 1989; Krieg *et al.*, 1987) finding neurophysiological differences associated with anorexia and others not (e.g. Palazidou *et al.*, 1990). And again it seems that whatever neurological differences may exist are most economically explained as effects of malnutrition (Krieg *et al.*, 1987).

The discursive construction of 'anorexia nervosa' as a natural disease category has, then, taken a number of forms. All manner of biological factors have been investigated. Yet, despite the long-standing and wide-ranging research programme that has accompanied this biomedical discourse, there is as yet no conclusive evidence of any organic aetiology. Despite promise-laden titles such as 'The neuronal basis of compulsive behaviour in anorexia nervosa' (Mills, 1985), the 'truth claims' that anorexia has any biological basis remain unfounded within the scientific, positivistic tradition that continues to constitute anorexia as a natural or quasi-natural disease category.

Why, then, does this medical construction of 'anorexia nervosa' continue to retain such a hold over our (popular, clinical and academic) understandings of girls' and women's distressing experiences around eating and not eating, and around gaining and losing weight? Why do we continue to buy into this medical perspective? For the discursive construction of 'anorexia' as natural disease entity is not only empirically unsubstantiated; by locating the hypothesized causes of 'anorexia' in the female body it also forecloses questions about the social or discursive production of women's distress around eating and not eating and around gender, subjectivity and embodiment. The positivist scientific credentials of biomedical discourse belie a profoundly ideological agenda. Despite the fact that many more women than men are diagnosed as 'anorexic', gender issues are rarely addressed in biomedical discourse which cannot provide any adequate explanation of the cultural-, historical-, class-, age- and gender-bound distribution in diagnoses (see Introduction).

This is not to deny that biomedical research can be useful to us. Nor is it to deny the physicality of the body. It would, of course, be foolish and irresponsible to deny corpo-*reality* of the female body or the 'anorexic' body when the disastrous physical consequences of women's self-starvation are all too apparent. Indeed, biomedical research may be useful in advancing clinical treatments of the physical effects of starvation. The low bone-mineral density associated with anorexia (Salisbury and Mitchell, 1991), for example, may require particular clinical interventions. Such research may also provide knowledge that would be useful in educating women about the health-related consequences of undernutrition. Conversely, however, the discursive construction of anorexia nervosa as organic disorder also has worrying implications for treatment of those diagnosed as anorexic. The postulation that 'anorexia nervosa is based on a hypersensitivity of the hypothalamus to oestrogens' leads to the advocation of drug treatment (Szmukler 1982: 166) rather than the advocation of psychological and/or social support which may be of more help to women experiencing distress around food, embodiment and identity.

The biomedical construction of 'anorexia' is profoundly problematic, not because it acknowledges the physicality of the body, but because it constitutes the body and our embodied experiences in a particular way. It severely restricts the kinds of research questions and the forms of methodology that may be deemed legitimate in attempting to understand 'anorexia'. Within this discourse there is no space in which to explore the political, socio-cultural or psychological aspects

79

of women's 'anorexic' experiences because women's experiences, women's distress about food, eating, embodiment and identity are presented as predominantly the effects of hypothesized dysfunctions of our bodies. As Jane Ussher (1992c) argues, we should be suspicious of such reasoning which relies on implicit beliefs about the female body's propensity for illness.

ANOREXIA NERVOSA AS GENETIC PREDISPOSITION

The 'discourse of genetics' shares much in common with biomedical discourse and might best be considered as a branch of the latter. It similarly constitutes 'anorexia nervosa' as a natural or quasi-natural disease category, but in this case is concerned with the hypothesized construction of 'anorexia' as genetic predisposition. The 'anorexic phenotype' is construed to be a consequence of genetic inheritance (and environmental risk factors).

Indeed, it has long been noted that children diagnosed with psychiatric problems often have parents who also have mental health problems (Rutter *et al.*, 1990). However, separating environmental from genetic factors remains problematic and the possibility of a genetic role in anorexia nervosa has frequently been discounted (Rutter *et al.*, 1990). Yet recently, a number of researchers (e.g. Elliott, 1985; Mitchell and Eckert, 1987) have argued that evidence from genetics studies suggests the possibility of genetic predisposition for anorexia nervosa. In fact, there are a number of studies (e.g. Holland *et al.*, 1988; Strober *et al.*, 1985) that have found higher rates of anorexia in the relatives of those diagnosed as anorexic than in the general population (see Rutter *et al.*, 1990). There are, for example, several reports of increased risk amongst siblings and of greater concordance rates for monozygotic (MZ) than dizygotic (DZ) twins (Garfinkel and Garner, 1983). Thus, the possibility of a genetic component in the aetiology of anorexia is suggested.

The construction of 'anorexia' as genetic predisposition is, however, problematic; first, because there is as yet too little evidence to substantiate adequately the claim in terms of its own positivist criteria (see Strober, 1991). Second, genetic and family studies have produced conflicting findings: in contrast with some other twin studies, Suematsu *et al.* (1986), for instance, found five of the seven MZ twins in their study to be discordant and even in the concordant cases the degree of 'anorexia' differed. And third, many of these studies are beset by methodological difficulties (Strober, 1991) with, for example, most of the probands being volunteers (Rutter *et al.*, 1990).

In addition to these problems and the problem of separating out possible genetic and environmental factors, it is also equally important to examine the way in which these supposedly empirically based arguments about a genetic predisposition to 'anorexia' are constructed within this discourse of genetics. It has, for example, been recently asserted that predisposing factors are best understood in terms of genetically transmitted dispositional traits (Strober, 1991). Yet the role of genetics in personality is highly controversial (Pervin, 1989) and is hardly empirical fact. Dispositional trait theory has been criticized as 'relatively atheoretical and tautological' (Snyder and Ickes, 1985: 892). It takes little or no account of the way in which people's behaviours may be situationally and temporally specific (Mischel, 1968; McAdams, 1992). 'Dispositional traits', then, are theoretical concepts, reified through particular psychological discourses and particular methodological techniques (see Tseelon, 1991). The proposition that heritable dispositional traits may predispose individuals to anorexia can thus be seen not as empirically verifiable 'fact' but as highly contentious discursive construction. Like the biomedical discourse discussed above, the discourse of genetics produces a predetermined research programme premised on a particular construction of 'anorexia nervosa' as natural or quasi-natural disease category.

ANOREXIA NERVOSA AS AFFECTIVE DISORDER

A third way in which 'anorexia nervosa' is discursively constituted by contemporary mainstream knowledges is as a variant of depression. It has been argued that 'anorexia' and 'depression' may be related in some way, since there is some degree of overlap in the symptomatologies of these two diagnostic categories. Clinical features of depression such as insomnia, weight loss and reduced libido are reported as also occurring in those diagnosed as 'anorexic' (Jampala, 1985; see also Strauss and Ryan, 1988), whilst 'anorexic' symptoms are reported in people with depression (Wolpert, 1980). Researchers have therefore investigated the possibility of some relationships between these two 'disorders' from a number of different perspectives.

Within biomedical discourse, for example, this relationship is construed in terms of a possible shared organic aetiology (e.g. Jampala, 1985), such as abnormalities in the hypothalamic–pituitary–adrenal axis (Schweitzer et al., 1990; see also Kolata, 1986). And within the discourse of genetics the relationship is construed in terms of an hypothesized, shared genetic risk factor. However, research investigating clinical phenomenology, course, outcome and epidemiology has proved inconclusive in identifying any relationship between anorexia and depression and indeed indicates greater divergence than overlap between the two diagnostic categories (Strober and Katz, 1987).[2] And, whilst girls and women diagnosed as 'anorexic' often feel 'depressed', it is not clear how the discursive construction of 'anorexia' as a form of affective disorder could help us to understand such distress, particularly when the theoretical status of 'affective disorders', like 'eating disorders', are open to dispute.

ANOREXIA NERVOSA AS COGNITIVE DYSFUNCTION

Within psychology one of the more dominant discursive constructions of 'anorexia' is as a cognitive dysfunction. Various psychological perspectives assign a central role to the meanings of body weight and shape for those diagnosed as 'eating disordered'. And within the discourse of cognitive psychology 'meaning' is conceptualized in terms of individual cognitions. The existence of a particular cognitive schema, it is argued, will produce systematic 'errors' in processing information relevant to that domain, and it is therefore hypothesized that such schemas may play a role in 'anorexia' and other eating disorders (Vitousek and Hollon, 1990).

Within the cognitive psychological discourse, then, 'anorexia' is construed in terms of individual cognitive deficits and 'constructs such as overvalued attitudes and dysfunctional beliefs' (Clark *et al.*, 1989: 377–378) which may either be causal or the result of physiological effects of starvation (Andersen, 1987). 'Anorexia' has, for example, been construed in terms of a lack of the capacity for abstract thought characteristic of the formal operational stage of cognitive development (Bruch, 1978); in terms of poor cognitive performance (Laessle *et al.*, 1989; see also Strauss and Ryan, 1988), and in terms of irrational beliefs (Ruderman, 1986), all-or-nothing thinking, superstitious thinking and ego-centric thinking (Garner *et al.*, 1982). Yet again, research findings remain inconclusive and contradictory, with some studies actually suggesting that 'anorexics' performed as well as, or better than, controls in some cognitive tasks (see Strupp *et al.*, 1986; Kowalski, 1986).

Primarily, however, cognitive discourse has constituted 'anorexia' as a manifestation of overvalued weight- and food-related schemata. And cognitive research has inevitably produced considerable evidence that women diagnosed as anorexic tend to be more preoccupied with food and weight than other women (e.g. King *et al.*, 1991; Mottram, 1985). In Stroop tests, women diagnosed as anorexic have, for example, been found to be significantly slower than controls in naming the ink colour of food- and weight-related words than of neutral words (Channon *et al.*, 1988).

The discursive construction of 'anorexia' as cognitive dysfunction or bias is clearly less reductive than the discursive constructions discussed above, as it attends to the psychological meanings that food and body weight may have for those diagnosed as anorexic. However, cognitive research has so far only succeeded in consistently distinguishing 'anorexic' from non-anorexic cognitions in terms of eating- and weight-related schemas (Vitousek and Hollon, 1990), and

> it is unarguable and ultimately uninteresting that someone who has organized her life around weight control will think a great deal about food and weight, will try to restrict her intake, and will experience considerable emotion as she encounters success and failure in pursuing her goal.
>
> (Vitousek and Hollon, 1990: 198)

The science of cognitive psychology seems only to have provided us with the knowledge that girls and women diagnosed as anorexic are particularly concerned about food and body weight. More importantly, however, in providing this knowledge cognitive discourse (and the research that accompanies it) constitutes 'anorexia' in a particular problematic way. It constitutes an individualistic knowledge of 'anorexia'; of 'anorexic cognitions' located within the *individual* woman rather than in her social context. 'Anorexia' becomes a problem of individual (mis)perceptions and biases rather than a socio-cultural or political issue. And, in investigating this individualistic construction of anorexia, cognitive research tends to look for differences between 'anorexic' and other girls and women. It (implicitly) draws on the biomedical construction of anorexia as a distinct clinical entity, seeking categorically to differentiate 'anorexic' from 'normal' cognitions. Yet preoccupations with food and body weight are hardly peculiar to girls and women diagnosed as anorexic. Neither are body dissatisfaction, negative reactions to weight or an idealization of 'slimness' (see pp. 89–94 below). What, then, of the similarities between 'anorexic' and 'normal' women? And what of the social/discursive contexts in which these 'biases' are manifested? Whilst cognitive psychology provides a knowledge of 'anorexia nervosa' as psychologically meaningful, it also constitutes 'anorexia' as a problem of *individual* cognitions, dissociating 'anorexic' experiences and behaviours from the experiences of other girls and women and from the social/discursive contexts in which these experiences are constituted.

ANOREXIA NERVOSA AND BODY-IMAGE DISTORTION

A further but related construction of anorexia nervosa is concerned with body-image distortion (BID). BID refers primarily to the observation that 'many patients [insist] that they are overweight when their bodies have become grotesquely emaciated' (Bemis, 1979: 490). It has been described as a central characteristic of anorexia, whose correction is critical for recovery (WHO, 1992; see also Introduction).

As with discursive constructions of 'anorexia' as cognitive dysfunction, 'anorexia' is similarly construed here in terms of *individual* misperception, in this case a misperception of one's body. And a number of studies have indeed found that those diagnosed as 'anorexic' (or 'bulimic') tend to overestimate the size of their bodies (Manley *et al.*, 1988; Steiger *et al.*, 1989) or body parts, such as waists and upper thighs (Fichter *et al.*, 1986; Sunday *et al.*, 1992). Yet, as with other lines of research in this field, there is a marked inconsistency in research findings (see Cash and Brown, 1987; Fraenkel and Leichner, 1989). Whitehouse *et al.* (1988), for example, found that, whilst 'anorexic' women significantly overestimated waist size, there was very little distortion in perception of the whole body. The extent to which (and the way in which) girls and women diagnosed as 'anorexic' do misperceive their bodies does not therefore seem consistent. Indeed, in a study of seven women hospitalized for anorexia, Brinded *et al.* (1990) found that BID fluctuated across and within individuals over a four-week period to different extents and in different directions. 'Feeling fat' may be a labile experience that varies with mood and context as well as actual weight (Fairburn, 1987).

Moreover, whilst many texts constitute BID as a central and defining characteristic of 'anorexia', several studies have found evidence of BID in 'normal' women (see Heilbrun and Friedberg, 1990). In this light BID becomes not so much a characteristic that distinguishes 'pathology' from 'normality' as a relatively common experience amongst women that is more complex, more variable and more widespread than many texts imply. Perhaps if we looked not for quantifiable differences between 'anorexic' and 'non-anorexic' women and explored instead the discursive contexts within which women's experiences of embodiment are located, we might understand better why some girls and women sometimes 'feel fat' even when emaciated.

FAMILY-ORIENTED AND PSYCHODYNAMIC DISCOURSES

Anorexia as familial pathology

Like cognitive psychological discourse, family-oriented and psychodynamic discourses also constitute 'anorexia nervosa' as psychologically meaningful. Paralleling work in other areas such as schizophrenia (Bentall, 1990), 'anorexia' has also been theorized and researched within the context of the familial environment. Within this field of knowledge it has been constituted not so much as biological disorder, genetic predisposition or cognitive dysfunction than as a psychological disorder, created and maintained within a dysfunctional family context. The psychological and behavioural characteristics of 'anorexia' are located within and explained in terms of various 'maladaptive attitudes', behaviours and interactional patterns of 'the anorexic family'.

One form of 'familial dysfunction' which has received considerable attention, not only in the academic and clinical literature but also in the popular media, is childhood sexual abuse (CSA). And several studies have indicated high rates of CSA amongst women diagnosed as eating disordered (e.g. De Groot *et al.*, 1992; Herzog *et al.*, 1993). Others have found strong associations between unwanted sexual experiences in women's pasts and particular 'eating disordered' behaviours such as purging (e.g. Waller *et al.*, 1993), whilst others have suggested a relationship between past sexual abuse and severity rather than type of disordered eating (e.g. De Groot *et al.*, 1992). Clearly such traumatic experiences as CSA may cause considerable long-term distress and for some girls and women disordered eating may be closely connected with the distress they continue to feel about past abuse. It would, however, be problematic to posit any generalizable or causal relationship between CSA and eating disorders. For such distress is an aspect of the lives of many girls and women, not all of whom will go on to develop an 'eating disorder'. And it is equally important to note that many of those diagnosed as 'eating disordered' do not report past experiences of CSA (see De Groot *et al.*, 1992). To suggest a generalizable or causal relationship between eating disorders and CSA thus seems unwise.

Family-oriented approaches to eating disorders are, however, concerned with a wide range of 'familial dysfunctions', often of a less emotive and contentious nature than CSA. Several studies have, for instance, reported high rates of overweight and underweight parents (Garfinkel and Garner, 1982) and of 'anorexia-like syndromes' in the adolescent histories of various family members (see Yager, 1982; Crisp *et al.*, 1980). Others have characterized 'anorexic families' as overvaluing thinness (Kalucy *et al.*, 1977), as having a propensity for odd diets (Dally and Gomez, 1979), and as focusing family conflicts around food, eating and appearance (Huon and Brown, 1984).

Such familial contexts, where they exist, clearly are important in understanding the experiences of family members. Families may indeed play an important role in mediating girls' and women's experiences of food, eating and body weight (Rakoff, 1983). Yet, as with other lines of research in this field, the evidence is not entirely consistent. Some studies have found no significant differences between the weights of parents of 'anorexics' and the weights of matched controls (Halmi *et al.*, 1978). And others have found no evidence that parents held particularly disturbed attitudes towards eating and body weight (see Garfinkel *et al.*, 1983). More importantly, perhaps, the discursive construction of 'anorexia' in terms of familial 'weight pathology' rests on an idealized concept of normality that has been assumed rather than demonstrated. The much-documented over-preoccupation of 'the anorexic family' with health, appearance and food is prevalent to some degree throughout contemporary Western society. The so-called 'anorexic family' may simply be the bearer of our culturally sanctioned values (Rakoff, 1983). And the value-judgement implicit in the pathologization of a family's 'weight-deviations' may itself be seen as a fetishization of cultural ideals about weight and appearance.

Family-oriented discourse has also sought to explain other psychological aspects of 'anorexia' in terms of 'the anorexic family'. Within this literature 'anorexia' is construed as a complex psychological disorder for which the more apparent symptoms of food refusal and weight loss act as a cover or pseudo-solution (Bruch, 1982). 'The anorexic' is portrayed as depressed, anxious, self-punitive, alienated, rebellious and hostile (Sheppy *et al.*, 1988); as ambitious (Guttman, 1986) and perfectionist (Humphrey, 1986), but also as feeling helpless and ineffective (Bruch, 1982; Humphrey, 1986). 'She' is lacking in self-esteem and has little sense of self as an autonomous individual (Sheppy *et al.*, 1988; Bruch, 1973).

Family-oriented discourse thus provides a detailed and often sensitive knowledge of the profound psychological distress associated with 'anorexia' and seeks to explain these problems in terms of a dysfunctional family context. Hence, like 'anorexics', 'anorexic families' are construed as psychologically disturbed (Sheppy *et al.*, 1988), as perfectionist and ambitious (Guttman, 1986), controlling (Rakoff, 1983) and hostile (Haggerty, 1983). 'They' are reported to have high rates of various psychosomatic and psychological disorders, particularly depression and 'addictive syndromes' (Kog and Vandereycken, 1985; see also Kalucy *et al.*, 1977). They are also often characterized as having high levels of unresolved conflict (Palazzoli, 1974); as tending to be socially isolated (Humphrey, 1986) and as having overly close or 'enmeshed' intra-familial relationships (Minuchin *et al.*, 1978).

Many texts leave the implied causal relationship between such 'family pathologies' and anorexia largely untheorized. However, the influential 'systemic theory' (Minuchin *et al.*, 1978) does provide an explanation of how dysfunctional families may be implicated in family members' 'psychosomatic illnesses' such as 'anorexia'. Within this discourse the 'anorexic' daughter (or son) is construed as an active participant of a dysfunctional family system. 'Her' symptoms are seen to play a functional role in, for example, diverting attention from parental conflict and thereby maintaining an appearance of family stability. Moreover, the anorexic or psychosomatic family is presented as typically very 'enmeshed': extra-familial contact is resisted, whilst intra-familial relationships are overly close and intrusive and the boundaries between different subsystems of the family tend to be blurred.[3] Such a system, it is argued, may result in a child giving primacy to interpersonal family proximity and loyalty over autonomy and self-realization. Hence, 'the typical anorexic-to-be' has difficulty in consolidating a separate, individual identity, distrusts the validity of her own feelings and perceptions, is overly dependent on parental approval and is thus unable to meet the demands of adolescent development. Within systemic theory, 'anorexia' is construed as a pseudo-solution to these intra- and interpersonal difficulties (see also Bruch, 1973, 1982).

Anorexia as psychodynamic disturbance

Minuchin *et al.*'s (1978) account of 'the psychosomatic family' converges with many of the above constructions of 'the typical anorexic family'. It also converges in part with psychodynamic and some psychoanalytic work in this field. Psychoanalysts have stressed the symbolic meanings of self-starvation in unconscious fantasy (Boris, 1984). Hence, anorexia has been construed as a defensive regression from adolescent sexuality (see Sayers, 1988) or from mature femininity (Plaut and Hutchinson, 1986) towards infantile orality. Refusal to eat has thus been interpreted as a fear of oral impregnation and as a response to unresolved conflicts in the separation–individuation process (Fischer, 1989) and to the greed and longing associated with that process. Boris (1984: 318), for example, argues that 'the anorexic is not to be found wanting, in both senses of the word', whilst Birksted-Breen asserts that 'anorexia' may be understood as a girl's attempt to have a body and sense of self separate from her mother:

as if maturing into adulthood is experienced as becoming the mother . . . The wish to be fused, the refusal to take and the attack on the representation of the mother's body through self-starvation are given fuel by feelings of envy . . . The anorexic is caught between the terror of aloneness . . . and the terror of psychic annihilation.

(Birksted-Breen, 1989: 30)

Psychoanalytic discourse thus constitutes 'anorexia' as a symptomatic manifestation of unresolved Oedipal and pre-Oedipal conflicts associated in particular with inadequate ego development and with a failure to accept female psycho-sexual maturity (see also Wilson *et al.*, 1983; Sours, 1980).

Although critical of psychoanalytic therapy, the extremely influential work of Bruch and of Palazzoli also draws on psychoanalytic discourse. And, as with much of the psychoanalytic literature (see Sayers, 1988), this work tends to focus on the role of the mother, particularly on disturbances in the early mother–child relationship which is viewed as an origin of the anorexic's poor sense of self. Bruch (1982: 1532), for example, interprets 'anorexia' as 'a defense against the feeling of not having a core personality of their own, of being powerless and ineffective'. 'Anorexia' is thus constructed as a 'self-pathology' (Geist, 1989) in which the body has become the focus of a psychological conflict and in which food refusal signifies greater control (over the body, the self and others).

Both Bruch and Palazzoli locate the origins of 'the anorexic's' 'ego-deficits' and subsequent anorexia in disturbances of the earliest mother–child relation-ship (Bruch, 1973), in terms of a real failure of the mother to respond appropriately to her infant daughter's needs.[4] Instead, it is argued, the mother superimposes inappropriate needs on the child, refusing to recognize and thereby legitimate the child's own needs (Bruch, 1973; Palazzoli, 1974). Hence

> If confirmation and reinforcement of his [*sic*] own, initially rather undif-ferentiated, needs and impulses have been absent, or have been contradictory or inaccurate, then a child will grow up perplexed when trying to differentiate between disturbances in his biological field and emotional-interpersonal experiences and he will be apt to misinterpret deformities in his self-body concept as externally induced. Thus he will become an individual deficient in his sense of separateness, with diffuse ego-boundaries, and will feel helpless under the influence of external forces.
>
> (Bruch, 1973: 56)

That is, the refusal or inability of the mother to confirm the child's perceptions of her own needs results in the child doubting the legitimacy of her self-perceptions. She becomes confused about appetite and satiety, focusing on what others want rather than what she wants, so that her desires become indistinguish-able from those of others. And her resulting lack of sense of self, her 'diffuse ego-boundaries', is later compounded by the imposition on the child of a role of submissive, high-achieving, perfect child (Bruch, 1982; Palazzoli, 1974). Adolescence further exacerbates her predicament because of its pressures to achieve independence, autonomy and separation from the parents and 'because it scotches the illusion of being a boy, of being able to achieve the same as boys. The anorexic's achievement-oriented response is to be "as good as a man", to be "super-special by being super-thin"' (Bruch, cited in Sayers, 1988: 366). Like the discourse of 'systemic theory', psychodynamic discourse constitutes anorexia as a pseudo-solution to the inter- and intrapersonal disturbances created and main-tained within a dysfunctional parent–child relationship.

Family-oriented psychological, systemic and psychodynamic discourses clearly produce very detailed and contextualized constructions of 'anorexia' as a psychologically meaningful disorder. Whilst these constructions are undoubtedly useful in understanding the complexities of the distress that many girls and women experience, they are not unproblematic. First, there is an implied causal relationship between family pathology and individual pathology. Yet much of this work is based on studies of 'anorexics' and their family *after* the onset of 'anorexia' and might not therefore be able to distinguish between those attributes caused by the stress of a daughter's 'illness' and those that may be causative (Hsu, 1984). A family's 'enmeshment', for example, may be interpreted as a reaction to, rather than a cause of, a daughter's distress (Yager, 1982).

Second, many texts present an overgeneralized picture of 'the typical anorexic' and the typical 'anorexic family'. Yet 'classic' descriptions of familial dysfunction are often based on relatively small, skewed samples (Yager, 1982). And the inconsistencies in research findings suggest considerable variation amongst the families of those diagnosed as anorexic (Yager, 1982). Indeed, family-oriented research clearly indicates that not *all* families of 'anorexics' are dysfunctional. And, even where they are, non-familial factors may also be involved (see e.g. Bruch, 1978). Moreover, the heterogeneity in the personalities and pathologies attributed to both the anorexic (Halmi, 1983) and her family (Rakoff, 1983; Yager, 1982) make any attempt to define a universal aetiology or to describe a typical 'anorexic' or 'anorexic family' somewhat implausible (see Hsu, 1984). There is no universal 'anorexic' personality and, as with most clinical problems, there are no universal patterns of familial aetiology (Yager, 1982).

More importantly, whilst family-oriented and psychodynamic discourses produce a contextual knowledge of 'anorexia', they also constitute that context in a particular problematic way. Although the importance of cultural factors is acknowledged (e.g. Bruch, 1978; Minuchin *et al.*, 1978), the emphasis is most often on an exclusively familial aetiology. These texts construct 'anorexia' as a consequence of familial environment but they often fail to locate the family within any socio-cultural context. Hence, the extent to which the pathologized 'anorexic family' can be distinguished from the 'normal' family or from other 'psychosomatic families' remains unclear and the possible reasons for 'familial dysfunction' remain largely untheorized. Public and private spheres are kept artificially separated (Goldner, 1989), thus precluding exploration of the reciprocal interplay between 'individual', 'family' and 'society' (Walsh and Scheinkman, 1989) and allowing an uncritical pathologization of familial characteristics such as (over-)preoccupation with food and weight or maternal (over)involvement.

Moreover, despite the fact that many more women than men are diagnosed as anorexic, the category of gender also remains undertheorized within this literature. 'The category of gender remains essentially invisible in the conceptualisations of family therapists' (Goldner, 1985: 33), and there is often a naive illusion of marital equality in patriarchal society (Goldner, 1989). Gender inequalities both within and outside of the family are often left unexplored and may be implicitly accepted as 'normal'. The influential Timberlawn group, for example, reported that women in 'adequate' or 'normal' families tended to be 'overwhelmed with responsibility, obese, psychosomatically ill and sexually dissat- isfied', whilst their husbands were 'functioning well'. Yet they concluded that 'the family is alive and well' (quoted by Luepnitz, 1988: 11). This patriarchal normal- ization of gender inequality within the family tends to preclude an exploration of its effects on (the daughter's) female psychosexual development. It also leads to an uncritical pathologization of parents who deviate from gender-stereotyped behaviour (see Luepnitz, 1988) and to an over-implication of the mother rather than the father in the daughter's 'illness' (see also Caplan, 1990; Sayers, 1988). As Bemis notes,

> mothers of anorexic patients are commonly depicted as dominant and intrusive, and the 'peculiar relationship' and 'striking ambivalence' between mother and child are frequently mentioned . . . In contrast to the unflattering prominence of the 'scolding and overbearing mother' in clin- ical reports fathers are briefly characterised as passive and ineffectual figures who play a minor role in the family structure.
>
> (Bemis, 1979: 491)

Thus, there is a slippage in the discursive construction of 'familial pathology' whereby the family becomes the responsibility of the mother, and 'familial pathology' turns into the 'failings' of the mother rather than the father.

In short, family-oriented and psychodynamic discourses produce a contextu- alized, detailed and often sympathetic knowledge of 'anorexia' as a psychologically meaningful 'disorder' and as a pseudo-solution to complex intra- and interpersonal difficulties. Problematically, however, in seeking to establish a universally applicable familial aetiology, many of these texts present an overly homogenized picture of both 'the anorexic' and her family. These texts also often rely on a notion of 'the family', first as something that can be considered in isolation from its socio-cultural context, and second as a system of ostensibly equal relationships. These texts' silences about gender, power and politics serves to normalize the gender inequalities (in family and society) which must surely have some bearing on the distress that so many girls and women experience in relation to eating, embodiment and identity.

ANOREXIA NERVOSA AND THE DISCOURSE ON RESTRAINED EATING

Many texts either implicitly or explicitly construe 'anorexia nervosa' as a natural or quasi-natural clinical entity, as something distinctly different from the experi- ences and (eating) practices of 'normal' girls and women. Yet, as we have seen, this categorical distinction is not entirely borne out by the research on which this distinction appears to be based. Women diagnosed as anorexic may not repre- sent a population entirely different from so-called normal women. And, indeed, eating disorders are increasingly viewed as being on a continuum with dieting and 'normal' eating (Butler *et al.*, 1990). Further support for this hypothesis comes from research into dietary restraint and from the many studies that have documented the high frequency of dieting and a preference for thinness in the general population.

Studies have indicated that as many as 75 per cent of undergraduate women diet to control their weight (Jacobovits *et al.*, 1977; see also Grunewald, 1985), and that perhaps as few as one-third would describe their eating habits as 'normal' (Mintz and Betz, 1988). A recent magazine survey (Unsworth and Shattock, 1993) similarly found that more than 10 per cent of respondents described themselves as having suffered from an 'eating related problem in the past year', whilst 22 per cent described themselves as 'always dieting', and only 30 per cent said that they had not dieted last year or that they had never dieted. And, not surprisingly, this worryingly high prevalence of reported dieting is paralleled by similarly high levels of body-dissatisfaction (Hall and Brown, 1982; Wardle *et al.*, 1993). It seems that a vast number of girls and women are struggling to become ever thinner and indeed to become underweight (see Huon and Brown, 1984; Freeman *et al.*, 1983). This distress around eating and body weight appears so widespread that many girls as young as 12 feel too fat and feel guilty about eating (Grunewald, 1985; see also Wardle and Beales, 1986), whilst girls as young as 9 seem already to be concerned with dieting (Hill and Robinson, 1991).

These figures are clearly very disturbing. Dieting and body-dissatisfaction seems to be more prevalent and therefore more 'normal' or normative than *non*-dieting amongst women and girls (Polivy and Herman, 1987). Yet this does not itself constitute an adequate explanation of the much-documented apparent increase in diagnoses of anorexia nervosa. We still need to ask why so many women and girls are dieting and how we should understand 'eating disorders' within this context.

One line of research that has investigated the continuum of women's experiences of eating is the work on restrained eating. This research has been informed by a number of theoretical models about how we regulate our food intake. Nisbett (1972), for example, proposed that each person has an individually determined, homeostatically defended 'set point' or ideal weight. Consequently, it is argued, societal emphasis on thinness may result in normatively, but not physiologically, overweight people attempting to suppress their weight. Thus, dieting is equated with biological deprivation, resulting in a number of behavioural responses such as increased responsivity to external cues to eat as a physiological attempt to regain the set point (Ruderman, 1986).

It follows from this that restrained eating will increase the likelihood of bingeing because binge eating may be understood as an attempt by the body to restore a more biologically appropriate weight (Polivy and Herman, 1985). And there is considerable evidence that bingeing and dieting co-occur (see Polivy and Herman, 1987). For example, in Keys *et al.*'s infamous research on normal-weight World War II conscientious objectors (Franklin *et al.*, 1948; Keys *et al.*,

1950), it was found that when these men were 'induced' to starve themselves to 74 per cent of their initial weight they later binged persistently when unlimited food and water was later made available to them. There are also a number of clinical reports (e.g. Garfinkel *et al.*, 1980; Pyle *et al.*, 1981) in which dieting and weight loss preceded the onset of 'bulimia'. And it has been suggested that bulimia often begins as 'a failure to control overwhelming hunger feelings in anorexia nervosa' (Casper *et al.*, 1980: 1034). An estimated 50 per cent of women diagnosed as 'anorexic' binge and purge (vomiting, laxative or diuretic abuse) fairly regularly (Polivy and Herman, 1985), and recent surveys have found quite high incidences of bingeing amongst women in general (e.g. Unsworth and Shattock, 1993; Halmi *et al.*, 1981).

Further research into restrained eating has investigated how cognitive and situational factors may influence eating behaviour. Much of this research is based on the 'disinhibition hypothesis',[5] which states that the self-control usually exhibited by dieters/restrained eaters may be interfered with cognitively, emotionally or pharmacologically. If a 'restrained eater' is induced to eat a large high-calorie meal (termed a 'pre-load'), this will act as a disinhibitor by causing the woman to feel that she has 'blown' her diet. Once disinhibited she would then eat larger quantities of food than non-restrained eaters. (The ethical problems in such research seem apparent.) Hence, it is predicted that unrestrained eaters/non-dieters will eat less food after a large pre-load than after either no pre-load or a small pre-load. Conversely, dieters/restrained eaters will eat little food after either no pre-load or a small pre-load but will eat a great deal after a large, high-calorie pre-load.

This 'counter-regulation' of food intake has been repeatedly confirmed in numerous studies (see Ruderman, 1986; Polivy and Herman, 1985). And several studies have also found that dieters/restrained eaters will also eat more when stressed, anxious, depressed or tired (Dewberry and Ussher, 1994; Polivy and Herman, 1987) or even when happy (Cools *et al.*, 1992). Other studies have also found that many of the psychological characteristics (such as BID, body-dissatisfaction and a desire for perfection) attributed to 'anorexics' can also be found in 'normal' dieters (Garner *et al.*, 1984; Dewberry and Ussher, 1994). Discourses on restrained eating thus present us with a causal *and* conceptual relationship between 'restrained eating' and 'eating disorders' such that 'normal' dieting may result in disordered and chaotic eating patterns and in many of those 'psychopathologies' that are frequently attributed to those diagnosed as 'anorexic'. And, hence, within this discursive context, 'eating disorders' are constituted not as discrete 'disorders' that can be neatly separated from the wider context of women's experiences of eating. Rather, they are presented as part of a continuum of eating behaviours.

Like other discourses on 'anorexia', the discourse of restrained eating does not simply reflect an objective reality but rather constructs reality in particular ways which are open to 'deconstruction'. Set-point theory, for example, sets up an implicit conceptual opposition between *natural* appetites and body weights

91

and *social* pressures to eat less and be thin, and interprets the research findings accordingly. Whilst not disputing the often devastating effects of these social pressures on many women's lives, I would also argue that a reliance on notions of *natural* bodies and appetites is also problematic.

Nevertheless, this research is clearly very useful in understanding 'anorexia' within the wider context of women's experiences of eating because it has indicated the high prevalence of restrained and disrupted eating amongst girls and women, and because it provides a (partially) contextualized knowledge of 'eating disorders' which thereby undermines the disease model of anorexia nervosa as a distinct individual pathology. Many of the 'pathologies' (such as obsessive concerns with weight and appearance) attributed to those diagnosed as anorexic are re-presented as experiences, attitudes and behaviours shared by 'normal' dieters (Polivy and Herman, 1987), and perhaps also by non-dieters (see Tomarken and Kirschenbaum, 1984). The terrain of 'disordered eating' is thus reconfigured so that 'terms such as *normal, acceptable,* and *overweight* can only be understood in the context of societal realities and ideals' (Polivy and Herman, 1987: 635).

ANOREXIA NERVOSA IN SOCIO-CULTURAL CONTEXT

As we have seen, there is considerable evidence to suggest that dieting or restrained eating is very prevalent amongst girls and women in contemporary Western culture and that a great many girls and women are preoccupied with and troubled by issues of food, eating and body weight and shape. If dieting and an attendant 'diet mentality' are now descriptively and prescriptively normative (Polivy and Herman, 1987), then it seems vital that we understand anorexia nervosa within this socio-cultural context.

There have been a number of studies documenting the increasing slimness of cultural stereotypes of feminine beauty as evidenced in the ever-decreasing size of models in women's magazines (Silverstein *et al.*, 1986) and 'Playboy centre-folds' (Garner *et al.*, 1980). Others have also noted the steep rise since the 1960s in the number of diet-related articles both in women's magazines and in the popular press (Woolf, 1990). And research also suggests that negative attitudes to fatness as well as idealizations of thinness, far from being peculiar to those diagnosed as anorexic, are culturally sanctioned and widespread. Popular images of obesity denigrate fat people as more psychologically disturbed, lacking in will-power and lazy (Harris *et al.*, 1991), and as less likeable (Richardson *et al.*, 1961) than thinner people.

Clearly there must be some relationship between these culturally entrenched prescriptions regarding the body (particularly the female body) and the recent apparent increases both in dieting and in diagnoses of eating disorders (see also Hsu, 1989). It is surely more than coincidence that societal changes in attitudes to female body shape and dieting have occurred at the same time that diagnoses of anorexia appear to have multiplied (see Bruch, 1978). Moreover, a fear of fatness and a preoccupation with body weight are relatively recent phenomena in anorexia (Russell, 1986). In fact weight-related fears in those diagnosed as anorexic were not reported outside of France until the 1930s (Habermas, 1989) and were rarely mentioned in the literature on anorexia before the 1960s (Casper, 1983), the decade in which the ideal of the thin female body significantly increased its hold in contemporary Western culture.

The specificity in the distribution of diagnoses of anorexia in terms of sex, age, ethnicity and socio-economic class, as well as its recent increase (Garner *et al.*, 1983b; Hsu, 1984), also suggests a cultural influence. 'Anorexia' appears to be a largely Western phenomenon (Edwards-Hewitt and Gray, 1993) and a problem associated in particular with young, usually white, 'middle-class' women (see Introduction). Some research, however, does indicate that diagnoses of eating disorders including anorexia are spreading across all socio-economic classes and ethnic groups (Pumariega *et al.*, 1984; Edwards-Hewitt and Gray, 1993). Asian English schoolgirls, for example, have been found by some to have higher EAT (Eating Attitudes Test) scores (see Garner and Garfinkel, 1979) than their Caucasian counterparts (Mumford and Whitehouse, 1988) and 'eating disorders' have been found in women of all ethnic backgrounds (Dolan *et al.*, 1990). Interestingly, it has also been found that 'eating attitudes' in young Hispanic American women were correlated with 'acculturation' to American culture (Pumariega, 1986). Thus, the spread of 'eating disorders' to all socio-economic and ethnic groups might be understood in terms of an increasing dissemination of Western cultural ideals of female beauty/thinness and dieting (Edwards-Hewitt and Gray, 1993).

The pernicious effects of the diet and fashion industries on many women's lives (and deaths) cannot be underestimated. Yet, it would be both superficial and simplistic to attempt to explain anorexia only in terms of cultural pressures for slimness, to characterize anorexia as a 'slimmer's disease' (Malson, 1992). Many socio-cultural explanations of anorexia are, however, limited to a documentation of the increased emphasis on a thin body and the increased prevalence of dieting in contemporary society. As such they tend to rely on a notion of internalization in which 'anorexics' are conceptualized as 'super-dieters' (e.g. Polivy and Herman, 1985), as over-adhering to omnipresent cultural ideals of feminine beauty as thinness. They therefore tend to focus on thinness and dieting to the exclusion of other aspects of anorexia and female subjectivity, and without exploring the complex cultural and political significances of female slenderness.

For 'anorexia' is also associated with low self-esteem, with a lack of sense of self, of independent autonomy and control, as well as with a 'fear of fat' or 'relentless pursuit of thinness' (e.g. Bruch, 1973). It has been described as 'a communicative disorder' which is experienced as a means of taking control over one's body, as a pseudo-solution to intra- and interpersonal difficulties (Bruch, 1978; Caskey, 1989). And culture may also play a role in the 'promotion' of such difficulties. The cultural dynamics of our Western post-industrial society may foster many of the psychosocial conflicts around gender, identity, self-esteem and autonomy (Appels, 1986) that have been associated with 'anorexia' (Malson, 1995a).

Furthermore, the high profile of anorexia both in the popular and the academic media suggests a cultural fascination with eating disorders (Malson and Ussher, 1996b). Anorexia is meaningful at a societal as well as a phenomenological level. Like some other illnesses (see Sontag 1978, 1989), it can be understood as a metaphor for, and a manifestation of, contemporary socio-cultural concerns and dilemmas (Turner, 1992; Orbach, 1993). Just as AIDS 'expresses' cultural concerns about the global spread of disease and about uncontrolled, anonymous sex (Sontag, 1989), so anorexia expresses, for example, a cultural conflict between mass consumption and normative thinness (Turner, 1987), between the indulging 'consumer-self' and the controlled, abstinent 'producer-self' demanded by capitalism (Bordo, 1990; Malson and Ussher, 1996b; Malson, 1995b, forthcoming): 'modern consumerism appropriates all forms of symbolism (including oppositional, anti-capitalist symbolism) to its own commercial purposes. Being hyper-slim, while in opposition to the signs of affluence, is also cool' (Turner, 1992: 221).

'Anorexia' may be expressive of societal concerns with consumption, personal display, feminist politics, the fashion for dieting and slimness and the individualistic competitiveness of late capitalism (Brumberg, 1988), and can therefore be construed as profoundly culture-bound (see Swartz, 1985a), representing public concerns as well as personal predicaments (Littlewood and Lipsedge, 1987: 291). And, as the distribution of diagnoses of 'anorexia' makes clear, a central dimension of this cultural context is gender.

ANOREXIA NERVOSA AND THE QUESTION OF GENDER

In *The Golden Cage*, Bruch (1978) argued that anorexia is in part a personal response to the confusion and contradictions of female maturation. Women are expected to have successful careers, to be intelligent, competent and ambitious. Yet they are simultaneously expected to be desirable and alluringly feminine (Guttman, 1986), particularly if they are heterosexual. Adult women are expected to be both autonomous and compliant, independent and needful of security, sexual and androgynously neutral (Turner, 1992). Consequently, some authors have suggested that recent increases in anorexia may be due to 'the new and often contradictory roles and expectations currently affecting women in modern society as well as the family's failure to adapt to the changing societal demands' (Palazzoli, 1974, quoted in Garner *et al.*, 1983b: 76).

Bruch (1978: ix) has similarly written that many of her patients 'expressed the feeling that they were overwhelmed by the vast number of potential opportunities available to them which they "ought" to fulfil, that there are too many choices and they are afraid of not choosing correctly' (cited in Garner *et al.*, 1983b: 77). Thus it is argued that women's roles are no longer as restricted as they had been in the past, and that our supposed increased freedom may be experienced as a difficulty by some individuals (e.g. Bardwick, 1971). Problematically, such explanations seem to attribute the apparent increased prevalence of eating disorders to the 'liberating' impact of 'second wave feminism', suggesting that women may have been 'safer' when more restricted. In this argument 'anorexia' is constituted as an unfortunate consequence of feminism, a manifestation of women's (implicitly) alleged inability to cope with our (alleged) equality. This subtext undermines, I think, the very basis of such arguments. How much equality do we have when such arguments, based as they are on a profoundly sexist construction of 'woman' as naturally inferior, still appear plausible, at least to some?

Alternatively, however, we can read women's contemporary social status quite differently and suggest that society has not progressed sufficiently towards gender equality; that women are expected to be simultaneously traditionally feminine *and* career-oriented; that we still 'ought' to fulfil a number of often contradictory roles – clearly an impossible predicament. Within this argument 'anorexia' comes to be constituted not as an effect of feminism but as a consequence of continued gender inequality. Moreover, contradictions in prescribed femininity are hardly new; the concept of feminine identity within patriarchy is fundamentally problematic (see Chapter 1). Indeed 'anorexia nervosa' emerged out of the wider category of hysteria (see Chapter 3), itself often described as epitomizing female sickness and as epidemic amongst women in the nineteenth century (Showalter, 1985) and often theorized in terms of the problematics and politics of feminine identity (e.g. Sayers, 1982). Feminist authors (e.g. Ussher, 1991) have repeatedly demonstrated a long historical link between femininity and illness, arguing that 'illnesses' such as PMS, depression and madness may be both consequences of women's oppression and expressive of patriarchal pathologizations of femininity: 'Social anxiety about sexuality [has been] directed against women and this anxiety has been expressed historically through a variety of medical categories which pinpoint and articulate the subordination of women to patriarchal authority' (Turner, 1987: 88).

Feminist theorists have been at the fore in examining the culture- and gender-bound nature of anorexia. Lawrence (1984), for example, provides a political analysis of women's control of their bodies in relation to their lack of power in other areas of life. Chernin (1983) similarly argues that prescriptive stereotypes of the female body as slim and childlike reflect gender power relations.

Within the feminist approaches to anorexia there is a considerable diversity of opinion about the relationships between anorexia and gender. For instance, Boskind-Lodahl (1976) argues that 'anorexics' strive to achieve an exaggerated ideal of patriarchally prescribed femininity, including a thin body. The psychological problems of 'anorexic' women are seen here as the result of an unquestioning acceptance of the prescription of femininity as beauty/thinness, passivity, dependency, a 'need' for validation of self by a man and a desire to please (see Swartz, 1985b). 'Our heritage of sexual inequality', Boskind-Lodahl (1976: 354) argues, is implicated not only in the aetiology of anorexia but also in the much-documented 'negative' attributes of the 'anorexogenic' mother. Conversely, Orbach (1979, 1993) asserts that anorexia reflects not so much an unquestioning acceptance as an ambivalence about, and a rebellion against, femininity; that the anorexic body is a *parody* of fashionable thinness (see Swartz, 1985b).

Drawing on psychoanalytic theories, feminist theorists have also provided more gender-sensitive and culturally contextualized explanations of how mothers may be implicated in their daughters' 'anorexia' (cf. 'Family-oriented and psychodynamic discourse', p. 87–89). Eichenbaum and Orbach (1983), for example, describe 'anorexic' women as typically feeling shameful of their needs and, like Bruch, they trace this feeling to the mother–infant relationship. They argue that the mother conveys this feeling to the daughter 'out of a sense that her daughter will have to learn this lesson in order to become properly socialised into the traditional female role of caring for others' (Bordo, 1992: 107), and because the girl represents for the mother 'the "hungry needy little girl" in herself which she denied and repressed' (Bordo, 1992: 108). That is, the mother conveys the contradictory message to her daughter that she must hide her needs if she is to get love and approval (Eichenbaum and Orbach, 1983). This message is then reinforced by cultural gender ideology so that the daughter comes to experience her needs and wants as wrong (see Bordo, 1992). Chernin (1986) has similarly focused on the mother–daughter relationship in explaining anorexia, arguing that 'women's eating disorders stem from the guilt women feel about becoming different from their mothers in a society that still accords this right less to women than to men' (Sayers, 1988: 365).

Referring to Klein's theory of infantile aggression and ambivalence, and to the mother's ambivalence about mothering, Chernin also argues 'the fat woman' evokes the terror and longing we experienced as infants:

> When we attempt to determine the size and shape of a woman's body, instructing it to avoid its largeness and softness and roundness and girth, we are driven by the desire to expunge the memory of the primordial mother who ruled over our childhood with her inscrutable power over life and death.
>
> (Chernin, 1981: 143)

Anorexia, she argues, represents this ambivalence towards the maternal body, 'towards regression and development and towards affirmation and denial of identification with the mother as female' (Sayers, 1988: 365). However, whilst both Orbach and Chernin locate the mother–daughter relationship within patri-archal society, they, like family-oriented theorists, tend to focus on the role of the mother to the exclusion of the father and others (Sayers, 1988).

There are, then, a range of feminist perspectives on 'anorexia', each of which constitute 'anorexia' in different and sometimes conflicting ways. However, these feminist analyses have clearly furthered understandings of anorexia by demon-strating the centrality of gender in relation to eating disorders. They have elucidated the relevance of gender power structures (Chernin, 1983; Lawrence, 1984; Sayers, 1988) and of the negativity and pathology of prescribed femininity (Orbach, 1979; Boskind-Lodahl, 1976) to anorexia as a predominantly female problem.[6] However, as Swartz (1985b) rightly argues, there is a problematic tendency in some feminist analyses to naturalize this life-threatening condition and to present anorexia as a reasonable expression of quasi-feminist discontent. And rather than adopt a multi-determinist position (see Garfinkel *et al.*, 1983, for example), some analyses tend to employ a model of unilinear causality in which the dysfunctional hormones, faulty thinking or 'bad' mothering of traditional theories are simply replaced by patriarchal society (Swartz, 1985b). In addition, there is often a conceptual opposition of 'nature' and 'culture', in which the woman's 'natural needs' are obstructed by cultural prescriptions of thin and passive femininity (Swartz, 1985b). While such prescriptions are undoubtedly oppressive, their analyses rest upon a false dichotomy – the natural female body versus its social oppression in which 'the body' is understood as outside of (rather than as constituted in) culture. Yet, as Riley (1988: 102) argues, 'the body is not, for all its corporeality, an originating point nor yet a terminus; it is a result or an effect'. That is, whilst our conceptualizations of the (gendered) body inevitably lean on corpo-reality, the body does not precede the social, but rather is socially and discursively constructed; there are no needs that we can know before culture intervenes (see Chapter 1). Hence, in understanding the female 'anorexic' body and the cultural symbolisms, identities and conflicts that are played out on it, it is necessary to explore how it is culturally, discursively constructed in its changing socio-historical specificities.

CONCLUSIONS: FICTIONING ANOREXIA NERVOSA

In Chapter 3 I explored how 'anorexia nervosa' first emerged as an object of medical discourse towards the end of the last century. In this chapter I have been concerned with its subsequent discursive development during the twentieth century, taking this genealogy of 'anorexia' up to the present day. In particular, I have explored the numerous academic and clinical institutional discourses which now converge on the anorexic body to produce a plethora of different 'anorexias'.

My aim in discussing these various perspectives on 'anorexia' has been twofold. First, I have sought to provide a brief overview of research and theory on 'anorexia' and to evaluate critically this literature, exploring the limitations and lacunae of these different knowledges; and second, I have sought to illustrate how these various fields of knowledge constitute their object in different ways so that we now have a number of different 'anorexias' constituted by the different disciplines and subdisciplines discussed above. In producing this genealogy I have thereby sought to illustrate the discursive nature of 'anorexia nervosa', to show that 'anorexia' is not an incontrovertible pre-given 'fact' existing independently of our knowledge(s) of it. It is not a natural or quasi-natural clinical entity but a socially (discursively) constructed category that, as an object of discourse, has changed quite significantly since its emergence in the late nineteenth century. The anorexias of the late twentieth century are constituted quite differently from the anorexia of the late nineteenth century. There are discontinuities in the causal explanations, in discursive constructions of the nature of this 'disorder', in the gender ideologies on which these 'anorexias' draw and even in the symptomatologies of these anorexias. And, as we have seen, during the course of the twentieth century 'anorexia' has become the object of an increasing number of knowledges, so that it is now variously constructed in terms of physiological dysfunction, genetic predisposition and cognitive deficits or biases. It is constructed as a consequence of familial dysfunction, of social prescriptions of female slenderness and of patriarchal oppression. We now have a multiplicity of competing constructions of 'anorexia nervosa'.

Paralleling developments in other fields, it has been suggested that 'anorexia' cannot be adequately understood from the perspective of any one discipline and that a multidimensional approach is needed in order to gain a 'fuller picture' of this complex phenomenon (Garfinkel and Garner, 1982; Sheppy et al., 1988).[7] This would combine all the different knowledges, the different discursive constructions of 'anorexia' to produce, so the argument goes, a more thorough and 'balanced' knowledge of 'anorexia'. Such an approach may seem appealing, but it is also problematic.

First, not all the perspectives discussed above are epistemologically compatible. How, for instance, can we reconcile a construction of 'anorexia' as a distinct clinical entity with a construction of 'anorexia' as part of a continuum of women's experiences around eating, embodiment and identity? And how can we coherently combine a biomedical construction of 'anorexia' as a physiological disorder with a feminist construction of 'anorexia' understood in terms of patriarchal oppression? From a post-structuralist feminist perspective, the physical reality of the body and of starvation must be acknowledged, whilst the 'absolute truth' of biomedical discourse must be challenged. Biomedical explanations of anorexia do not simply and objectively describe the physical reality of the anorexic body (Malson, forthcoming). Rather, they discursively constitute anorexia in particular ways which lean on, but do not objectively reflect, the extra-discursive reality of the body (see Malson, forthcoming). The notion that 'anorexia' may be caused by dysfunctional (female) hormones is profoundly sexist as well as reductionist. The various constructions of 'anorexia' cannot simply be added together to produce a 'fuller picture'. And, indeed, the very notion of a 'fuller picture' leans on a positivist concept of a total and objective Truth which, as we have seen (see Chapters 1 and 2), is itself problematic.

Second, by combining these different knowledges of 'anorexia' we cannot thereby simply eliminate the problems of each – the reductionism of biomedical discourse or the individualism of cognitive psychology, for instance. The various discourses on anorexia discussed above tend to lean uncritically on a medical or quasi-medical construction of 'anorexia' as a distinct individual pathology

(Hepworth, 1991). Yet the research that accompanies these discourses indicates no such clear-cut distinction between 'anorexic' and 'normal' women. And, whilst psychological discourses attend to some of the meanings of 'anorexia', thereby moving beyond the reductionism of biomedical accounts, they nevertheless re-produce 'anorexia' as an *individual* pathology. Whether anorexia is explained in terms of cognitive biases, maladaptive attitudes or physiological dysfunction, the origin of the problem remains firmly located within the individual woman rather than her social context (Malson and Ussher, 1996a). Yet, as we have seen, 'anorexia' is expressive of cultural concerns as well as personal predicaments.

Psychological discourses which attribute anorexia to such factors as the family, maternal influence or the media do move the focus away from the individual woman and on to her immediate environment (Malson and Ussher, 1996a). Nevertheless, they still tend to adopt an empiricist or positivistic stance, assuming that anorexia exists independently of the language in which it is described; assuming that it can be objectively identified through empiricist research. Yet the notion that we can gain some objective knowledge of 'anorexia' is profoundly problematic. For, as Foucault (1972) argues, discourses are social practices that systematically form their objects. Medical and psychological discourses do not simply describe 'anorexia' more or less objectively, but rather construct it in particular ways (Foucault, 1972, 1979). These discourses reify 'anorexia nervosa' as pre-given 'fact' rather than as a socially (discursively) constructed category. (And these problems apply as much to multidimensional as unidimensional perspectives.) 'Anorexia nervosa' thus comes to be seen as a distinct entity which *causes* many of the problems experienced by 'anorexic' women, rather than as a socially constructed diagnostic label with particular connotations and consequences for girls and women. Moreover, as power/knowledges, these different institutional perspectives on anorexia not only constitute our understanding of girls' and women's experiences, they also regulate those experiences. The different discursive constructions of 'anorexia' have particular implications for the treatment of eating disorders (see Jarman, 1996). Each discourse brings with it a set of discursive practices, of judgements and treatment regimes of varying efficacy in alleviating the distress of those diagnosed as anorexic (see Hsu, 1980). And, in constituting 'anorexia' as pre-given fact, as objectively existing clinical entity, these discourses also tend to produce universalistic knowledges. They flatten out the lived differences between girls and women diagnosed as anorexic (see Yager, 1982; Halmi, 1983) to produce 'anorexia nervosa' as an homogeneous category.

Moreover, socio-cultural research has amply demonstrated the dominance of a cultural idealization of the thin female body and the prevalence of body-dissatisfaction, dieting, and weight- and food-related concerns amongst Western women. Within this context the distinction between 'normal' and 'abnormal' eating becomes problematized and the importance of locating 'anorexia' within its socio-cultural context becomes clear. For 'anorexia' also has a high profile both academically and culturally, thus suggesting a cultural fascination with 'anorexia'; that 'anorexia' is of cultural as well as personal significance. It is expressive of cultural and political concerns about, for example, mass consumption and normative thinness, personal display and the individualistic competitiveness of late capitalism (Turner, 1987; Bordo, 1990; Brumberg 1988). And, as other feminist theorists have repeatedly argued, 'anorexia' is expressive of gender-political issues. Gender ideologies are as deeply imbricated in the problem of 'anorexia' in the twentieth century as they were in the nineteenth. The discourses and discursive practices in which we live as gendered subjects infuse our knowledges of 'anorexia', just as they are also imbricated in the lived experiences and in the distress that many girls and women experience around eating and not eating, losing and gaining weight, being fat or thin, and being a woman in contemporary Western society.

Part III

WOMEN'S TALK?

Productions of the anorexic body in popular discourse

5

THE THIN/ANOREXIC BODY AND THE DISCURSIVE PRODUCTION OF GENDER

In Part II of this book I discussed a genealogy of 'anorexia nervosa', exploring the institutional discourses that first constituted the thin woman as an object of medical discourse and that have then continued to constitute and regulate the category of 'anorexia nervosa' into the late twentieth century. In Chapter 3 then I explored how women's self-starvation gradually came into the remit of the medical profession and how 'anorexia' first emerged towards the end of the nineteenth century as distinct clinical entity. I continued this genealogy up to the present day in Chapter 4, focusing in particular on how, during the twentieth century, 'anorexia' has become a multiply constituted object of an increasing number of academic and clinical discourses. In the third part of this book I shall turn my attention from these institutional discourses to look at popular discourses, the everyday discourses that constitute and regulate women's experiences of eating and not eating, of losing and gaining weight, of embodiment, gender and identity.

In this and the following three chapters I shall, therefore, be exploring a variety of different discourses that converge upon the female body and the 'anorexic' body to constitute and regulate women's experiences of gender, subjectivity and embodiment. In exploring these different discourses I shall be drawing on a series of semi-structured interviews that I conducted with 23 women, 21 of whom had been diagnosed as anorexic and 2 of whom were self-diagnosed.[1] As with other discourse-analytic studies, these interviews were not viewed as a means of eliciting facts about anorexia. Rather, they were social and emotional interactive processes (see Griffin and Phoenix, 1994) in which we discussed experiences and ideas about 'anorexia' and about femininity and in which my own subjectivities both as interviewer and as fairly thin woman were also significant. First, the sharing of various subject positions may have diminished the inevitable power differential that exists between researcher and researched. And these shared discourses, subjectivities and experiences will have had some effect on the dynamics of the interview process, on the ways in which the interviewees articulated their ideas and experiences and later on the ways in which I analysed the interview transcripts. The discourses by which I am interpellated have inevitably conditioned and delimited my readings of these texts just as the discourses by which you are interpellated will effect your reading of my text here.

This is not to suggest, however, that the interview process was thereby distorted, since I was not concerned with the positivistic endeavour of revealing some putative objective or universal 'truth' about anorexia. I am not concerned here with identifying some underlying cause of 'anorexia' nor with attributing these women with particular psychological characteristics that might be presented as 'typically anorexic'. It is not these women *per se*, but rather the discourses and discursive resources that they deploy, that I shall be concerned with. My aim here is to explore those discourses and discursive resources deployed in women's everyday accounts about anorexia, femininity, subjectivity and embodiment. What I hope to illustrate in this and the following three chapters is that the many discourses that converge upon the female body and the 'anorexic' body, that interpellate these women, are discourses that are profoundly embedded in contemporary Western culture and that permeate all our lives.

CONSTRUING THE FAT AND THE THIN BODY

One of the most prominent ways in which the female body is discursively constructed and regulated in contemporary Western culture is through the social significations accorded to body weight and shape (see Woolf, 1990). Numerous studies have shown that negative constructions of fatness and a concomitant desire for a thinner body are not restricted to those diagnosed as 'anorexic' or eating disordered (see Chapter 4). Rather, fat and thin bodies are saturated with cultural meanings. As Wetherell's (1996) discourse-analytic study of young women's talk about eating, dieting and body image demonstrates, fat and thin bodies are frequently construed within cultural narratives that imbue these bodies with particular personological and moral values. Amongst the discourses identified in the young women's talk, Wetherell (1996) describes a 'personological discourse of fatness and thinness' in which a fat self was constructed as unattractive and shameful and was associated with introversion and lack of self-esteem. Conversely, a thin self was construed as highly desirable and was associated with extraversion, self-confidence and happiness. Inevitably this discourse could also be identified in the interviews that I conducted (see also Malson and Ussher, 1996b). As the following extracts illustrate, both fat and thin bodies signify a variety of personal characteristics, systematically divided into negative 'fat' and positive 'thin' attributes.

LAYLA: I thought if I lost some weight I would look much nicer and attractive /H: right/ (.) and then I would be more happier /H: right/ because then I would have confidence in myself. (.) I would be able to do things I've (.) never dreamed of doing because /H: mm/ I was ashamed of the way I look and of the way *I was* /H: right/ (.) altogether. /H: mm/ So I thought if I could change the way I look I might be better able to (.) do things that I want to /H: right/ and I'm afraid to do.

JANE: So I just wanted to get rid of all this weight an' /H: right/ (.) it made me feel I was better cos there was less fat /H: mm/ as if there was less /H: mm/ bad.

H: Mm yeah what about um fatness or a more curvy figure? [. . .]

JACKIE: (laughing) gluttony (laughter) you know, that sounds awful uh (laughter)

TRICIA: I s'pose for me it was (.) I felt being clumsy and being ugly, /H: right/ (.) being out of control, (.) /H: mm/ but I think uh as far as a woman goes, being (.) sexually so desirable by men and not being able to say no.

These extracts illustrate, amongst other things, that discursive constructions of 'the fat body' are consistently negative and that this negativity is produced in a variety of ways. 'The fat body' is construed as ugly, unattractive, disgusting and shameful. It signifies gluttony and uncontrolled sexual availability. The 'fat self' is unhappy and lacking in control and self-confidence. 'Fat' seems to be a 'metaphor without brakes'.[2] The 'personological discourse of fatness and thinness' (Wetherell, 1996) can thus be understood as the effect of an intersection and entanglement of various themes 'borrowed' from a number of different discourses, an effect of which is to consolidate and reconsolidate the disciplinary power of the discourses that surround the female body.

GENDERING THE THIN/ANOREXIC BODY

Fat is ugly – thin is beautiful

One very dominant way in which the idealization of thinness and the negativity of fatness is produced in these texts as well as in the wider social sphere is through the construction of fat as ugly and thin as beautiful (Malson, 1995a; Malson and Ussher, 1996b). The fat body is despised as unattractive, and conversely the thin body idealized as perfection and beauty.

EMMA: I can't bear it and especially when I see somebody who really doesn't have to pay very much attention to what they eat. /H: mm/ You know and they're still so slim and they're and they're so beautiful.

ZOE: Well I think ads like told me you know like: OK, being thin was like beautiful, or slim. And when I looked at all the pictures of myself when I was an adolescent I *was* really thin. And you know, so I thought: oh OK I was beautiful and thin then. Like what happened to me.

This construction of fat-as-ugly and thin-as-beauty is so dominant and normalized that it often appears to be an unquestionable prescription of some law of natural aesthetics; that fat *is* ugly and thin *is* beautiful. Yet, prescriptions about what constitutes a beautiful body have fluctuated from the Rubenesque to 'the beanpole' (Orbach, 1993). Beauty is a concept whose specific expression differs both historically and culturally (Malson, 1992). And, as several of the women commented, these aesthetic values have regulated the female much more than the male body (Woolf, 1990).

BARBARA: It's not so bad to to be fat as a man. It's more accepted.

LAURA: The ideal men don't have to necessarily be attractive to women
/H: no/=

=PENNY: Exactly, it's OK for men to be a bit overweight /H: mm/, you know it's okay for men, That's allowed [. . .] I don't mean to generalize, but men do get away with a hell of a lot more when it comes to you know what you have to look like.

These extracts construe men as exempt from prescriptions of physical perfection. Masculine ideals are neither defined through the male body nor are they dependent on women's validation. It is women's, but not men's, duty to attain a beautiful, i.e. thin/slim, body (see also Ferguson, 1983). This is not to argue that men in their totality *are* exempt from any prescriptions of physical perfection or concerns about others' opinions of their bodies. Indeed, many men are clearly troubled by the disparity between their own bodies and ideals of, for example, phallic muscle-bound masculinity. Nevertheless, the discursive construction of 'men' articulated here forms a significant part of the plural collectivity of 'men'. Masculinity can be more easily defined independently of physical appearance than can femininity. And one of the most dominant ways in which femininity, rather than masculinity, is currently regulated is through standards of physical perfection, through slimness (Woolf, 1990). This gender asymmetry is evident both in discursive constructions of men as exempt from this disciplinary discourse and in directly equating femininity with thinness, in defining female beauty and (heterosexual) attractiveness in terms of a thin body (see also Malson and Ussher, 1996b).

ZOE: Like I felt like um guys didn't like me or guys never paid any attention to me as much as they did to like my room mates who were like gorgeous. And I, and I just felt ignored, like no, like they didn't look at me because I was *fat*.

Thus Zoe contrasts herself with her 'gorgeous' room mates. Men, she says, ignored her because she was fat. One dominant meaning of feminine beauty/thinness, then, is being heterosexually attractive, the object of a male desire.

WENDY: It was all tied up with the image that it was good to be slim and you'd attract the boys if you were slim.

This construction of the thin female body is, I think, firmly embedded within a romantic cultural narrative in which the beautiful woman gets a perfect life and lives happily ever after.

CATHY: Things like the media /H: mm/ they seem to connote that (.) um (.) that if you're slim then you're successful, you're intelligent, beautiful, you get the man of your dreams /H: right/, dream children, dream house, money whatever. And I think there's an awful lot of pressure /H: mm/ whereas with men it's less pressurized.

H: Like personality characteristics or I mean do you think it's portraying anything other than slimness to you or?=

=ZOE: Yeah, oh sure. It seems like yeah they're beautiful. There's no doubt they {fashion models} have the perfect lives like, you know everything's cool, like *great*, like what more could you ask for, that sort of thing.

This narrative which structures numerous fairy-tales and romantic fictions constructs a beautiful (thin/slim) heroine who will, after some trials and tribulations, be rewarded with 'the man of {her} dreams [. . .] dream children, dream house, money whatever'; 'Like what more could you ask for'.[3] Physical beauty does not simply connote heterosexual attractiveness, since it thereby represents the passport to a 'perfect' life. As Margaret Wetherell (1991: 2) has argued, romantic discourse 'presents an image of redemption, of salvation and rescue through the gaze of the Other. Usually, but not necessarily this is presented as a heterosexual passion.' Within romantic discourse a beautiful slim body is necessary to attract a man who will 'rescue' the woman, providing her with a perfect life and happiness ever after. The catch is that women are required to be the 'perfect' shape if they are to fit into this romantic and patriarchal story.

In short, romantic discourse idealizes the thin female body, equating thinness with female beauty and defining female beauty in terms of heterosexual attractiveness. Being thin is thus construed as a signifier of romantic femininity, a means of achieving 'redemption' and happiness through a heterosexual passion.

Thinness and the petite woman

The thin body may then signify a romantic femininity. But femininity is traditionally associated not just with a particular appearance but also with a variety of psychological characteristics. Femininity and masculinity are frequently conceptualized as fixed and categorically different sets of individual traits:

Big boys are made of – independence, aggression, competitiveness, leadership, task orientation, outward orientation, assertiveness . . . Big girls are made of – dependence, passivity, fragility, low pain tolerance, non-aggression, non-competitiveness, inner orientation, interpersonal orientation, empathy, sensitivity, nurturance . . .

(Bardwick, 1971, cited in Wetherell, 1986: 79)

Rosenkrantz *et al*.'s Sex-Role Stereotype Questionnaire (see Broverman *et al.*, 1970) re-produces a similar image of femininity, including items such as 'very dependent', 'very passive', 'very submissive', 'very subjective', 'very emotional', 'very illogical', 'very quiet', 'very strong need for security', 'very excitable in a minor crisis', 'not at all aggressive', 'not at all competitive', 'not at all self-confident' and 'not at all adventurous' on their 'feminine pole'. And these 'traditional' feminine characteristics are precisely those required of women in romantic narratives. Indeed, dependency and passivity are central features of romantic femininity, since woman's self-validation and redemption is achieved here only through the intervention of man. And these traditionally feminine characteristics are, I would argue, also signified by the thin/anorexic body as it is constructed within romantic discourse. In the extracts below, for example, 'anorexia' and the thin body are produced as signifiers of a childlike, meek, delicate femininity.

LYNN: I wanted to look like a 12-year-old [. . .]
=JANE: And buying children's clothes, it made you feel you were really successful /SIMONE: yeah, quite/ (laughter) oh god yeah. (laughter)
LYNN: And petite and feminine, /JANE: yeah/ you know really delicate. It made you feel like that.

ELAINE: I would think of it (a slim female body) as being *meek* (.) /H: right/ and childlike. /H: mm/ I mean when I think of Kate Moss, for instance, who's always portrayed as, who's always said to be *the waif*, the child-waif /H: yeah/ kind of and that's exactly how she comes across.

Thinness in these extracts signifies a delicate, meek, childlike femininity. The extreme thinness of many women diagnosed as anorexic may make these infantilizing significations more accessible, since breasts and hips are reduced in size and menstruation often ceases.[4] The very thin female body can thus be seen as a particularly efficient signifier of traditional romantic femininity. It is presented as both physically attractive and as a signifier of the requisite psychological characteristics. But, whilst idealized, this form of femininity is also perilously disempowered and dismissible. Popular media presentations of 'anorexia' as a trivial affliction of childish and vain girls bear this out. A recent discussion of eating disorders in *The Guardian* (Hattersley, 1993), for example, suggested that 'it is in the hope of looking like [top models] that girls refuse to eat their rice pudding'. The phrase is, I would argue, reminiscent of A.A. Milne's (1924: 48–51) poem *Rice pudding*, in which a little girl refuses to eat her pudding despite being 'perfectly well'. His text thus creates an image of 'anorexic' women as childishly petulant; an image which also parallels nineteenth-century descriptions and treatments of 'hysterical' women discussed above (see Chapter 3). And, as Orbach (1993: 4) argues, 'once seen as a child, the anorectic woman becomes much less of a threat'; her symptoms and opinions become discountable because, like her, they are immature. How, though, can we justify describing 'anorexics' as immature when images of childish and childlike women are idealized and constructions of 'child-waifs' abound in the fashion media? Recent images of Madonna, Naomi Campbell and Courtney Love dressed up as sexualized little girls demonstrate the prevalence of cultural figures of infantilized femininity.

These media images emphasize one of the many profound contradictions in the category of 'woman'. For 'womanhood' is an ostensibly adult status and yet the heterosexually attractive woman is frequently portrayed as child-like, dependent and passive. Cultural representations of this perversely infantilized femininity, of this diminutive child-woman thus add to the discursive productions of 'woman' as inferior. For in a phallocentric society it is size that counts and:

PENNY: I think I always found that to look feminine you have to be a size eight and then you know, /H: mm/ just like the kind of society always kind of dictates it to me. I think femininity is not, you know, bigger than size eight or ten.

Femininity is small, and small is inferior. The thin/anorexic body again becomes a very efficient signifier of this (inferior) femininity.

SIMONE: I always felt much bigger than anybody else and wanted to be smaller than, than *men* and feel like a subservient, stupid little girl (laughter) or whatever. I always wanted to be fragile and it's it was rather a nice feeling /H: mm/ (.) for a while.

MANDY: There is this um image of um being smaller /H: right/ in every way /H: mm/ and being the the second-class citizen to the male /H: right/. So I think that probably, possibly is, is a factor. /H: right/ But there is this, this image that women are somehow less important and are behind, physically, /H: yeah/ behind, you know, the male.

Femininity is defined here by size, by not being 'bigger than size eight or ten', and size itself signifies the inferior social status of women that is implied in constructions of femininity as childlike. An important meaning of thinness is, therefore, not only beauty but smallness. Thinness signifies a delicate fragile 'petite' femininity, a woman who is 'less important' because 'she' is an inferior diminutive of man.

'The thin body' can thus be understood as culturally overdetermined in its signification of feminine 'perfection', since it is not only 'beautiful'; it is also small and therefore petite and inferior. As Lacan, like Derrida, insists, 'no word is free of metaphoricity' (Sarup, 1988: 12). The signified is always commutable, always becomes itself a signifier.[5] The thin woman is not only beautiful; her smallness again metaphorically signifies that she is 'petite' – dainty, fragile and delicate but also 'of lesser importance' (see *Concise Oxford Dictionary of Current English*, 1990). The thin body thus signifies several aspects of a femininity that are simultaneously idealized and belittled. The ambivalence entailed in the term 'petite' parallels a social ambivalence towards a 'femininity' that is indicated by the smallness of the thin female body.

As a diminutive object this 'woman' might also be understood as an analogue of grammatical diminutives. Like a pet name, 'woman' is an abbreviation, cut short, lacking. She is 'castrated' and has meaning only in relation to the proper term/phallus/man from which 'she' is derived. 'The petite woman' is therefore an exemplary of 'the woman' of psychoanalytic theory in which 'femininity' emerges as a lack, defined negatively in relation to a masculine signifier – the phallus (see Chapter 1). As Freud's theorization of psychosexual development makes clear, size (of the penis versus the clitoris) is of central importance in the determination of sexual identity within patriarchal society. In relation to the phallus, woman's gender is assigned on the basis of her 'castration'. It is precisely the smallness of her clitoris that, for Freud, symbolizes her inferiority. Whilst Freud argued that the clitoris is inferior because it supposedly affords less pleasure, his texts also suggest a symbolic significance of size (see Nagera, 1969) which is repeated in discursive constructions of the thin body as a signifier of a 'traditional' femininity that is simultaneously idealized and denigrated.

Anorexia: a convergence of femininity and sickness

The dependency, fragility and inferiority of 'the petite woman' are further consolidated by constructions of the thin/anorexic body as sick. The location of 'anorexia nervosa' within medical discourse (see Chapters 3 and 4) is clearly central to constructions of anorexia as pathology. Indeed, terms such as 'slimmer's *disease*' indicate the widespread conceptualization of anorexia as an illness. This medicalization and pathologization of 'anorexia' was both resisted and accepted by the women I interviewed. The transcripts contained constructions of anorexia as an illness and some women also described the physical damage to their bodies that had resulted from prolonged self-starvation. In the extract below this pathologization is explicitly gendered. The discursive construction of the thin body as feminine, 'petite', fragile and inferior is extended so that the thin body also signifies a sick body.

ELAINE: It seems to be the big thing that that a pop star can say: well I was anorexic ten years ago. It's like: /H: right mm/ poor you kind of thing /H: mm/ (.) or something like that. I'm not exactly sure what they want. *They want to be seen* as having had this illness /H: right/ for some reason. [. . .] And it was the same with Mandy Smith (.) that she (.) I mean she was shown to be so frail and like she was getting very ill. /H: mm/ I mean I I think through all that, I think her problem was anorexia or whatever but there's this whole /H: mm/ glamorous thing about (.) you know (.) /H: this/ this poor yeah /H: yeah/ poor ill creature /H: mm/ (.) seems so glamorous to the world for some reason. (.)

110

/H: yeah/ And it was the same with Princess Diana. Everybody wanted to *know* about (.) /H: mm/ this poor (.) creature.

In her account of the media coverage of eating disorders Elaine describes a media image of 'the sickly anorexic' as glamorous, as an identity for pop stars and princesses. Both Mandy Smith and Princess Diana are portrayed as pitifully ill and yet simultaneously glamorous and feminine. This convergence of 'femininity' and sickness, epitomized by the nineteenth-century cult of female invalidism (see Chapter 3), may seem at first to be of little relevance in the late twentieth century. Yet 'anorexia' appears to be a site in which it re-emerges. In the representation of Mandy Smith as 'glamorous' and as a 'poor ill creature', 'sickness' and 'femininity' become entangled in a morbid spectacle that '{e}verybody wanted to *know* about'.

This entanglement of femininity and sickness is consolidated by its similarities with the fragile and delicate 'woman' of romantic discourse. It is a construction which in turn reaffirms both the femininity and the inferiority of the petite woman. In signifying 'femininity', fragility and sickness, the thin female body can be read as a site in which quasi-medical and medical discourses converge with romantic discourse to consolidate 'femininity' as at once 'ideal' and pathologized, as 'properly' inferior.

My discussion here might be interpreted as an endorsement of the notion that women diagnosed as 'anorexic' tend not to question 'traditional' gender ideologies and that they seek to fulfil a traditional feminine stereotype (see Boskind-Lodahl, 1976). However, the discourses that construct the thin/anorexic body as feminine do not simply reflect particular people's attitudes and beliefs or identities. Like other people, women diagnosed as anorexic inhabit a multiplicity of subject positions. They articulate a variety of different discourses which constitute the female body and the anorexic body in multiple, often conflicting ways. The thin/anorexic body may then signify quasi-feminist and non-feminine subjectivities as well as 'traditional' femininity.

BE MORE BEAUTIFUL: A DISCOURSE FROM MAGAZINES

One discourse that both converges and diverges from romantic discourse in its construction of the thin body is a 'be more beautiful' discourse promulgated in women's magazines, where physical beauty is frequently presented 'less as an aspirational ideal, more as a holy commandment' (see Ferguson, 1983: 59). In these texts beauty figures as a state of salvation achieved through ritualistically following 'the "step-by-step" instructions, the day-to-day diets' for beautification (ibid.: 59).

This 'be more beautiful' discourse converges with romantic discourse in their mutual themes of salvation or rescue as well as in their emphasis on female beauty. In the 'be more beautiful' discourse, however, the beautiful thin body is not construed as a requirement for attracting a man who will save the woman.

Rather, it *is* the state of salvation. And this 'salvation' is achieved through the woman's efforts rather than through male intervention. Indeed, women's magazines contain surprisingly few references to the 'benefits' of female beautification in attracting and holding a man's attention (Ferguson, 1983). Thus, whilst retaining a romantic theme, this discourse displaces the masculine position and offers a less 'traditional' subject position of 'woman who is beautiful for herself'.

The absence of men from this discourse does not, however, necessarily signify their lack of importance here. It may be that being heterosexually attractive is so culturally important that it goes without saying that women's beautification is for men (Ferguson, 1983). Nevertheless, the apparent absence of men from this discourse does also emphasize the extent to which physical appearance constitutes an integral part of femininity so that narcissism becomes the explicit norm in the pages of women's magazines (see Coward, 1984). Thus, whilst feminine beauty remains equated with thinness, the pursuit of this 'ideal' is presented as a form of self-care rather than a means of attracting a man. Whilst within romantic discourse the thin/anorexic body signifies a traditionally heterosexual femininity, within this 'be more beautiful' discourse it signifies a more self-possessed woman who is beautiful 'for herself' rather than for another. This latter 'reading' of the thin female body cannot entirely escape patriarchally imposed meanings, but it does suggest the possibility that that body sustains a variety of meanings, not all of which conform to patriarchally defined ideals of 'femininity'. The disciplinary power of discourses about the body is produced through the entanglement of these different discourses through which the multiple meanings of fat or thin bodies continually slip. And it is within this entanglement and slipping of significations of 'the body' and 'the woman' that alternative and often contradictory meanings are consolidated.

THE ANOREXIC BODY AS A STRUGGLE OVER MEANING

If the thin or anorexic female body sustains a multiplicity of meanings then we can understand the texts, talk and social practices that surround that body as sites of struggle over the meanings of the body and over the forms of subjectivity that that body signifies. If we accept that the body is not the origin of its meanings, and that knowledges and meanings about the body are, rather, produced in discourse, then it follows that discourse is an arena in which these different meanings are asserted, contested, accepted, resisted and subverted. The following extract, in which Michelle describes a discussion with her father about a supermodel, illustrates such a struggle over some of the entangled meanings of thinness and femininity.

MICHELLE: I remember having lots of chats about her {a supermodel} with my dad (.) and my mum and everything (.) and um my dad was saying: oh she's all right but you know she's she's terribly thin. /H: right hu/ You know: I hate hate women that look so thin an' (.) /H: mm/ you know she should, she doesn't really look like a woman an' hu (.) /H: (laughing) right/ *But* I admit I didn't really agree with him and I don't think (.) if there were ever any women in the room (.) when (.) he was saying this I don't think they would either. /H: right/ But /H: mm/ (.) he just said (.) he preferred to see women that looked like women, women /H: right/ woman-shaped [...] But I didn't think so. I thought that she was (.) really perfect [...] I just thought she looked beautiful generally /H: right/ um (.) And (.) that I mean I I knew quite a lot about her personality. I thought she was a nice person. She was very (.) she was very how I thought (.) at the time I thought women should be. She was (.) she was quite quiet really and um (.) (laughing) you know she behaved herself. (laughter) Yeah she was very um (.) I don't know how to put it really (.) um. She was kind of dignified really [...] I think yeah /H: mm/ I could be like her.

In this account the model is construed as 'really perfect'. She was 'thin', 'beautiful', 'a nice person', 'quite quiet really', 'she behaved herself' and was 'dignified'. Ostensibly she constituted a manifestation of traditional femininity. Yet Michelle's account of her father's contribution to the discussion also suggests a different reading. In contrast with Michelle's admiration, 'he' argues that 'she doesn't really look like a woman' and that he preferred women to be 'woman-shaped'. Thinness thus comes to signify not-woman as well as perfect femininity. And this difference of meaning is also explicitly gendered by Michelle's comment that it is not only herself that would disagree with her father. If there were ever any women present they would also disagree with him. Her account not only introduces the possibility that 'thinness' may signify 'non-woman' as well as 'perfect woman'. By juxtaposing this 'male'-voiced possibility with her own description of the model, Michelle thereby also alters the meaning of her construction of the thin body. Her definition of the thin body as feminine perfection now involves a conflict with 'male' opinion rather than a desiring of 'male' approval. The account can thus be read as a discursive struggle over the multiple competing meanings of the thin female body. The romantic construction of the thin female body is contested and thereby subverted at the same time as many of the romantic meanings of that body are also affirmed.

Discourse can thus be seen as a site in which these multiple and often conflicting meanings of the thin or anorexic body are produced and contested. The thin body connotes feminine fragility, defencelessness, and lack of power ('ideal' characteristics for a heroine of heterosexual romantic discourse). But it also signifies a more self-possessed femininity where women are beautiful 'for themselves'. And at the same time it may signify not-woman and perhaps a liberation from the oppression of traditional domestic femininity (see also Bordo, 1990). The thin female body signifies a multiplicity of femininities *and* a rejection of femininity. It signifies a conformity to patriarchal femininity but it also indicates a differing from, and a deferring of, prescribed gender positions.

DIFFERING WITH GENDER

Construing the thin body as boyish

Why can't a woman be more like a man?

(My Fair Lady)

As we have seen, talk about 'the thin body' can be viewed as a site of struggle over the multiplicity of its meanings. It can, for example, be 'read' as signifying non-woman as well as 'perfect femininity'. It resists as well as embodies patriarchal gender identities. And one way in which the femininity of 'the thin body' is most clearly resisted is in its discursive construction as androgynous or boyish.

This quasi-feminist signification of the boyish body ideal has also been paralleled in some modernist elements of women's fashion. As Evans and Thornton (1991: 50) argue, a fashion item 'negotiates the terms of sexual difference and constructs the feminine . . . [The] work *actively* negotiates difference and generates meaning.' Like bodies, fashion is located in a significatory system in which its meanings are produced and re-produced. The 1920s work of Chanel, for example, adopted the style of masculine clothes so as to signify power and control just as women's power-dressing did in the 1980s. Whereas the 'excess and folly' of flowing, decorative, non-functional dresses, exemplified in the 1930s works of Schiaparelli, can be read as an 'appropriation of female masquerade', so the clean straight lines of Chanel's suits represent a cultural rejection of the feminine and an 'appropriation of masculine power' (ibid.: 50).

Like women's 'masculine' clothing, the thin body may also signify a cultural rejection of the feminine. It may be construed as boyish. And, in appropriating the masculine, it thereby disrupts the gendering of the female body. It resists a patriarchally imposed feminine identity and can thus be 'read' as signifying a quasi-feminist, 'liberated' subjectivity of the late twentieth century (Bordo, 1990). It might even signify masculine power and control. Yet, this discursive construction of the thin body as boyish is also highly ambiguous and problematic:

ELAINE: Uh (.) well women are always so (.) portrayed so petite like (.) not not even like girls. They're portrayed like little boys. (.) /H: right/ Men are always like this muscular, /H: mm/ big, almost, almost to make (.) one protective over the other.

The boyish female body may signify a liberation from oppressive patriarchal gender (im)positions. Yet this construction also resonates with constructions of the thin body as childlike, as powerless, dependent and femininely fragile; a construction which seems far from liberatory. Women, even if boyish, are construed in Elaine's account as 'petite' and defenceless in contrast with men who are 'big', 'muscular' and 'protective'. The primary signification here is that the body is little and childlike and *then* it is differently gendered. Patriarchal gender relations remain intact. Moreover, the portrayal of women's bodies as boyish is articulated here as an imposition rather than as a liberation. This is how women are 'portrayed', not how they are. Whilst not denying the more liberatory meanings of the boyishly thin body, we must also acknowledge some of the problematic ambiguities of 'the boyish body'.

Yet the fact that the thin female body signifies a 'boyish' non-femininity as well as a feminine subjectivity does open up further semiotic fields in which the gendering of that body can be played out. For this androgynous body, in signifying femininity and non-femininity, is doubly gendered and can therefore be understood as signifying a bisexual gender identity. And if bisexuality indicates the precariousness of subjectivity (Rose, 1982), then the discursive construction of the thin female body as boyish is inevitably ambiguous and perhaps subversive. It involves a precarious balancing between significations of masculine power and petite femininity. The meanings of this doubly, or bisexually, gendered body is then endlessly differed back and forth between these two significations. The thin (boyish/feminine) body refuses to 'line up on one or other side of the divide' of gender difference (see Rose, 1982). It refuses and thereby subverts the illusory possibility of a unitary, stable gender identity by refusing the closure and difference of the phallic mode of identity (see also Benjamin, 1985).

As Lacan argues, within the Symbolic order 'sexual difference is a legislative divide which creates and reproduces its categories' only in relation to the phallus (Rose, 1982: 41). And the 'boyishly' thin female body can be read as subversive in that it signifies a differing with, and deferring of, this difference.

Yet this construction of the thin female body as boyish also resonates with 'the woman' described by Lacan. For 'the woman', Lacan argues, there is 'something unacceptable' about an order which produces difference only in relation to the phallus. 'Her' position (in relation to the phallus) is inevitably 'fundamentally conflictual' and 'insoluble' (Rose, 1982: 45). And, like 'the woman', the discursive construction of the thin female body as boyish is profoundly conflictual and impossible. It unsettles the very notion of categorical difference and unitary, stable identity.

The theme of masquerade produces further resonances between the subjectivity signified by the boyishly thin body and the category of 'woman' theorized by Lacan. Discursive constructions of the thin/anorexic female body as boyish produce that body as something that it is not, as a masquerade. Women, Elaine argued, are 'portrayed like little boys' (my emphasis). And 'for Lacan, masquerade is the very definition of "femininity" precisely because it is constructed with reference to a male sign' (Rose, 1982: 43). Joan Riviere (1929) similarly described the 'failed femininity' of the hysteric as a masquerade. 'To "her" "femininity" really seems to equal the gap indicated by castration . . . it is enacted as "a masquerade" to cover it' (Mitchell, 1984: 308). And if, as Freud argues, 'the feminine . . . was in part a hysterical formation' (Mitchell, 1974: 48), then femininity and masquerade are again equated. Thus, like Chanel's 'masculine' clothes, the 'boyishly' thin female body collapses into the very category that it rejects. It becomes feminine masquerade. Whilst the two significations of 'the thin body' –

romantic femininity and boyishness – appear directly contradictory, they are also simultaneously (and impossibly) compatible.

Discourses of femininity and the amenorrhea-ic body

As we have seen, the extreme thinness of the 'anorexic' body renders it a particularly effective signifier of traditional or romantic femininity. But this very thinness simultaneously renders it a very effective signifier of non-feminine subjectivities. As the body becomes progressively thinner, so breasts and hips are reduced and menstruation ceases. Thus, whilst 'the anorexic body' may be (multiply) constructed as hyper-feminine, it may also be (multiply) constructed as non-feminine, as boyish or as an evasion of the femininities signified by the post-pubertal female body.

Amenorrhea (the absence of menstruation) is now considered to be a major diagnostic symptom of anorexia nervosa (Halmi and Falk, 1983). And, as we have seen (see Chapter 4) this is frequently considered as a biological matter. Yet, menstruation (and therefore its absence) is also a socially embedded phenomenon surrounded by 'superstitions', rituals and taboos (Ussher, 1991; Millett, 1971). Menstruation and amenorrhea are located within sets of discursive (and material) practices through which they acquire particular meanings. And usually (but not always) these meanings have been negative (see Malson and Ussher, 1996a). 'The menstruating woman' has often been figured as incapacitated, dangerous and dirty (Ussher, 1991). 'She' has been barred from religious and sexual activity, from preparing food and from sleeping in the family home (Ussher, 1991).

The recent controversy over television advertisements for sanitary products suggests that constructions of menstruation as a shameful 'curse' are still deeply entrenched in society, whilst the medical concept of PMS similarly re-produces an image of a debilitated and often dangerous, biologically labile woman governed by her menstrual cycle (Malson and Ussher, 1996a). Despite the lack of satisfactory supporting evidence, 'PMS' has lent scientific authority to the notion that women are rendered unreliable, debilitated, accident-prone, mentally unstable, violent and dangerous (Ussher, 1989; Parlee, 1989), and that woman's supposed inferiority is rooted in her body (Ussher, 1992a).

In short, the menstruating woman has been negatively construed as dirty and dangerous within a variety of socio-cultural contexts. Hence, the physical and discursive production of the female body as an anorexic/amenorrhea-ic body has particular consequences for the gendered significations that that body can sustain. The amenorrhea-ic body is inevitably construed in relation to those discourses and discursive practices that surround menstruation. Within this context menarche represents an imposition of the negatively construed femininities that are signified by the menstruating body (see Malson and Ussher, 1996a).

NICKI: It was like uh when like when my periods started and that was when

116

I first sort of you know realized that I was becoming a woman. /H: right/ And I can remember being really angry. /H: mm/ And it was more, it was very specific [. . .] I just wanted to be *young* again.

In this account menstruation is constituted as a source of anger and as a signifier of an adult femininity, of 'becoming a woman'. Consequently amenorrhea may be construed positively as a rejection of this unwanted femininity.

ELAINE: What what they would be trying to do through their anorexia?
H: Yeah. (.)
ELAINE: A lot of things. /H: mm/ They'd be isolating themselves. They'd be (.) stopping their periods and not being a woman any more. (.) /H: right/ They'd be (.) avoiding emotions. (.) /H: mm/ All kinds of things like that /H: mm/ in that range.

CATHY: And um (.) I suppose when I started my periods, I mean I don't have periods any more, /H: right/ I haven't had for years. But when I started um (.) I felt angry and I wanted to be a boy.

The amenorrhea-ic, anorexic body thus acquires the positive connotations of 'not being a woman any more', of escaping the femininity signified by menstruation. Thus, like the 'boyishly' thin body, it is discursively constituted as non-feminine. Anorexia has been interpreted by a number of authors as a psycho-biological retreat into childhood (see Crisp, 1970) and as a refusal to be an adult woman (Plaut and Hutchinson, 1986). Goodsitt (1985), for example, describes anorexia as a symptomatic manifestation of a failure to accept female psychosexual maturity: 'Pubertal body changes panic her because they mean becoming a self-sufficient adult woman' (Goodsitt, 1985: 75). In the interview extracts above, the amenorrhea-ic body does signify non-feminine subjectivity. The physical production of the amenorrhea-ic body is clearly constituted discursively as a rejection of womanhood. 'They'd be (.) stopping their periods and not being a woman any more.' It is not so clear, however, that what is being rejected here is adult femininity in its totality. For femininity is not an unproblematic, unitary category and might be better understood as a plural collectivity of often contradictory representations (see Chapter 1). And, as we have seen, the culturally sanctioned discourses surrounding menstruation most frequently present the menstruating woman not as self-sufficient adult but as dirty and dangerous, as biologically labile. Perhaps then the amenorrhea-ic, anorexic body signifies a rejection of this particular denigrated femininity rather than a rejection of femininity *per se* (Malson and Ussher, 1996a).

In Elaine's extract above, amenorrhea is associated not simply with a refusal of womanhood but also with 'avoiding emotions' and 'all kinds of things like that'. The extract suggests, therefore, a stereotypical association between femininity and emotionality (see Nicolson, 1992). In the following extract, this association is again apparent but there are also other attributes associated with the particular discursive construction of femininity that is signified by the menstruating body.

TERESA: It {anorexia} was about not having feelings, not having periods, not being (.) /H: mm/ emotional, not being vulnerable. /H: right/ I mean vulnerability is just the one thing I couldn't afford. /H: right/ And um, although I'm sure in a lot of ways I was vulnerable but I mean it /H: yeah/ um and I was very asexual. I mean I'd sleep around but I didn't have orgasms.

Menstruation is associated here with emotionality, sexuality, vulnerability, danger and lack of control. The account reproduces a socially prevalent, polyvalent figure of the 'biologically labile' woman (see Ussher, 1991). It produces a *particular* negative construction of femininity so that amenorrhea as a symptom of anorexia is construed as a refusal of this specific version of 'woman' rather than of femininity *per se* (Malson and Ussher, 1996a).

The amenorrhea-ic body and a discourse of Cartesian dualism

In the extracts above the menstruating body is produced as a signifier of a particular 'biologically labile' femininity that is emotional, sexual, vulnerable and dangerous. This femininity is also firmly located in the female (menstruating) body. The very thin, amenorrhea-ic body is construed, then, as a rejection of this particular femininity. It is both physically and discursively dissociated from the menstruating body and from the subjectivity that that body signifies (Malson and Ussher, 1996a).

NICKI: It was very specific. It was involved with my periods starting and I hated them /H: right/ and I was very annoyed and I sort of saw my body as a separate thing, like it wasn't me. /H: right/ It was a separate thing and I was very angry /H: right mm/ and I wanted to sort of distance myself from it. [. . .] It felt, well it felt scary /H: mm/ cos it felt like I wasn't secure [. . .] all of a sudden it was doing something that was out of my control /H: mm right/ and I saw it as being not me /H: mm/ and I couldn't relate to it and I wanted to sort of get rid of it.

The menstruating body is construed here as uncontrolled and dangerous, as 'scary' and as a source of insecurity. The negative attributes signified by menstruation are firmly located in the body which is then presented as alien to the self. 'It was a separate thing . . . it was doing something that was out of my control . . . and I saw it as being not me . . . and I couldn't relate to it.' I would argue that the extract draws on a discourse of Cartesian dualism in which mind and body are bifurcated. Subjectivity is constituted as a disembodied mind/self, dissociated from the body which is produced as lacking in control and as alien and threatening to the mind/self: 'the body is the locus of all that threatens our attempts at *control*. It overtakes, it overwhelms, it erupts and disrupts' (Bordo, 1992: 94).

This discourse of Cartesian dualism constructs the body as unruly and threatening and, at the same time, produces a disembodied subjectivity of mind/self dissociated from the (menstruating) body. Hence, the 'biologically labile' femininity signified by (and located in) the menstruating body is construed as other of the self. Amenorrhea can thus be read as a physical and discursive consolidation of this dissociation.

Bruch (1978) has commented that many women diagnosed as anorexic talk of two 'warring' selves – one spiritual, intellectual, strong-willed and 'male', and the other bodily, uncontrollable, impure, weak-willed and 'female'. This aspect of anorexia might be better understood, however, not as individual pathology but as the interpellation of the subject by a socially pervasive discourse of Cartesian dualism. Discourses of mind/body dualism have a long history in the traditions of Christian asceticism and stoicism (Foucault, 1988). They are also manifested in a variety of contemporary cultural representations of the body, for example, in the division between mental and physical illness (Turner, 1987); in the images of bulging, unruly fat promoted by the diet industry (Bordo, 1990, 1992) and in the horror film genre's concern with the alien, eruptive and disruptive body (Bordo, 1990). They set up an antagonism between mind and body which informs a variety of cultural practices such as dieting and exercise, as well as self-starvation and purging (Bordo, 1990, 1992), ideals of being without a body (Chernin, 1981) and the constructions, articulated above, of the (menstruating) body as alien and threatening (Malson and Ussher, 1996a).

The above extracts deploy, then, a discourse of Cartesian dualism to construct a disembodied mind/self that transcends the femininity signified by the menstruating body. Yet, as indicated above (see Bruch, 1978), this mind/body duality is also distinctly, systematically gendered. 'Woman' has frequently been made to signify otherness (Mitchell and Rose, 1982) and bodily-ness (Crowley and Himmelweit, 1992), particularly the sexualized body (see de Beauvoir, 1953; Ussher, 1992a), the pathologized, defective and disruptive body (see Ussher, 1991; Showalter, 1985) and the excluded body (see Sayers, 1982). And dualist discourse rearticulates these patriarchal dichotomies that equate woman with the body, with weakness, irrationality and lack of control and man with the mind, with rationality, strength and control (Malson and Ussher, 1996a). That is, the body of dualist discourse is frequently figured as a feminine body. It is homologous with constructions of the menstruating body articulated above.

In short, the discourse of Cartesian dualism, evidenced in the extracts above, interpellates the subject as a disembodied mind/self dissociated from the biologically labile femininity signified by menstruation. But it simultaneously consolidates the discursive construction of the (feminine, menstruating) body as eruptive, threatening and alien to the self. Ironically, menstruation can be seen as signifying both the uncontrollability of the 'biologically labile' woman and the self-division produced by dualist discourse. Like eating and purging, menstruation transgresses the body's boundaries and can be read as a metaphor both of uncontrolled bodily eruption and of a disrupted self. Within a discourse of

Cartesian dualism the amenorrhea-ic body, like the 'boyishly' thin body, is construed as non-feminine. It signifies a dissociation both from this uncontrolled and threatening body and from the 'biologically labile' feminine subjectivity that that body signifies.

CONCLUSIONS

In this chapter I have sought to explore how the thin/anorexic body is multiply constituted, focusing on the ways in which that body is differently gendered by different discourses. Within romantic discourse, for example, the thin/anorexic body is constituted as feminine and heterosexually attractive, a signification which is consolidated by constructions of the thin/anorexic body as childlike, as small and petite, as fragile and sick. Yet this body may also signify a more self-possessed femininity or a non-feminine subjectivity. As a boyish body, the thin or anorexic female body may signify a differing with, and a deferring of, patriarchal gender (im)positions. Or as an amenorrhea-ic body it may signify a rejection of a particular negatively construed 'biologically labile' femininity.

The different discourses that converge upon the female body and the anorexic body thus constitute that body in quite different ways. They locate it within different power/knowledge relations (Foucault, 1979); and it is through such discourses that power permeates the body, its movements, it routines, its sensations, its sexuality, its meanings (Foucault, 1977b, 1979). These popular discourses that converge upon the female body constitute and regulate our experiences of gaining and losing weight, of embodiment, gender and identity. They conspire to consolidate and reconsolidate the appeal of the thin female body as they produce and reproduce the thin female body as an ideal which sustains a multiplicity of meanings, even a multiplicity of gendered subjectivities. Within this context it becomes increasingly difficult to think of 'anorexia' as an individual pathology, as a category of experience that can be neatly separated from its social discursive contexts. What I have sought to do in this chapter is to show how popular discourses – texts, talk and social practices – can be understood as sites of production of bodily meaning and as sites of struggle over the multiplicity of meanings of the body and over the differently gendered subjectivities that that body signifies.

6

SUBJECTIVITY, EMBODIMENT AND GENDER IN A DISCOURSE OF CARTESIAN DUALISM

In the previous chapter I discussed how the thin or anorexic body may be differently gendered by the different discourses in which it is constituted. One of the discourses that I identified in this analysis was a discourse of Cartesian dualism, which produces the body as uncontrolled and threatening and alien to the disembodied subject position of mind/self. This chapter continues with this theme of mind–body dualism, exploring how issues of control, subjectivity, embodiment and gender are discursively constituted within this Cartesian dualist discourse (see also Malson and Ussher, 1996b; Malson, forthcoming).

THE DISCURSIVE PRODUCTION OF CONTROL

'Anorexia nervosa' has frequently been interpreted as a response to feeling out of control and as an attempt to assert control by controlling the body (Bruch, 1974). And this theme of control is clearly a prominent aspect of the discourses surrounding eating and embodiment. The extracts below, for example, illustrate the commonplace construction of the thin body as a controlled body.

H: Was there something that say being thin meant to you?
WENDY: Yes, it made me feel successful as if I was kind of (.) I don't know, in control.
ZOE: I felt like such a loser because *I* felt like *I couldn't control my weight because I was overweight.* /H: right/ *So there must* be something wrong with me because you know: oh well, I didn't have enough self-control.

The thin, anorexic body is discursively produced here as a controlled body, whilst conversely being overweight signifies a lack of self-control. Being overweight is equated with a lack of weight control and thereby signifies that there is 'something wrong' with Zoe because she 'didn't have enough self-control'. The discursive constructions of fat and thin bodies evidenced here differ again from the various constructions discussed in Chapter 5. They do, however, converge in reproducing and thereby consolidating idealizations of thinness and denigrations of fatness. The thin or anorexic body here signifies not romantic femininity, passivity, fragility, sickness or inferiority but control – weight control, self-control and control over one's life. And the value of this control, like the value of thinness, appears as self-evident truth.

NICKI: There are a lot of characteristics that I admire like being slim [. . .]
It's the kind of idea of being in control of your life and doing all your
work and sticking to deadlines and /H: mm/ you know /H: being
competent/ sort of perfection, yeah the perfection ideal.

Being thin is construed as part of 'the perfection ideal' of being in control. The
thin body seems to signify far more than weight control alone. It signifies 'being
in control of your life'. But how is it that the thin body appears as the only body
that is controlled? How does being thin come to signify a wider control over
one's life, and why does this control seem to be such a good thing?

A CONTROLLED BODY – A CONTROLLED LIFE

The thin body is so frequently presented to us as the desired end-product of
dietary restraint. And dietary restraint, so we are told, is a form of virtuous self-
control. To eat less than we want to, to go hungry is, apparently, to exert control.
And to be thin is both the proof of that virtuous exertion and the reward for it.

MICHELLE: There are so many things in magazines (.) um about (.) diets
you know how /H: right/ how you should make an effort with yourself.
You should be really tough /H: mm/ and (.) /H: right/ um you know
after Christmas the first thing you've got to do is go on this diet to get
back (laughing) some of your /H: (laughing) right/ self-control or whatever.

The thin body is valued here not so much for its beauty as for its being the
product, the proof, of self-control. It is proof that you have not (over)indulged in
food; that you have gone 'on this diet to get back some of your . . . self-control'.
Control is discursively produced in a specific way here. It is construed as something achieved through abstinence, particularly through food refusal, so that not
eating becomes an assertion of individual control because

JACKIE: However much people try and make you eat no one can (.) /H:
right/ you know control *that*. I mean it's sh' it's *me* doing what I want.

The thin body thus signifies a positively valued subject position of self-controlled,
autonomous individuality. Yet this construction is also permeated by a theme of
restricted control in which food and body weight feature as the *only* arenas in
which control is possible.

DENISE: I didn't like myself so I saw myself as a failure, can't do anything
right. /H: right/ And in in a way (laughing) that losing weight or having
troubles around food was sort of saying: well I can do this. /H: right/
You know: I'm in control of *this*.

122

PENNY: Nothing was ever good enough. Every half a stone I lost I wanted
         to lose another one. /H: mm/ And I kept saying: no I'll stop when I get
         to six stone, you know. It carried on so you know, it just took a snowball
         and I couldn't let go cos I wanted /H: mm/ that control that I thought I
         didn't have over my life.

The defiance of taking control through food refusal is immediately undercut by
the articulation of food and body weight/shape as perhaps the only aspects of
life where control is possible. The positive subjectivity signified by the thin body
here is accompanied by a subtextual subjectivity of 'failure' in all other aspects of
life.

The thin/anorexic body may signify the quasi-feminist subjectivity of an
autonomous woman who is in control of her life but 'her' control is restricted to
the traditional arena of female domesticity, to food and the body (see Brumberg,
1988).

Paradoxically, however, this theme of restricted control is overwritten by a
theme of control that extends far beyond the body and food. The controlled
body becomes a metonym of a controlled life, so that not eating and being thin
quite explicitly signify a total control.

NICKI: If I'm feeling that everything's getting on top of me /H: mm/ like I
         was in my room last night and it was a tip and I was tired and I've got
         all these deadlines and I hadn't done the work. /H: right/ So I hadn't
         done the work and also I'd had a row with someone and I just felt sort
         of out of control /H: right/ and everything and then the thought of
         being hungry felt so nice /H: right mm/ cos it'd mean, I mean if like if
         I lost weight then everything else'd be solved as well /H: right/ cos I'd
         be in control.

In Nicki's account of the previous evening, she describes *everything* as getting on
top of her. There is nothing that she is in control of. The description of her
room as 'a tip' works as a metaphor for the rest of her life at that moment which
seems overwhelmingly cluttered with problems. She is tired. She hasn't done her
work. She isn't going to meet the deadlines she has been set and she has just had
a row with someone. In contrast, 'the thought of being hungry felt so nice'. The
'solution' is simple: if she lost weight, then 'everything else'd be solved as well'
because that would mean that she was in control. Losing weight signifies not just
weight control but *total* control.

These very powerful significations of thinness and food restriction appear
plausible because, I would argue, they are embedded in the culturally dominant
discourse of Cartesian dualism. That is, the (over)valuing of control and the
equation of control with thinness cannot be adequately understood in terms of
individual pathology (Malson and Ussher, 1996b). Rather, the thin/anorexic
body is produced as a controlled body within a discourse of Cartesian dualism
which produces the concept of control in a specifically idealized way.

As we have seen, this discourse produces human existence as essentially dichotomized into the spiritual (or mental) and the physical (see also Chapter 5). Whilst the mind is privileged, the body is constructed as alien, as an enemy that threatens our attempts at control and must itself be controlled (Bordo, 1990). The hegemony of this discourse of Cartesian dualism is apparent in a variety of cultural practices. It has, for example, long been manifest in Christian literature (see Martin *et al.*, 1988) and its central theme of mind divided from body is apparent in divisions between physical and mental illness (Turner, 1987). Dualistic concerns about managing the alien, disruptive and eruptive body are also evidenced in popular culture; in, for example, films such as *Alien*, *A Teenage Werewolf in London* and *The Thing* (Bordo, 1990). Cartesian dualist discourse similarly informs popular narratives such as *Flashdance* and *Rocky*, where people succeed in life through persistent control and mastery of the body (Bordo, 1990). Dualistic concerns are manifested not only in the prevalence of eating disorders and dieting, but also in a contemporary stance towards health and exercise

> which, although preoccupied with the body and deriving narcissistic enjoy-ment from its appearance, takes little pleasure in the *experience* of embodiment. Rather, the fundamental identification is with mind (or will), ideals of spiritual perfection, fantasies of absolute control.
>
> (Bordo, 1992: 97–98)

One of the most dramatic aspects of this dualistic fiction of subjectivity and embodiment is the fantasy of dictating one's own body shape, a fantasy that manifests itself not only in anorexia and in dieting but also in normal/obsessive exercise and body-building, in the fantasies of halting the ageing process and dictating body shape that pervade numerous advertisements for cosmetics and cosmetic surgery (Bordo, 1990).

In short, Cartesian dualist discourse produces the body as alien to the mind/self. As eruptive Other, the body threatens to overwhelm the self and to disrupt self-integrity. This discourse thereby discursively produces the need for control over the body and at the same time constructs 'control' as a form of war against the body. The body is produced as the prime target of control, and body management acquires immense significance because self-integrity requires control over the body.

A DUALISTIC CONSTRUCTION OF EATING

It is, then, within the socio-cultural context of this discourse of Cartesian dualism that the body is construed as alien and in need of control, and that the thin/anorexic body is constructed as *the* controlled body. It is construed as a proof of self-control and integrity and metonymically signifies an absolute will and total control over one's life. Within this discourse eating becomes constituted as a bodily and therefore alien desire, a temptation that must be resisted at all costs (Malson and Ussher, 1996b).

EMMA: You know everything that you're forbidden to have and you have to
        eat it *all* at once [. . .] and it's just the franticness that I hate /H: mm/
        because you do. In a way it feels like it's not me. It feels *it* takes over. /H:
        mm/ It's not me saying: oh, you know do it. /H: right/ It's something
        completely (.) something completely dissociated from me /H: right/ that
        just kicks in and says: yeah do it you know. But I'm not thinking about it
        at all. /H: right/ I have to clear up the mess once I've done it and sort
        out you know what's been going on /H: mm/ because I haven't been
        there all the time that that's all been happening.

The subjective experience of eating is constituted here in clearly dualistic terms.
Mind and body are dichotomized and eating is construed as a bodily desire,
entirely alien to the mind/self. 'In a way it feels like it's not me. It feels *it* takes
over . . . It's something completely (.) something completely dissociated from me.'
Eating becomes an alien activity that belongs to the body rather than the
mind/self. It is something that happens only when the mind/self is not vigilantly
in control of the body and its desires.

ZOE: I would just run into the like kitchen and like four o'clock in the
        morning, like have a bowl of cereal, like *two* muffins and like toast, like
        and would eat so much and then I couldn't like, I felt like I had eaten
        half of it before I'd even realized what I was doing. You know /H: mm/
        and I was like, you know, this is so weird [. . .] my body was just eating
        it before my mind could /H: could think about it/ was awake enough to
        stop it from doing it.

Within this discourse subjectivity is radically split so that the (bodily) experience of
eating becomes dissociated from the experience of self. The relationship between
the self/mind and the alienated body is discursively produced as a relationship of
conflict. The desire to eat is construed as the body's invasion of mind/self
integrity. Like 'the menstruating body' (see Chapter 5), 'the eating body' is
constructed as Other and as 'the locus of all that threatens our attempts at
control. It overtakes, it overwhelms, it erupts and disrupts' (see Bordo, 1992: 94).

FOOD AS AN OBJECT OF DUALISTIC DISCOURSE

It is within this discursive context that I would argue one might understand
better the immense significance of thinness and food refusal as signifiers of self-
control. For body management becomes central to the maintenance of
self-integrity, and eating becomes an occasion when the body, something that is
'not me', 'takes over' and triumphs in the discursively produced conflict between
mind/self and body. As an object of bodily desire, food similarly takes on very
powerful significations within this discourse. It is simultaneously wanted (by the
body) and forbidden (by the mind/self). Food becomes constituted as a
profoundly threatening temptation.

H: What did what did um food mean to you? Did=

=LAYLA: *Huu! Wherr!* /H: uh/ (.) *Enemy* /H: right/ I loved food. I *loved* food
    (.) but that meant (.) fat bellies, /H: mm/ (.) fat legs, fat bottom, ugliness,
    (.) unaesthetic, /H: right/ dangerous.

LYNN: Used to think it was something *dirty* and disgusting [. . .]

SIMONE: There was also that little part that really wanted it as well /JANE:
    yeah/ wasn't there, little part that and then you'd be *so* cross with your-
    self for feeling that /JANE: mm/ and actually thinking: (laughing) God
    that would be quite nice actually.

Food is constituted here as 'quite nice actually'. It is 'liked' and '*loved*' but it is also
'dangerous', '*dirty* and disgusting'. There is an enormous tension in these discursive constructions of 'food' – a love–hate relationship.

ZOE: Like I would love, like if I felt bad I realize I'd love to just go eat [. . .]
   but then I saw food, yeah, food's my enemy and I like hated it.

Food is constituted as a simultaneously desired and feared object. And in the
discursive space created by this tension 'food' assumes enormous, almost myth-
ical importance. Within this discourse the dangers of food extend far beyond
weight gain *per se*. Given the significance accorded to the mind–body battle,
'food' becomes an extremely dangerous and powerful temptation.

PENNY: In the beginning the food, it was a love–hate relationship /H:
    right/ um really more hate. It just, it was just that I was interested in
    everything you know, food magazines, TV, anything. /H: mm/ A discus-
    sion with food you'd guarantee I'd be on it, in on it. Diets. It was all, so
    food became the centre of my life. First thing, wake up, what do I think
    of? Food. /H: mm/ Food, food, food. But then almost towards, you
    know as it progressed food became almost poison to me. I thought I'd
    be poisoning /H: right/ my system if I was going to allow myself to
    have anything [. . .] I didn't see the food as life-sustaining. I saw it as
    life-threatening.

'Food, food, food' is the centre of Penny's life, but it is a dangerous obsession. For
food is construed here as poisonous and life-threatening. In the context of dualistic discourse, to give in to this bodily temptation is to lose control. It is to
pollute the purity of the mind/self and disrupt or even destroy self-integrity. As a
bodily temptation, food is simultaneously loved and hated, desired and feared; a
discursive tension which is further amplified by its construction as both life-
threatening and life-sustaining. In Penny's extract above, this latter aspect is
suppressed: 'I didn't see the food as life-sustaining. I saw it as life-threatening'.
The discursive construction of food as poisonous and life-threatening cannot,
however, entirely escape the obverse construction of food as life-sustaining and
indeed physically necessary for survival.

NICKI: I know that you have to eat to live but um (.) when at the time it
       seemed like an awful thing to do /H: mm/ and re' like a disgusting
       thing to do.

Because 'you have to eat to live' the tensions created in the dualistic construction
of food are inescapable. Our inevitable physical dependence on food produces
resonances with other forms of dependence so that food can function as a
metaphor for the ambivalences of social and emotional relationships that similarly may be both desired and feared. Like food, a relationship may be construed
as both necessary and dangerous. The discursive construction of food as simultaneously life-sustaining and life-threatening resonates with cultural
representations of heterosexual relationships, with adages such as 'Can't live with
them, can't live without them.' It also brings to mind a 'standard' psychoanalytic
interpretation of anorexia as a fear of (oral) impregnation (see Chapter 4). One
of the many meanings of food refusal might, then, be a resistance to constructions of 'the self' as (femininely) dependent.

   The dualistic construction of food as temptation can also function as a
metaphor for the ambivalence of mother–daughter relationships. As we have
seen, the 'anorexogenic' mother has frequently been imbricated in the daughter's
'anorexia' (see Chapter 4). Bruch (1973), for example, attributes disordered
eating to disturbances in the early mother–child (feeding) relationship.
Universalistic and mother-blaming accounts are, as I have argued above,
profoundly problematic (see also Malson, 1992). However, the prominence of
'the mother' in much of the literature on anorexia does indicate a cultural dominance of discourses which constitute 'the mother' as provider of food, as almost
wholly responsible for her children's welfare and as potentially dangerous (in this
case, to her daughter). It also indicates the cultural importance of 'the mother',
and hence the mother, in the constituting of our identities as daughters, as
women. It is significant, then, that Bruch (1973) argues further that disturbances
in this mother–child relationship result in a curtailed development of individuation, in a lack of sense of autonomy in the child, in 'diffuse ego-boundaries'. The
mother is thus a culturally overdetermined presence in women's gendered and
problematized relationships to food (see also pp. 87–89).

   Within Cartesian dualist discourse food is constructed as both necessary and
threatening; an object of temptation and a metaphor for (potentially dangerous)
dependence. In Michelle's extracts below, this construction of 'food' as fearful is
very apparent.

MICHELLE: Now that I know the calorie value of everything it's sort of
       makes things (laughing) very scary. /H: right/ A cream cake's /H:
       (coughs)/ a cream cake can be really threatening and frightening [. . .]
       I know that food's got a lot of power over *me* because if I start (.) if I
       start eating and sort of (.) if I don't have that control then I could quite
       easily (.) blow it. (.) That's a day's dieting gone.

JACKIE: I mean when I came in here *every* food, even literally an orange (.) /H: right/ I couldn't *eat* (.) anything. I mean even I was (.) could hardly even drink. I was so terrified of the fact that I would put on weight (laughing) if I had any /H: right mm/ (.) anything in me. (.) /H: yeah/ I think before I was like that as well, /H: mm/ I mean terrif', I mean before I would eat fruit, (.) I wouldn't eat vegetables because I was too scared of them.

In these extracts the discursive construction of 'food' as temptation, as simultaneously 'nice' and 'horrible', is still apparent but it is predominantly construed as 'frightening', as having 'a lot of power over *me*'. 'It' is scary, 'poison' and 'suspect'. Even the words 'food' and 'eating' become taboo.

CATHY: You'll find that I never say f-double-o-d uh. There are certain words /H: right/ that are just taboo uhm such as e-a-t-i-n-g as well. I wouldn't say that to save my life. Uhm.

H: What is it that you dislike about all those words?=

=CATHY: Cos they connote *nice* things. And the whole process is horrible. I don't like having, I look at these things (indicates the Ribena carton she is holding) as being poison and I don't want poison in my body and I want to be cleansed inside. Even if I have water I get really paranoid, you know.

These accounts might be described as manifestations of individual pathology, of 'dysfunctional beliefs' or faulty cognitions (see Chapter 4). Yet constructions of 'food' – cream cakes, vegetables and even water – as profoundly threatening temptations are also homologous with more mundane formulations of food as 'naughty but nice', discursive constructions that pervade popular cultural representations of food. Cathy's refusal to say the words 'food' or 'eating' might similarly be described as obsessional. Yet, her account becomes more understandable if we read it within its cultural and discursive context. Her spelling out of these taboo words evokes a number of analogous cultural phenomena: for example, cultural or religious prohibitions against the use of particular words such as sexual words or God's name; situations where adults spell out words to prevent children from understanding 'forbidden' subjects; or Oscar Wilde's reference to 'the love that dare not speak its name'. Each of these involves objects or desires that are also forbidden and fearful. The object whose name is taboo is construed as tempting and threatening. It is controlled through a prohibition against naming it. A refusal to say the words 'food' or 'eating' might therefore be understood as a deployment of a particular cultural, discursive practice in a further attempt to control one's body and food, to control the temptation that threatens the integrity of the mind/self.

DUALISTIC CONSTRUCTIONS OF BODY FAT

The discursive construction of 'the thin body' as a controlled body can thus be understood as an element of a dualistic discourse in which 'food' represents temptation and 'eating' is construed as a bodily desire which threatens self-control. Within this discourse 'the body' is both a counterpoint to, and a metaphor for, the mind. Thinness signifies the mind's triumph over the body and its desires (see Bordo, 1992). It signifies control and therefore the integrity of 'the self'. In contrast, fatness is construed negatively, as it is in the extracts below, where the dualistic theme of the alienated body is explicitly centred on body fat (Malson, forthcoming; Malson and Ussher, 1996b). 'Fat' comes to signify the body. It is flesh, both 'the human body and its physical or sensual nature as opposed to the soul or spirit' and also 'excess weight; fat' (*Collins Dictionary and Thesaurus*, 1987; *Collins English Dictionary*, 1986).

EMMA: I want to lose the fat. /H: right/ And that's the only way that I ever look at it. I don't think to myself: right if I could get rid of the fat then, you know, people would look at me in the street, *then* everybody would find me more attractive. /H: mm/ It's just I (.) I hate it. I hate it being in me and it feels completely alien /H: right/ and I just want it away. You know. I want it *off*. /H: right/ But I don't really know (.) what it is, the goal of it at the end of it /H: mm/ you know. Because I'm not going to be able to change me intrinsically and I can't change my face which is what's on show most the time anyway. /H: yeah/ It's just, it's just the fat. I just hate it. It just doesn't feel like it should be part of me /H: mm/ you know. It feels all wrong. /H: yeah/ And I feel to a certain extent that something I did a few years ago has forced it to be there and now I've got to force it to go away again /H: right/ you know.

One of the dominant features of this extract is that 'fat' is construed both as bad and as 'completely alien'. It is a hated enemy to be got rid of: 'I just want it away . . . I want it *off*'. And it is also a cause of ontological anxiety and estrangement of 'the self' from the body. Emma describes fat as something that 'just doesn't feel like it should be part of {her}'. Like the body, body fat is produced as other of the self. That Emma's desire 'to lose the fat' is constituted as a dualistic desire is further reinforced by her refusal here of other possible interpretations. She does not want to lose the fat so that 'everybody would find {her} more attractive'. Yet she cannot produce an alternative motivation. She does not know 'the goal of it'. Losing body fat appears to be a goal in and of itself. Noticeably, however, Emma concludes that maybe the fat is 'forced . . . to be there' because of something she has done in the past and that she must therefore 'force it to go away again'. Her statement evokes a sense of penitence, a struggle against evil/fat in which the fat was forced on her as a form of punishment for which she must make amends by losing it. Losing fat, then, is constructed as a means of self-salvation; a construction which resonates with the themes of salvation and rescue of romantic discourse. But Emma's account also deploys a moralistic theme of punishment and atonement (see also Malson, forthcoming; Malson and Ussher, 1996b). The state of 'the body' is both a counterpoint to, and a metaphor for, the state of the mind/soul. (Body) fat is other of 'the self' but it also symbolizes 'the self'. Fat signifies that 'the self' is bodily, rather than controlled and 'spiritual'. Hence, getting rid of fat is construed as a quasi-spiritual struggle against the body.[1] Within this discourse of Cartesian dualism body fat becomes a moral issue.

JANE: I just wanted to get rid of all this weight an' /H: right/ (.) it made me
feel I was better cos there was less fat /H: mm/ as if there was less /H: mm/ bad. /H: mm mm/ And then once a nurse, I was in hospital, I went down to three stone twelve (.) and she stood me in front of this full-length mirror and said: look at you, for goodness sake. You know and I stood there and said: but I've got to lose another stone cos look at all the fat and the evil in my eyes. She sort of like: *What*. (laughs) She didn't quite know what to say /H: mm/ and I mean I was really serious /H: mm/. I just wanted to get down to like a stone or something [. . .] I used to (laughing) hate myself. I used to think I was a really bad and evil person. And I thought the more weight I lost the more evil I could get rid of so /H: right/ the better pers' (.) the better a person I'd be.

In Jane's disturbing account of her increasing emaciation, body fat is dramatically construed as morally bad. The negativity of this construction resonates with the numerous other negative constructions of 'fat' in the various discourses that converge on the body, consolidating and reconsolidating 'the fat body' as a negative term. Despite being so thin, Jane describes wanting 'to get rid of all this weight' because the more weight she lost 'the more evil {she} could get rid of'. In the slipping signifying chain of fat–flesh–body, body fat metonymically stands in for the body as a whole, epitomizing all that is (morally) wrong with the body of dualist discourse (see also Malson, forthcoming). Within this discourse losing weight has little to do with becoming more physically attractive. Rather, it constitutes an attempt to become a better person by eliminating as much of the body, as much fat/evil as possible.

NICKI: My whole self-like-worth was based on how small I was /H: right/
and each pound like increasing was like I was worse /H: right/. And it's *that* important.
H: Mm, is there some, was there something that you could say why it was that that each pound made you feel worse?
NICKI: I s'pose it was more of me living in the world or more of my body.

However emaciated one may be, there is still a desire to lose more weight. The 'ideal' body here is a non-body (see also Bordo, 1990) rather than a physically beautiful body.

To construe one's *whole* self-worth in terms of how small one is, on 'each pound', to construe fat so explicitly as morally bad or even evil might be interpreted as 'a "side show" experience, separating the "normal" audience from those on view' (see Bordo, 1990: 85). Yet, the discursive construction explicated here of 'fat' as alien and as morally bad (and therefore of the 'fat' person as bad) is a cultural discursive construction rather than an individual aberration. Constructions of fat, flesh and the body as other of the self/soul and as morally corrupt can be found in a variety of culturally sanctioned discourses. Within medical discourse, for example,

> the body still has an ambiguous location despite the secularization of medical viewpoints . . . While the current medical view is less dogmatic about the negative effects of obesity, especially in relation to stress and heart disease, there is still a widespread moral condemnation of obesity as indicative of an absence of personal control. ·
>
> (Turner, 1987: 26)

That is, Cartesian dualist discourse informs a variety of institutional and popular discourses and discursive practices including medicine and other contemporary forms of body management. This discourse has also quite clearly informed various 'technologies of the self' (see Foucault, 1988) from pagan and early Christian practices to the present which have, as Foucault argues, 'been diffused across Western culture through numerous channels and integrated with various types of attitudes and experiences so that it is difficult to isolate and separate it from our own spontaneous experiences' (Foucault, 1988: 17).

The construction of 'fat' as morally bad, as corrupt and corrupting, can be found in Christian doctrine, for example. In 'The Book of St Thomas', Jesus claims that those 'who have not received the revealed doctrine are ignorant and, thus, renounced. Their soul has been corrupted by the body and by the world' (from Martin, 1988: 56). Similarly, St Paul states: 'In the name of our Lord Jesus Christ, when ye are gathered together, and my spirit with the power of our Lord Jesus Christ, to deliver such a one [a sinner] unto Satan for the destruction of the flesh, that the spirit may be saved in the day of the Lord Jesus' (1 Corinthians 5: 4–5); 'Meat for the belly, and the belly for meat: but God shall destroy both it and them' (1 Corinthians 6: 13). The apparently extreme construction of fat/flesh/body discussed above can therefore be located within a long-standing history of mind–body dualism that is embedded in a variety of cultural practices and 'technologies of the self'. And we might understand women's distressing experiences of food, eating and embodiment better if we locate them within their cultural contexts rather than attempting to characterize these experiences as peculiar to, and originating in, a particular group of pathologized girls and women.

In particular I would argue that this aspect of the dualistic construction of 'fat' can be traced to the technology of Christian asceticism with its 'theme of the renunciation of the flesh' (see Foucault, 1988: 17). And these traces of Christian asceticism are also evidenced in the discursive construction of 'control' itself; that is, in the construction of 'control' as denial of the body rather than as just conscious and deliberate self-determination.[2] Controlling one's food is about resisting temptation, denying the body and its desires and 'never, never allowing myself . . . to have any of it'. 'Controlled' eating is about not eating or, at least, eating very little. It is a construction of 'control' which precludes the possibility of describing a fat body as controlled however consciously or determinedly that fatness is acquired or maintained. It refuses the possibility that eating a lot could be anything other than a lack of control. This discourse of Cartesian dualism, informed by a Christian asceticism, is so prevalent that now

> Food for literally millions of women – and here I wish to stress that, horrifying as it is to confront this reality, I do mean millions of women – is *a combat zone, a source of incredible tension,* the object of the most fevered *desire,* the engenderer of tremendous *fear,* and the recipient of a medley of projections centring round notions of *good and bad.*
>
> (Orbach, 1993: 43, my emphasis)

One might now argue that the unease and hatred that many women feel towards their bodies has become 'a cultural norm' (Chernin, 1981). Recent surveys have found not only that many girls and women diet in an attempt to get thinner (see Chapter 4), but also that for many women 'getting fat' constitutes their greatest fear (Chernin, 1981). And this fear can be understood as a culturally, discursively produced fear: Ferguson, in her study of women's magazines between 1949 and 1974, found that:

> 'self-control' was the most frequent and visible value held up to females . . . Towards the self it was associated with beauty admonitions against 'letting yourself go' – putting on weight or looking a mess, or sexual commandments 'not to let yourself go'.
>
> (Ferguson, 1983: 68–70)

Constructions of 'fat' as morally bad, and of weight reduction as a quasi-spiritual struggle against the body, are also evident in the jingoistic phrases used by the diet industry such as 'fight the flab', 'burning off' calories or fat, and 'fatbuster' diets (see Bordo, 1990) and in the widespread moral condemnation of fat as a signifier of lack of personal control (Turner, 1987). The construction of 'fat' as a negative term is a cultural commonplace, evidenced in a variety of discourses. That 'it' is repeatedly reproduced as bad in different discourses not only consolidates its negativity. It also allows its construction as morally bad to appear mundane.

ZOE: Like if you're, if you're not super-slim you're not as good a person as someone who is.

ALISON: It's not easy you know /H: right/ (.) with food and things an' (.) when you've been on a diet an' you've been sort of strict with yourself and you (.) you've been good to lose the weight (.) you you feel guilty because you (.) it's sort of been sort of hard work and then (.) to have something you know (.) sort of sort of high in calories would be like um (.) sort of like um (.) a defeat for like your diet sort of thing.

In contrast with some of the extracts discussed above, these extracts appear unremarkable. It is 'good' to be 'strict with yourself' and 'to lose the weight'. Such formulations may appear more familiar, more 'normal', but they nevertheless articulate the same moralistic theme identified in more dramatic constructions of 'fat' as morally bad.

THE 'IDEAL' OF THE NON-BODY

The discursive construction of 'fat' as morally bad can, then, be culturally located in a discourse of Cartesian dualism and in a tradition of Christian asceticism that have diffused across Western culture and may perhaps have become more sharply focused in recent years. As Bordo notes,

> the construction of the body as an alien attacker, threatening to erupt in an unsightly display of bulging flesh is a ubiquitous cultural image. Until the last decade excess weight was the target of most ads for diet products: today, one is more likely to find the enemy constructed as bulge, fat or 'flab'. 'Now' (a typical ad runs) '. . . Have a nice shape with no tummy.' To achieve such results (often envisioned as the absolute eradication of the body: e.g. 'no tummy') a violent assault on the enemy is usually required.
>
> (Bordo, 1990: 89–90)

The dualistic construction of fat/flesh/body as alien to the mind/self and as morally corrupt and corrupting, and the Christian ascetic theme of 'the renunciation of the flesh', produce an 'ideal' of a non-body (see also Malson and Ussher, 1996b):

H: What did slimness mean to you when you started to become anorexic? (.)
LAYLA: Uh (short laugh) um (.) first of all (.) having no tummies or no great bottoms /H: mm/ and having nice (.) thighs, thin (.) thighs.

Here the ideal is not merely a thin body but 'no tummies', 'no great bottoms'; not just a reduction but an *eradication* of the body. However emaciated one might be, there is still a desire to lose more weight. This culturally entrenched discourse produces (for some) the desire literally to eradicate the (female) body. The 'ideal' body becomes a very dangerous impossibility since it is a non-body, a predicament expressed by Ellen West, who wrote: 'I must now be able to look at my ideal, this ideal of being thin, of being without a body and to realize: "It is a fiction"' (quoted by Chernin, 1981: 20). Noticeably, however, there is a slippage between 'thinness' and non-body. In Layla's account, *'no* tummies' is interchangeable with *'thin* thighs' (my emphasis). The impossible fiction of the non-body is signified by the possible, by the very thin, anorexic body. Whereas the fat body signifies bodilyness, the very thin/anorexic body comes to signify a non-body, representing a triumph of the self/mind over the body. And, whilst fat is a material, bodily substance, thin is not. Getting thinner involves a literal dematerialization of the body, so that the very thin body may signify an entirely disembodied and 'spiritual' subjectivity construed as if that body did not exist.

TRICIA: Except for (.) I mean I'm still trying to sort of get myself really down here but uh /H: right/ I mean at one time I remember feeling (.) I was so up really *out* of my body /H: mm/ that I remember sort of (.) looking in a mirror and being actually surprised that I saw a form in the mirror /H: right/ and not just a nothingness.

This discursive construction of the thin body as a signifier of a non-body might also be read in parallel with psychoanalytic interpretations of 'anorexia' as an attempt to reduce the body to a phallic symbol (Sayers, 1994, 1995). The discursive construction of the thin/anorexic body as a phallic symbol rather than as a body converges with both the dualistic construction of the non-body discussed above and with constructions of the thin/anorexic body as non-feminine or masculine. Its construction as *phallic* symbol also consolidates the power accorded to the thin/anorexic body within the discourse of Cartesian dualism.

THE ANOREXIC BODY AS SIGNIFIER OF TRANSCENDING POWER

As we have seen, within this discourse of Cartesian dualism the body represents both a counterpoint to and a metaphor for the mind, spirit or will. And, as a metaphor for the mind/self, the idealized anorexic body signifies the mind's triumph over the body. It signifies the control and integrity of the self. Thus, whilst this discourse produces a subjectivity divided into mind and body, it also firmly consolidates a positive construction of the thin/anorexic body as a controlled body and as a signifier of power.

ELAINE: When I actually started to to starve it wasn't because I wanted to diet. It was because I wanted to starve. (.) /H: mm/ And I don't know when I started getting on the scales all the time but (.) /H: right/ losing weight suddenly became a (.) I suppose a powerful thing you know like (.) /H: right/ I really liked it. It made me feel good.

NICKI: If I didn't have it {anorexia}, if I wasn't thin /H: mm/ then I wouldn't have an identity. I'd just be this big bad blob.

H: Righ' mm. What sort of identity did you feel it was or it is or whatever?

NICKI: It was um it was very powerful. /H: mm/ It made me feel good and in control.

In these extracts 'starving' is constituted as a practice that is entirely different from 'dieting'. It signifies not the pursuit of feminine beauty but the achievement of power. Whereas the fat body signifies an identity-less 'big bad blob', the subject position of 'anorexic' is articulated here in strongly positive terms as 'very powerful . . . good and in control'. It is a construction which converges with readings of 'the anorexic body' as phallic symbol. Here, the thin/anorexic body is proof of denial of the body and its desires and it thus signifies the mind/self's control, strength and integrity: 'It' is an affirmation of 'the self'. The thinner the body, the stronger the soul/mind/self.[3]

In this respect the dualist discourse articulated in the accounts above differs significantly from the technology of Christian asceticism and more closely resembles a Stoic technology of the self (see Foucault, 1988; Martin, 1988). That is, 'in Christianity asceticism always refers to a certain renunciation of the self and of reality because most of the time your self is a part of that reality you have to renounce in order to get access to another level of reality' (Foucault, 1988: 43). The renunciation of the flesh and penitence 'of sin doesn't have as its target the establishment of an identity but serves instead to mark the refusal of the self . . . Self-revelation is at the same time self-destruction' (Foucault, 1988: 43).

In contrast with this ascetic theme of self-renunciation, however, the extracts above present the thin/anorexic body as a signifier of a powerful identity. Whereas the fat body signifies a lack of identity, being a 'big bad blob', the thin/anorexic body signifies a powerful identity. Being very thin provides identity (Malson and Ussher, 1996b). Self-starvation is discursively constituted here as self-productive rather than (or perhaps because it is also) self-destructive.

Thus, whilst the dualistic discourse that I have been discussing evidences traces of Christian asceticism, it is not synonymous with an ascetic technology of the self. In its construction of the thin/anorexic body as a signifier of a powerful identity this discourse also evidences traces of Stoicism in which 'practices of abstinence . . . establish and test the independence of the individual with regard to the external world' (Foucault, 1988: 37). This discourse interpellates the (thin/anorexic) abstinent subject as powerful, strong-willed, controlling and independent.

We can begin to see, then, how thinness is culturally overdetermined as a positive term. Within the different discourses that converge on the body it is produced as beautiful and feminine, but also, conflictingly, as powerful, controlling and independent. Within both romantic and dualistic discourses the thin body is positively construed despite the fact that these discourses produce this body in very different ways. In romantic discourse the thin/anorexic body signifies a feminine subjectivity that is defined in terms of the (beautiful) body. In a discourse of Cartesian dualism, however, it signifies a subjectivity which is construed in antithesis to the body which is, therefore, at least ostensibly, genderless. In signifying a transcendence of the body it may also signify a transcendence of femininity

TERESA: It was something to do with not, not being in my body [. . .] transcending, /H: mm/ transcending my position, my sexuality /H: mm/ cos my sexuality was vulnerable [. . .] There's something about being anorexic can be powerful.

Within Cartesian dualist discourse the thin/anorexic body signifies a powerful, independent and disembodied subjectivity. And in transcending the (female) body it also transcends the problematic femininities that that body signifies. It transcends the vulnerabilities of patriarchally defined heterosexual 'woman' and can thus be read as a rebellion against these gender (im)positions, a reading that is consolidated by constructions of the anorexic body as 'too thin' to be attractive and as a parody, rather than an affirmation, of contemporary prescriptions of 'feminine beauty' (see Selig, 1988). Within dualistic discourses the anorexic body signifies a (fictional) subjectivity that appears to transcend or refuse the (fictional) gender identity signi-fied by the female body. As Riley (1988: 103) argues, 'the body is only periodically lived and treated as sexed'; there are different 'densities' of gender. And Lacan (1972–1973, quoted by Rose, 1982: 27) similarly questions whether 'woman' 'takes on anything whatsoever of her fate'. The production of the thin/anorexic body in dualist discourse provides, I think, a subject position that, at least ostensibly, tran-scends the problems of gender and hence of 'feminine' identity:

> The question of how far anyone can take on the identity of being a woman in a thoroughgoing manner recalls the fictive status accorded to sexual identities by some psychoanalytic thought. How could someone 'be a woman' through and through, make a final home in that classification without suffering claustrophobia?
>
> (Riley, 1988: 6)

In short, this discourse of Cartesian dualism appears to provide an escape from the culturally/discursively produced problems of embodiment and from the claustrophobia, limitations and vulnerabilities of patriarchally prescribed 'femininity'. It produces a subjectivity that is not only powerful, independent and controlling, but also disembodied and hence genderless. Yet these problems of embodiment and femininity are problems that are precisely constituted in this discourse (and elsewhere). It is this discourse which interpellates the subject as fundamentally divided into mind and body and which predicates the integrity of 'the self' on the denial of the body. It is in this discourse that the 'ideal of being thin, of being without a body' (Ellen West, quoted by Chernin, 1981: 20) is reproduced. It is also in this discourse that the already-existing problem of femi-nine subjectivity is further compounded.

THE EXCESSES OF 'WOMAN' AND 'THE BODY' OF DUALISTIC DISCOURSE

This discourse of Cartesian dualism appears to provide a disembodied and hence gender-neutral subject position signified by the thin/anorexic body. Yet gender is nevertheless profoundly imbricated in this discourse in that it re-produces patriarchal dichotomies of male/female, mind/body, controlling/ uncontrolled, good/bad (see Jordanova, 1989). It re-produces the subject/other, I/not-I divide that structures gender identity within the Symbolic order (see

Chapter 1). Within this dichotomization 'woman' signifies bodilyness: 'when woman is given over to man . . . he demands that she represent the flesh purely for its own sake. Her body is . . . a thing sunk in its own immanence' (de Beauvoir, 1953: 189).

The alien, uncontrollable, corrupt and corrupting 'body' of dualist discourse is a body that has frequently figured as a feminine body in a variety of contexts. For instance, 'the biologically labile woman' that may be signified by menstruation is construed as alien and uncontrollable (Malson and Ussher, 1996a). Havelock Ellis (1897, cited in Ussher, 1991: 19) similarly described 'woman' as 'a temple built over a sewer', whilst Baudelaire (quoted by Ussher, 1991: 19) wrote that he often thought 'of the female organ as a dirty thing or as a wound, . . . dangerous in itself like all bloody, mucous, contaminated things', and described woman as 'that obscene and infected horror'. In misogynistic discourses 'women are objectified, associated with danger and temptation, with impurity, with an uncontrollable sexuality' (Ussher, 1991: 21). 'Woman' is discursively produced as bodily and 'her' body is constructed as homologous with 'the body' of dualistic discourse (Malson, forthcoming).

This construction of 'the female body' as defective, uncontrollable and dangerous is deeply embedded in a variety of discourses and cultural practices. It is, for example, evident in the nineteenth-century construction of 'the female invalid' (see Chapter 3) and is currently reified in medical concepts such as PMS, PND and menopausal syndrome where women's 'raging hormones' are construed as a cause of madness (Ussher, 1991). Our distress, we are told, is the fault of our bodies rather than of society. These constructions of 'the female body' as defective and disruptive have served to 'justify' constructions of 'woman' as Other, as hysterical, mad, weak, dangerous and incapable, as bodily, psychologically and morally inferior (Ussher, 1991; Showalter, 1985). They have served to exclude women from education, politics (Ehrenreich and English, 1974; Sayers, 1982) and employment opportunities (Marshall and Wetherell, 1989) whilst simultaneously naturalizing these exclusions; making socio-political forms of gender oppression appear to be part of a natural order. The dualistic construction of the female body can thus be seen as part of a wider patriarchal discursive order which serves to denigrate, exclude and oppress women in a variety of different contexts.

This relationship between 'woman', 'the female body' and 'the body' of dualistic discourse has a long genealogy evident, for example, in the misogyny of Christian Pauline doctrine where '*It is* good for a man not to touch a woman' (1 Corinthians 7: 1) and where marriage is valued only in that it prevents fornication: 'But if they cannot contain, let them marry: for it is better to marry than to burn' (1 Corinthians 7: 9). In the anti-sex dictums of the Church it is most frequently 'woman' who is constructed as morally and bodily polluted and polluting. Thus, 'the cycle of fleshly life derives finally from intimacy with women and polluted intercourse' (quoted by Martin, 1987: 56). Similarly, de Beauvoir, in her discussion of cultural myths, writes of 'woman' as the siren whose song lures sailors upon the rocks; she is Circe, who changes her lovers into beasts, the undine who draws fishermen into the depths of pools. The man captivated by her charms no longer has will-power, enterprise, future; he is no longer a citizen, but mere flesh enslaved to its desires, cut off from the community, bound to the moment, tossed passively back and forth between torture and pleasure.

(de Beauvoir, 1953: 197)

Not only has 'woman' signified 'the body', but 'the female body' has also often been constructed as alien, uncontrollable and dangerous. 'It' is a source of temptation that is both corrupt and corrupting. Like 'the body' of dualistic discourse, 'the female body' is constructed as Other and as 'the locus of all that threatens our attempts at control. It overtakes, it overwhelms, it erupts and disrupts' (Bordo, 1992: 94). The female body becomes constituted as a site and source of denigrated (feminine) bodily excess.

This figure of 'woman as excess' is exemplified in particular in discursive constructions of the sexualized woman and of the mother (Malson, forthcoming). The romantic ideal of the heterosexually attractive woman, as we have seen, is almost ubiquitously signified by the thin female body. Nevertheless, the fat female body may also signify a sexualized femininity. The whore, the woman of Pauline doctrine, 'the nymphomaniac', 'the femme fatale' and 'the man-eater' are culturally prevalent images of 'the sexual woman' as excessively bodily, uncontrollable, overwhelming and dangerous (see Ussher, 1991). And such images of dangerous and excessive female sexuality are more easily signified by the fat (voluptuous?) rather than thin female body which, as we have seen, already connotes an uncontrolled bodily excess.

This discursive relationship between female sexuality and body fat is further consolidated by symbolizations of sexuality in terms of food and eating, apparent in references to 'consuming passions' or to women as sweet foods such as 'honey' or 'sugar'. Such constructions of 'woman' as food-like commodity to be consumed produce 'feminine sexuality' as something vulnerable as well as dangerous (see Ussher, 1994).[4] The cultural significance of such symbolization is demonstrated by, for example, the popularity of *Like Water for Chocolate* (Esquivel, 1993) – a 'worldwide bestseller – now a major film', according to the cover – in which a woman communicates erotically with her forbidden lover through the food she cooks for him and in which the minutely detailed recipes function as a central element in this romantic narrative. Recently, renewed interest in vampire films such as Coppola's *Dracula* and novels such as Anne Rice's *Vampire Chronicles* may also be interpreted in terms of a deeply embedded cultural preoccupation with symbolizing an uncontrolled and dangerous sexuality in terms of food and eating:

The exploration of contemporary slenderness as a metaphor for the correct management of desire becomes more adequate when we confront the fact that hunger has always been a potent cultural metaphor for female sexuality, power, and desire – from the blood-craving Kali ... to the language of insatiability and voraciousness that mark fifteenth century discourse on witches, to the 'Man Eater' of contemporary rock lyrics: 'Oh, oh, here she comes, watch out boy, she'll chew you up'.

(Bordo, 1990: 101)

Like 'the sexual woman', 'the mother' is also a profoundly significant element of a variety of different discourses that constitute and regulate our experiences of femininity (see Hirsch, 1989; Malson, forthcoming). 'She' figures, for example, in medical, religious, psychological and political discourses. 'The mother', we are repeatedly told, is responsible for the physical, psychological and moral well-being of her child (e.g. Bowlby, 1969, 1973) and her family (see Bemis, 1983). Consequently 'she' is also held responsible for the 'moral fabric' of society (see McGoldrick *et al.*, 1989). 'Her' cultural significance cannot be overestimated. 'The mother' is held up as a 'natural destiny' of women and revered in images of the madonna and in the traditionalist discourse of family values. Yet 'she' is also reviled as the domineering or rejecting mother, as the 'schizophrenogenic' or 'anorexogenic' mother (see Caplan, 1990; Yager, 1982), as the 'irresponsible' single mother and as the butt of numerous mother-in-law jokes.

As a plural collectivity, this category of 'the mother' is, then, organized along a deep fissure, for 'she' is either good or bad (cf. Klein, 1968), either the nurturing mother or the abandoning or punishing mother. But she is rarely both. Yet, whether positive or negative, these images of motherhood are most frequently centred on the body. 'The mother' is discursively produced as 'the maternal body', as a source of (mortal) life and thereby of (psychological and physical) death (see de Beauvoir, 1953). The mother's body both nurtures and engulfs her child's individuality. 'She' is both necessary and threatening to identity and is thereby implicated in the problematics of subjectivity and embodiment articulated in dualist discourse. In Teresa's discussion of 'the mother', these themes of maternal subjectivity and bodily excess are particularly explicit:

TERESA: I did quite a lot of work on that in my therapy about (.) being able to sort of, wanting this very um autonomous power /H: mm/ and quite a male power /H: right/ but not being able to (.) to do it. /H: right/ So I mean for me there is this sort of, there is this terrible (.) fear, anger of femininity in terms of passivity. /H: right, mm, right/ You know, kind of images of the kind of, the mother figure as this sort of cow-like unintelligent person that like, that just feeds. /H: mm/ You know the um figure out of *The Bell Jar* Dodo Conway [...] I mean Sylvia Plath's just very um (.) I mean awful about her. She paints this awful picture of this very unintelligent working-class American mother who just feeds the kids on ice creams and ice cream and marshmallows cos that, just has them like one after the other like this /H: mm/. She presents her as this cow without a /H: mm/ without a brain /H: mm/

139

who's just massively fat and unattractive. /H: mm/ Her, her whole um motive in life is just to have, mindlessly have more children and breed more, /H: right/ more and more and more. And not have any life of her own. All that is just like devoted to caring for other people. /H: mm/ And that is I s'pose an image of horror for me.

'The mother' is constructed here as feminine, passive and caring and yet 'she' is 'an image of horror'. And what is so horrifying is 'her' uncontrolled excess, 'her' engulfing bodilyness and 'her' absolute lack of individual subjectivity. 'The mother figure' is produced as 'cow-like', 'unintelligent' and 'awful'. 'She' is a 'cow without . . . a brain'. 'She' is 'massively fat' and 'mindless'. 'She' is an 'image of horror' that leans on dualistic discourse in its reproduction of the mind/body, self/other dichotomy. 'The mother' is constructed as entirely bodily rather than spiritual, wilful, or intelligent: she is 'mindless' and her maternal body with its excess fat and uncontrolled fecundity symbolizes this entirely bodily, feminine excess.

Within this discursive context we might re-evaluate how 'the mother' and hence the mother may be implicated in her daughter's 'anorexia'. Both the perceived failings of the mother and the 'pathogenic' role allotted to her in clinical and academic theories can be read as manifestations of the damage of patriarchal fantasies and their symbolization (see Sayers, 1995). As we have seen, the negatively (patriarchally) constructed 'mother' represents a site at which gender is imbricated in dualist discourse; an exemplar of the construction of 'woman' as bodily excess; uncontrollable, engulfing, dangerous, an antithesis to the mind/self. 'She' is thereby discursively imbricated in her daughter's 'anorexic'/dualistic rejection of 'the body', an entanglement that is further consolidated by the construction of 'the mother' as an embodiment of 'the traditional female domestic role'.

In short, these two negative constructions of 'woman' – as 'the sexual woman' and as 'the mother' – represent 'extreme cultural expressions of woman-as-too-much' (see Bordo, 1992: 103). But this polyvalent figure of 'woman as excess' is also more widespread (Lacan, 1982b). It is evidenced in constructions of woman as talking 'too much' and having 'too much emotion, too much need, [being] too loud and demanding' (see Bordo, 1992: 103). 'Women' take up 'too much' space, are 'too much *there*' (Bordo, 1992: 103). Eating less, taking up less space, having less body fat thus become dualistic ideals that are particularly salient for women. For, as we have seen, within this discursive context body fat acts as a signifier of excess (flesh) and thus represents a point at which gender is imbricated in dualist discourse, since it also resonates with these constructions of 'woman' as excess. Where dualistic discourse converges with misogynistic themes they become enmeshed, consolidating and reconsolidating a patriarchal and particularly damaging construction of 'woman' as bodily, uncontrollable, disruptive, and polluted, as Other.

CONCLUSION

In this chapter I have explored how this discourse of Cartesian dualism consti-tutes the body as threatening, eruptive and alien to the mind/self. And, in constituting the body as potentially eruptive, it produces the necessity of control-ling/denying the body. Dualistic discourse, I have argued, produces both the problem – the need to control and ultimately eradicate the (female) body – and the (fictional) solution – the construction of a disembodied and hence gender-neutral subjectivity signified by the very thin 'anorexic' body. Within this discourse the thin/anorexic body is constituted as a controlled body and as the signifier of a powerful, disembodied and ostensibly genderless subjectivity. Yet the body of dualistic discourse is also figured as a female body. Ideological constructions of 'woman' as bodily and of 'the female body' as alien and dangerous have a long history and are deeply embedded in contemporary Western culture. The discourse of Cartesian dualism consolidates the negative figure of 'woman' as bodily, alien and dangerous, of 'woman as excess'. It produces the desire to control, deny and ultimately to eradicate the body, partic-ularly the female body. That so many girls and women now engage in this process of bodily destruction through self-starvation is clearly an overly deter-mined cultural practice. In this chapter I have sought to illustrate how this discourse of Cartesian dualism forms a significant part of the cultural discourses and the discursive practices of bodily destruction in which 'anorexia' is currently constituted.

7

ANOREXIA AND THE
DISCURSIVE PRODUCTION OF
THE SELF

In the preceding two chapters I have drawn on a series of interviews with women diagnosed or self-diagnosed as 'anorexic' in order to explore some of the discourses and discursive resources deployed in the constructions of 'anorexia', 'femininity' and 'the body'. I have aimed to demonstrate that both within and across the women's accounts there is a variety of entangled discourses which produce these discursive objects in multiple, often conflicting ways. That is, the meanings of these objects differ between discourses and, whilst some constructions are mutually consolidating, others are conflictual. The thin/anorexic body may, for example, be construed as heterosexually attractive, as a signifier of a patriarchally defined romantic femininity. And this signification is consolidated by other constructions of the thin body as small, childlike and ill. However, this same body may also be construed as androgynous or boyishly thin. It may signify a resistance to or rejection of 'traditional femininity', and it may be produced as a controlled body, signifying a powerful and disembodied subjectivity. The thin body thus sustains a multiplicity of meanings and may signify a variety of (often conflicting) subjectivities. The discursive and physical management of the thin/anorexic body and the discursive struggle over its meanings can thus be understood as a management of identity. The production and maintenance of the thin/anorexic body through dieting, self-starvation and/or purging can be viewed as facilitating interpellation in certain subject positions and as resistance to others.

Yet, whilst self-starvation or dieting may be interpreted as a technique of self-production, it is also self-destructive. And it is these mutually conflicting themes – self-production and self-destruction – that I shall explore in this and the following chapter. In this chapter I shall begin with a discussion of the diversity of discursive constructions of 'anorexia' itself, analysing the different discursive relationships of 'the self' to this shifting category.

ANOREXIA AS DISPUTED CATEGORY

The thin/anorexic body, as we have seen, is discursively constituted in a variety of different ways. Similarly, the concept of 'anorexia' itself sustains a multiplicity of meanings constituted within the different discourses of which it is an object. It may, for instance, be discursively produced as an illness, as an extreme diet, as self-starvation, as a coping mechanism, as a means of achieving a positively construed identity or as a form of self-punishment. The discourses within which these various meanings are produced each interpellate the subject in different ways and, as the extracts below illustrate, some of these 'anorexic' subject positions may be resisted and rejected, so that talk about 'anorexic' experiences may be viewed as a site in which subjectivity is constantly negotiated.

DENISE: I would definitely not call myself anorexic. /H: right/ Yes, I lost a lot of weight but (.) I didn't, /H: it's um/ I wouldn't put it down to anything to do with anorexia. /H: mm right/ So when people say to me: Oh you're anorexic, or, you're in the anorexic unit, /H: right/ it just makes my back prickle. I hate it. /H: mm right/ I really do. I think it's uhh (.) in a way it's because even in *my mind*, even though *I've* been with people who who are, who would call themselves anorexics, /H: mm/ still in my mind is the old stereotype of (.) what *the media* portray as (.) as anorexic, /H: right/ sort of um self-inflicted, spoilt brat, /H: right/ selfish, um (.) unnecessary. You know: Well why can't you just eat, /H: right mm/ things like that. Um (.) and other people sort of see it as pathetic and that /H: right/ and so it just, it really does make my my back prickle.

In this extract Denise describes a fairly common stereotype of 'anorexia' as self-inflicted, pathetic and unnecessary. She articulates this as an *other*'s construction, which she rejects as a potential self-description. She is similarly reluctant to identify other women in the Eating Disorders Unit as anorexic: her statement that they *are* anorexics is repaired to one in which they 'would call themselves anorexics'. In the extracts below, Laura and Nicki also discuss a media-promulgated construction of 'anorexia', in this case as a 'slimmer's disease'. It is a construction which they both reject and dispute.

LAURA: Now I know about it {anorexia}, it makes um I wish there was more sort of, not education about it but it's not a slimmer's disease. It's not just you know, /H: yeah/ it doesn't have, it doesn't always start out as a diet. Well it often does but it's not just vanity. /H: right/ It's not just girls who want to be you know particularly thin. /H: right/ You know, it's not a vain thing.

NICKI: They {doctors} think it's to do with vanity and the media /H: right/ but it's so much more deeper than that. /H: right (inaud.)/ Like it's called the slimmer's disease which is a load of rubbish anyway.

In these accounts both Laura and Nicki discuss the construction of 'anorexia' as a 'slimmer's disease', as a trivial issue about dieting, vanity and the media. The subject position offered to them by this construction is resisted by their disputing

143

its validity and by countering this 'media construction' with an alternative construction of 'anorexia' as a 'deeper' issue. Tricia's extract below similarly produces 'anorexia' as a disputed category. Like Denise, Tricia also refuses the term 'anorexia', which she locates within a medical discourse that positions her as a pathological 'specimen'.

H: When you think of the label anorexia (.) what what do you think about? (.)

TRICIA: I s'pose I I still feel (.) some of the projections onto me (.) from society (.) /H: right/ and it's correlated with the professional view [. . .] I was continually labelled when I was out of (.) you know like home as well /H: right/ (.) and treated like a specimen [. . .] I feel that eating distress is something that a normal (.) majorit' I would say I'm afraid the majority of women go through at some period of their lives /H: right yeah/ (.) um far more frequently than actually /H: mm/ comes to light /H: right/ and it's *not* a pathological state.

Tricia describes how medical discourse positions her as a 'specimen', a subject position that she rejects by locating herself within an alternative discourse of survivor/user groups. In contrast to the pathologized subject position of 'anorexic' offered by medical discourse, Tricia reconstructs her experience in terms of a more normalizing concept of 'eating distress' (see also Pembroke, 1993).

These extracts illustrate, then, a discursive struggle over interpretations of 'self' and 'anorexia'. The constructions of 'anorexia' as 'selfish' and 'pathetic', as a pathology, or as a 'slimmer's disease' are presented as others' constructions and are rejected and/or disputed. They are potential 'anorexic' identities that are resisted. In other extracts, however, whilst 'anorexia' is constructed as separate from the self, the self is also implicitly construed as 'anorexic'.

LAURA: I found a sort of friend which was my anorexia really [. . .] When you're anorexic you tend to you know really isolate yourself and become really lonely. /H: mm/ But also I used it to sort of fill up my loneliness. It just fed on me being really lonely.

LAYLA: I used to think when I first came to realize how strongly it was living in me I thought people used to describe it as a friend or as a /H: mm/ an enemy (.) but I realized that (.) it's a creature (.) getting hold of my body to survive *in the body*.

These accounts again illustrate a multiplicity of discursive constructions of 'anorexia'. In contrast to the previous extracts, however, the self is produced here as anorexic, although a dissociation between 'self' and 'anorexia' remains. 'Anorexia' is constructed here as 'a friend', 'an enemy' or 'a creature (.) getting hold of my body'. 'It' is an entity to which one is somehow related but which is simultaneously separate from the self: '*It* just fed on *me* being really lonely'; '*It* was living in *me*' (my emphasis). Whilst 'the self' is construed as 'anorexic', 'anorexia' is construed as an entity that is *not* the self.

This discursive relationship between 'self' and 'anorexia' parallels a biomedical model of illness in which disease invades and affects the body but is not considered as part of the person: a patient generally *has*, rather than *is*, an illness. And this discursive relationship is supported by parasitic images of 'anorexia' as 'a creature' surviving in the body, feeding on Laura's loneliness.[1] The use of such imagery also emphasizes the construed autonomy of the 'anorexia' itself. 'Anorexia' is constituted here as something that has an existence independent of the 'anorexic'. 'Its' effects are not 'hers'. In contrast with the dualistic construction of 'anorexia' (see Chapter 6), being 'anorexic' is construed here not as a form of control (over the body) but rather as a state in which 'the self' may lose control (to the anorexia). In the collision of these two discursive constructions 'anorexia' becomes an excess of control, a form of control that is itself out of control.

PENNY: Nothing was ever good enough. Every half a stone I lost I wanted to lose another one [. . .] it just took a snowball and I couldn't let go cos I wanted /H: mm/ that control that I thought I didn't have over my life.

ANOREXIA, RESISTANCE AND IDENTITY

There is, then, a multiplicity of contending constructions of 'anorexia'. And the relationship of the speaking subject to this shifting category also varies both within and across transcripts. 'Anorexia' may be construed as something entirely dissociated from the self or as something that 'invades' and affects the self but that is simultaneously separate from the self. Alternatively it may be construed as an identity. And, as we shall see, the category of 'anorexia', like 'femininity' (see Riley, 1988), is a plural collectivity, signifying a multiplicity of shifting and often contradictory subjectivities.

H: Do you remember how you felt when you, when you were first diagnosed as anorexic?

OLIVIA: Happy [. . .] I liked it (.) because it really made me feel like I had a sense of control over my life and my eating which was always a problem for me. And I was *skinny* and I loved that so much [. . .] I loved (.) I loved the sensation of the bones [. . .] And I I had every intention of staying anorexic.

CATHY: This is probably going to sound very crude but um on many occasions I'd actually said: I wish I was {anorexic} because then I'd know that I was slim.

JACKIE: I mean when I'm um (.) when I'm in an anorexic state it means success. (.) /H: right/ I really do get a feeling of achievement from what I'm doing to myself.

Whilst Olivia, Cathy, and Jackie articulate different relationships to 'anorexia', each construes 'it' here as a positive term. 'Anorexia' signifies success and achievement, that one is sufficiently skinny or slim, that one is in control. To be 'anorexic' connotes that one has at least some desired attributes. In Jackie's extract below, 'anorexia' is, in addition, constituted as a means of differentiating herself from others. 'It' makes her different and thus provides her with an identity.

H: What is it that you feel you're achieving?
JACKIE: Well in some ways it's being different from other people. (.) /H: right mm/ It's you know it's something that was my, this is what I find quite difficult now. It's something that's my own [. . .] I achieve also control /H: mm/ definitely cos /H: right/ you know no none of my (.) however much people try and make you eat no one can (.) /H: right/ you know control *that*. I mean it's sh' it's *me* doing what I want.

In this context the 'control' achieved through 'anorexia' also functions to produce identity. Jackie is the subject as well as the object of control: 'it's *me* doing what I want'; no one else can make her eat. Anorexia is discursively produced as 'something that's {her} own', *her* control and *her* property that marks *her* identity.

This construction of 'anorexia' as 'my own', as an identity/possession, might also be read in the context of the doctor–patient power relationship, since 'anorexia' is presented here as Jackie's property rather than as an illness to be controlled and cured by the medical profession. This construction confers on her greater rights over 'her anorexia' than would be the case within a medical discourse. In the extract below, Lynn's articulation of 'anorexia' as something that is hers is explicitly located within this context of medical power relations.

LYNN: In the end I did like the label. I thought that's something that's me, that's mine. /H: right mm/ You know and I haven't got anything else /H: right/ so that's the one thing I have got and but /H: (coughs)/ I was like frightened of people trying to feed me up /H: mm/ you know. Like doctors would give me a sheet of paper saying: eat all this. An' you know an' I thought /H: yeah/ they're going to take over /H: yeah/ and be more powerful than me. And I just wanted to run away and /H: mm/ not let anyone take it away from me, /H: right/ sort of protect it and look after it as if it was mine.

Here the doctor–patient relationship is presented as a contest for control over the anorexia. Lynn's construction of 'anorexia' as her possession thus functions to position her as 'its' owner, a more powerful subject position than that of a patient whose illness is under the remit of the medical profession. And, as in Jackie's account above, this construction simultaneously functions to mark her identity: 'that's something that's me, that's mine'. 'Anorexia' is both her possession and her identity, as it is in these accounts.

H: So how how did it feel when when you went for help and they said: this is, you have anorexia or bulimia or?

NICKI: I thought they're probably right. /H: mm/ But at the same time they were looking at it as being such a problem. /H: right/ And I thought: well it isn't really a problem for me. It's a way of life. /H: right/ And it was like, well it was like me. It's like it was a way to have an identity.

TRICIA: I don't feel that anorexia *is* a pathological state. /H: right/ I mean my feeling is that it's it's a desperate search to find one's own identity /H: right/ to put it in a nutshell.

These accounts dispute the constructions of 'anorexia' as problem, pathology or superficial issue and posit instead constructions of 'anorexia' as 'a way of life' and as 'a desperate search to find one's own identity'. They are therefore accounts that can be read intertextually in terms of their rhetorical function as instances of discursive resistance to potential 'anorexic' subjectivities. And, whilst there is a diversity in these oppositional constructions, the accounts also converge on the issue of identity. That is, 'anorexia' is construed as a possession or process that marks one's identity; it is something 'that's mine', 'something that's me'.

ANOREXIA, IDENTITY AND LACK

'Anorexia' may, then, be positively construed as a means of finding or marking an identity for oneself or as itself constituting an identity. Yet these accounts also indicate a concomitant negative construction of 'the self' as otherwise lacking an identity.

JANE: It {anorexia} was like the one thing in my life, the part that I could control and that was mine. /H: mm/ And it was like a security to me. /H: mm/ I didn't think I'd be able to live without it /H: mm/ if anyone took it away.

Hence, Jane describes how she 'didn't think {she}'d be able to live without it'. The construction of 'anorexia' as identity suggests not only that one has an (anorexic) identity but also, conversely, that without 'anorexia' one would have no identity at all.

TRICIA: And the physician there refused to listen to all my bantering on about food or anything like that [. . .] And it was as if he he said well you know: yeah OK I don't want to hear about your anorexia. I want to hear about *you*. And I started thinking: But I am the the anorexia. /H: mm/ This is my identity [. . .] it had actually become my identity /H: mm (.) yeah/ and I think that's that's a problem with it. /H: mm/ I think it becomes (.) can become an all-consuming identity.

H: Right (.) that that you feel you're you're nothing else outside of it?

TRICIA: Nothing else *but* anorexia. That /H: yeah/ that's my name (.) you know. /H: right (.) yeah/ And *then* it's very hard to get out of /H: mm/ because (.) it's like if I give up that name what else is there? /H: right/ I'm still this this shell inside.

NICKI: It's like it was a way to have an identity. /H: right/ And I didn't care if people saw it as bad cos it was how I was. /H: right/ And if it, if I didn't have it, if I wasn't thin /H: mm/ then I wouldn't have an iden- tity. I'd just be this big bad blob. [. . .] It was my thing. /H: right/ Before I'd felt just like nothing. /H: mm/ Now I had something to focus on and something to be.

These extracts again evidence a very psychologically oriented construction of 'anorexia' as identity: 'I am the the anorexia . . . This is my identity.' For Tricia 'anorexia' was her name. But there is also another text running through these accounts, in which 'the self' seems lacking in identity: 'if I wasn't thin . . . then I wouldn't have an identity'. Without anorexia one would be devoid of identity, nameless because one is '{n}othing else *but* anorexia'. 'The self' is discursively produced as simultaneously having an 'all-consuming' ('anorexic') identity and obversely as otherwise lacking identity. 'Anorexia' is 'something to be', but without it one is 'nothing', a 'shell'.

This construction of (anorexic) identity leans on at least two metaphors about personhood. The first is illustrated by Nicki's construction of the thin/anorexic body as 'something to be'. It signifies an identity whereas the fat body signifies an absence of identity. If Nicki was not thin she would 'just be this big bad blob'. The production of these dichotomies – thin/fat, identity/lack of identity – leans, I think, on a construction in which the body's physical boundaries function as a metaphor for the self/other divide. In this context the amorphous and loosely defined flesh of the fat body contrasts with the taut well-defined hard contours of the thin body. The softness and fluidity of body fat blurs the defining borders of the body and submerges the boundary between self and outside world.[2] Hence, to be fat signifies a lack of definition of the self, a lack of identity, that one is merely an amorphous 'blob', whereas to be thin/anorexic signifies that one has a clearly defined identity. These discursive constructions thus converge with and consolidate the negativity of many other constructions of 'the fat body' and the positivity of 'the thin body', perhaps, in particular, the dualistic construction of the thin/anorexic body as a signifier of a powerful and independent identity.

The second metaphor deployed in these extracts is again a spatial metaphor and is apparent in Tricia's description of herself as a 'shell *inside*'; in Lynn's account of herself as becoming a 'deeper' person now and in her hope that people will know her for what she is '*deep* down' rather than basing their judge- ments on her *superficial* appearance (my emphasis):

LYNN: I feel a stronger character /H: mm/ now than I was then. Didn't feel I had a character at all /H: right/ then. I was just a like a shell (.) /H:

mm/ but now I'm a more deeper person. /H: right/ And I you know I hope people get to know me for what I am now /H: right/ deep down than what they see.

This spatial metaphor of selfhood is also evident in many texts in which 'anorexia' is constituted as a *superficial* and vain condition, and in the extract discussed above, in which such constructions are resisted by constructions of 'anorexia' as a *deeper* issue about identity. Such talk and texts deploy a commonplace topographical metaphor of identity based on the spatial aspect of the individual–society relationship conceptualized as an internal/external dichotomy. 'The individual' is construed in terms of (internal) spatial levels, from his/her most superficial (and often more malleable) aspects to her deepest, most profound, and perhaps essential, characteristics which may not be immediately *visible* to others.

WOMAN, IDENTITY AND LACK

These spatial metaphors of identity pervade both academic and popular discourses concerning identity. They are apparent in, for example, psychological concepts such as 'internalization' and 'core personality', in which individual identity is construed as being *inside* (the body) and as consisting of progressively *deeper* layers of selfhood. This geography of personhood appears at first sight to be benign, perhaps even banal. Yet, as Foucault (1977b) has illustrated, space is a medium in which power/knowledge operates, and the metaphorical space of personhood is no exception. For these metaphors interface with constructions of 'feminine' identity in particularly problematic ways. For instance, one culturally dominant construction of 'femininity' is in terms of physical appearance (see Chapter 5). And this superficiality of 'femininity' is profoundly at odds with the deep internality of identity, so that, in terms of this geography of personhood, 'femininity' (as appearance) becomes the other of identity.

LYNN: I always admired Ma' uh Maria Helvin, is it?

H: Oh right, yeah I know, with the hair.=

=LYNN: Cos there was a picture at the health club and I used to look at it. I'd think: Oh she's so attractive. I wish I could look like that [. . .] (Now) I've got no desire to look like Marie Helvin. I I'm more interested in developing *myself*. /H: right/ I want the in' the inner me rather than a picture of someone an' aiming for that.

OLIVIA: I had no identity or individuality of my (.) self. So I decided to give up on trying to look nice, just wore baggy clothes and didn't care.

'Femininity' is constituted here as something superficial. It is about *looking* nice. It is 'a picture of someone', an image rather than an 'inner me'. It lacks the depth and internality of 'identity or individuality'. In this scheme of things femininity is only skin-deep – an unlikely place for any serious (deep) identity.

This metaphorical geography of identity thus becomes yet another element of a (patriarchal) discursive order which constitutes and regulates women's lives, problematizing their/our experiences of subjectivity, gender and embodiment; contributing to women's 'deep' distress and simultaneously serving to dismiss that distress as trivially superficial.[3]

Gender politics also pervade the 'body boundary' metaphor of identity in which fat represents a blurring of this boundary: first because constructions of 'woman' and of 'fat' are discursively related through the concept of excess (see Chapter 6; see also Caskey, 1989), and second, as Lacanian theory has illustrated, the category of 'woman' can be understood as epitomizing the impossibility of phallocentric notions of unitary identity (see Chapter 1). As the Other of (masculine) identity, 'woman' unsettles the I/not-I division (Rose, 1982) and thus highlights the problematic nature of the self/other boundary. Within the Symbolic order 'the woman' is in excess of this boundary (see Lacan, 1982b).

H: What at the time did um being fat mean (.) to you? Why was it something that you didn't want?

TRICIA: I s'pose for me it was (.) I felt being clumsy and being ugly, /H: right/ being out of control (.) /H: mm/ but I think as far as a woman goes, being sexually so desirable by men and not being able to say no [. . .] And also maybe it (.) more of a link with my mother [. . .] And the other thing as well is that being quotes normal is something about (.) maybe I'd just be submerged into sort of the rest of of womanhood /H: right/ and totally lose my identity /H: yeah/ in amongst everyone else. It's like needing needing some, to keep some sort of specialness in myself, /H: mm/ some identity.

H: Yeah yeah, I remember having that feeling that uh (.) /TRICIA: mm/ you had to do *something* to to stay yourself cos otherwise (.) you'd end up not *being* your mother but (.) not being you=

=TRICIA: Just being a woman /H: mm/ or something. I don't know (inaud.)

H: Yeah some sort of (.) generic something.

TRICIA: *Blob.*

Here Tricia associates being fat with being clumsy, ugly and out of control. And 'fat' also signifies motherhood and an uncontrolled female sexuality which, as we have seen (see Chapter 5), may function as tropes of feminine bodily excess. But fat is also associated with a fear of becoming a normal woman; that becoming a normal woman would entail being 'submerged into sort of the rest of of womanhood'. To become a woman is construed here as a total loss of identity, as becoming a 'generic something', a blob. 'Woman' is produced here as the Other of identity, as not-I (see Chapter 1). Just as Nicki construed 'the fat body' in opposition to identity, as being a 'big bad blob', so 'femininity' is produced here as the Other of identity, a generic 'blob' lacking in both depth and definition. This metaphorical geography of identity is, then, a geography of exclusion which both problematizes feminine subjectivity and consolidates the desire to be thin, to achieve ever firmer body boundaries. It produces a metaphorical space in which the female body becomes a battleground.

IDEOLOGIES OF SELFHOOD AND A DISCOURSE OF INDIVIDUALISM

These spatial metaphors of identity can also be read as elements of a 'discourse of individualism' which interpellates the subject as a sovereign and unitary individual. It is a discourse which constructs the notion of 'person' as a given entity separate from society and which is dominant throughout contemporary Western society (Henriques et al., 1984). It is, for example, pervasive in the social sciences and is written into social organization, into concepts of justice, social order and human rights (Hirst and Woolley, 1982). It is a discourse based on a liberal ideology, setting up as its ideal 'the autonomous, self-directed, self-governing individual who stands separate from society and social influences' (Wetherell and White, 1992: 6).

Within this discourse of individualism 'being your own woman' is the ideal. But this ideal can make it difficult to explain why one wants to be thin:

If you say that it is weak to be influenced by others, then it is difficult to present the desire to be thin as reasonable ... To admit to being influenced by social pressure [to be thin] jeopardizes the ideal of being an independent autonomous individual.

(Wetherell and White, 1992: 10)

Succumbing to social pressures (to be thin) abnegates the independence of one's inner self. Hence, within the bounds of this discourse, if women wish to retain their/our (already problematized) individuality then we must explain our desire to be thin in other ways. Women might therefore explain this desire using a 'discourse of natural body processes' which reconstrues the cultural imperative to be thin as a natural imperative to be healthy (Wetherell, 1996); a discursive construction which we see repeatedly promulgated by the fashion and diet industries, where health and beauty are frequently conflated. This discursive manoeuvre allows women to retain an individualistic subject position even whilst dieting (Wetherell, 1996). But it thereby naturalizes, i.e. depoliticizes, women's restrained eating. It obscures the social pressures that compel women to diet and that produce a widespread distress about eating and not eating for many women (Wetherell, 1996).

This dilemma about how to account for wanting to be thin applies just as much to those girls and women diagnosed as anorexic as it does to women generally. In this case the problem involves the avoidance of potential constructions of oneself as suffering from a 'slimmer's disease', as being (overly) motivated by social pressures to be attractively thin/slim.

NICKI: I never ever looked at like slim women in magazines and thought:

> Oh I'd like to be slim /H: right/. It was something that you know I just didn't bother about and then when my periods started I was very angry and then um and I sort of noticed that I was starting to lose weight and then /H: right/ I sort of, you know, just focused on that, /H: mm/ not in relation to like the media. /H: mm right/ Not earlier on anyway.

Here Nicki explicitly dissociates her losing weight from media images of slim women. Emulating 'slim women in magazines' was something that she 'just didn't bother about'. Her losing weight was something she notices, not something prompted by the media. It had nothing to do with social pressures on women to be thin.

Within the framework of a discourse of individualism, accounting for one's 'anorexia' in terms of social pressures to be thin further undermines one's already precarious interpellation as a sovereign and unitary individual, as 'one's own woman'. However, the women I talked to rarely articulated a 'discourse of natural body processes', perhaps because all but two of these women had been medically diagnosed as 'anorexic'. To construe one's (non-)eating and weight loss as healthy when one is under medical supervision for an eating disorder appears implausible. Instead, the construction of 'anorexia' as a 'slimmer's disease' was most frequently countered by construing it as a deeper issue about identity. Yet, whilst this discursive opposition curtails (others') negative constructions of the self as *superficial*, as a 'fashion victim' swayed by social pressures, it also curtails one's ability to construe 'anorexia' as a socio-political issue since the desire to be thin is individualized as a personal psychological search for identity.

Whilst this discourse of individualism curtails politicized explanations of women's desire to be thin, it also produces a positively construed subject position of 'rebel'. By rebelling against social norms 'the rebel' emphasizes the self-directed individualism of liberal ideology (see Wetherell and White, 1992). Might not this subject position constitute a site from which women can resist social prescriptions of female thinness? Could women not explain being 'fat' in terms of a rebellious disregard for the dictates of the diet and fashion industries? It seems not (see Wetherell, 1996).

Women's rebellion against cultural dictates to eat less and be thinner seems to be socially unacceptable. 'Defiantly fat' female rebels are not tolerated. As Millman (cited in Bordo, 1990: 99) notes 'the obese elicit blinding rage and disgust in our culture', particularly if an obese woman claims to be happy, as is amply demonstrated by the audience of a recent Phil Donahue talk show featuring an obese woman:

> I can't believe you don't want to be slim and beautiful, I just can't believe it, . . . I heard you talk a lot about how you feel good about yourself and you like yourself, but I really think you're kidding yourself, . . . It's hard for me to believe that Mary Jane is really happy . . . Mary Jane, to be the way

you are today, you had better start going on a diet soon, because if you don't you're just going to get bigger and bigger and bigger. It's true.

(from the transcripts of a *Phil Donahue Show*, cited in Bordo, 1990: 100)

Similarly, Jane Walmsley, author of the recently published *Thin Think*, writes that she

refuse[s] to regard Roseanne Arnold as a heroine for the Nineties . . . Only her wallet weighs more than she does . . . She ODs on junk food and is unapologetically obese . . . She is an undisciplined, ungrammatical big-mouth, an unreconstructed porker-and-proud-of-it. . . . What a con . . . She has simply made a polemic out of bad manners, self-indulgence and uncouth behaviour. She has turned vulgarity into an art form, gluttony into a political statement – and she has cleverly created a myth around herself.

(Walmsley, 1994: 46)

This myth, Walmsley claims, is that Roseanne Arnold is happy with her weight. That Arnold could take up an individualistic rebellious stance, discursively constructing herself as defiantly fat, is construed by Walmsley as both outrageous and unbelievable. In these two quotes, Mary Jane and Roseanne Arnold are construed as appalling, enraging and unbelievable, not only because they are fat but particularly because they present themselves as happy with being fat. To take up a rebellious subject position in a discourse of individualism, to construe oneself as defiantly fat rather than as a pathological failure, is dismissed here as illegitimate. Despite the social idealization of the subject as a self-directed, self-governing individual unswayed by social pressures, the interpellation of the fat, female subject within a discourse of individualism may itself be construed as unacceptable. This social proscription against locating fat women as rebels in a discourse of individualism ensures that the 'failure' to be thin is construed within an equally individualizing discourse of pathology. The 'body boundaries' metaphor of identity, discussed above, further compounds the problems for any woman wanting to articulate a positive fat identity for herself. In this metaphor body fat blurs the defining borders of the body, submerging the boundary between the self and the outside world so that the fat (female) body signifies a lack of distinction between self and other, a lack of identity. Taking up the subject position of a defiantly or happily fat woman becomes distinctly difficult. It seems, then, that there is no obvious way out of this trap that we find in the discourses that converge upon fat and thin female bodies. It is socially unaccept-able to be fat, yet this discourse of individualism also dictates that it is unacceptable to explain one's desire to be thin in terms of social pressure. Whether we are 'too fat' or 'too thin', patriarchal discourses present our often distressing experiences around eating and body weight as a problem of *individual pathology* rather than as a consequence of social oppression.

This problem of pathologization is clearly heightened for those women diagnosed as anorexic who have already been institutionally pathologized as eating disordered and who have often experienced the discursive and material consequences of medical intervention. However, being *too* thin also makes available certain 'solutions' to some of the dilemmas posed by individualistic discourse. Being 'anorexic' does not only signify a pathologized subject position. It also confirms that one is (more than) sufficiently thin. And, at the same time, being '*too* thin' is rebellious. The discursive construction of the (very) thin/anorexic body as unattractively thin, as a parody of prescribed female slenderness, provides a subject position in which the desire to be thin seems to oppose rather than conform to social pressures. In being *too* thin, 'the anorexic' is discursively produced as both thin and rebelliously individualistic.

NICKI: I started losing weight and I think people say to you: Oh you're losing lots of weight. What's going on? [. . .] then you have the media images as well which you may never have noticed before but you know you start looking at the people and then you start feeling thin. So you just want to get smaller and smaller. /H: mm/ And then any comment that people say, if they say you look really dreadful today that just makes you feel good /H: right/ and reinforces /H: mm/ your behaviour.

Nicki's account is heavily informed by a discourse of individualism. Whilst it does not provide a reason for Nicki's weight loss it produces her as a sovereign individual: she lost weight because of internal, individual reasons rather than because of external social reasons. The strongest construction of Nicki as a self-governing, self-directed individual is, however, where she construes herself as rebellious: that 'any comment that people say, if they say you look really dreadful today that just makes you feel good'. If she feels good when she is told that she looks dreadful, then it follows that she is not swayed by social pressure but is losing weight *despite* such pressures on women to strive to conform to a current ideal of feminine beauty. Through the physical and discursive production of herself as *too* thin Nicki is positively constituted as thin *and* as a self-directed, autonomous individual.

Individualistic discourse might be understood as politically problematic because it interpellates the speaker as the author of her acts and feelings and thereby depoliticizes the desire to be thin (or to conform to other social ideals). The imperative to construe oneself as governed by an *internal* self rather than by *external* society curtails a more political construction of the self as socially pressured to be thin. Yet the recent challenges to the individualistic concept of the person – most notably by French theorists such as Althusser, Barthes, Derrida, Foucault and Lacan (Hirst and Woolley, 1982) and by feminism (Henriques *et al.*, 1984) – have been denounced by academics of the Left (e.g. Thompson, 1978) as well as the Right. Individualistic conceptualizations of the subject have informed the Civil Rights and Liberation Movements of the 1960s and 1970s and were established as a defence against 'inhuman' empiricism and behaviourism in the social sciences (Henriques *et al.*, 1984). Anti-humanist philosophies thus appeared to undermine the conceptual basis of these humanistic politics.

The 'progressive' nature of these political movements might lead one to assume that a humanistic variant of individualistic discourse could be usefully deployed in undermining the disciplinary power of discourses which insist on the necessity of a thin (female) body. Humanistic discourse dictates that it is the inner self, an individual's character rather than their appearance, which is important and should be valued. Yet, as the extract below demonstrates, the deployment of humanistic discourse does not necessarily lessen the imperative to be thin. It may instead result in a negative interpellation of the subject as irrational and superficial, as being too concerned with appearance.

EMMA: And if I wasn't fat and ugly then there wouldn't be a problem /H: mm/ which I know is probably quite irrational /H: mm/ and that I would hope that the person that I'm with is actually looking beneath my fat (laughter) you know to see somebody underneath it. /H: right, yeah/ I do tend to hook everything on that /H: mm/ when things are going bad [. . .] It sounds so stupid and I hate myself for saying it because I know that it's probably wrong but it's purely physical characteristics /H: right/ that just turn me over with jealousy. They really do [. . .] I even know that one of the qualities that I would want in friends or in relationships is for somebody to be able to disregard the physical to a certain extent and really /H: right/ be able to appreciate somebody's underneath character /H: mm/ which is something that I hope I do. And yet I've got this totally other, you know other side /H: right/ that really can't bear to see somebody else who I consider to look so beautiful. /H: mm/ Yeah, I don't understand why I do it [. . .] And I don't think I would like to be friends with somebody like me who's constantly, you know worrying about really petty things which in you know the grand scheme of things really you know are insignificant.

In this extract Emma deploys a spatial metaphor of identity, producing an individualistic notion of the person. 'The self' is 'underneath' the appearance; it is internal and implicitly dichotomized from (external) society. However, the extract can also be read as deploying a humanistic variant of individualistic discourse; the individual is valued for their *inner* self. Appearance is construed as unimportant; it is petty and should be disregarded so that 'somebody's underneath character' can be appreciated. Yet the deployment of this humanistic discourse does not lessen Emma's concern with being thin. Rather it interpellates her negatively for being concerned with the apparently trivial issue of appearance. Just as the discourse of individualism excludes the person who is influenced by social pressures from the idealized subject position of sovereign individual, so this humanistic variant produces Emma as less than ideal, as weak and superficial.

It seems, then, that whilst humanistic discourse was effective in furthering the progressive liberation politics of the 1960s and 1970s, it is rather less effective at countering the oppressive social pressures on women to be attractively thin *individuals*: 'what counts as positive action and resistance is not fixed once and for all' (Henriques *et al.*, 1984: 5). Not only does individualistic discourse proscribe depoliticized explanations of the desire to be thin, but its humanistic variant both fails to undermine the disciplinary power of discourses which insist on thinness and negatively constructs the subject who is interpellated by such discourses.

How we conceptualize 'the person' is, then, a political issue with distinct consequences for the ways in which we experience and understand our feelings and behaviours. And despite its progressive liberal credentials humanistic discourse is perhaps not the best discourse through which we can resist the imperative to be thin. The non-humanism of feminist post-structuralism might provide a better strategy. For

> Politics and the metaphysics of the 'person' are closely entwined. The opponents of 'anti-humanism' were wrong to suppose that it presages a descent into savagery. What is challenged is not the *status* of person, free agent, or subject of right but rather the claimed ontological foundations of that status. The notion that men [*sic*] are 'free agents', directed by a sovereign and integral consciousness, is a metaphysical 'fiction'.
>
> (Hirst and Woolley, 1982: 131)

The non-humanist challenge to the metaphysical fiction of 'the person' of individualistic discourse is not an attempt to reduce 'the person' to a mere effect of the social or to disregard concepts of human dignity or freedom (Hirst and Woolley, 1982: 131). Rather, it is an attempt to understand the notion of the sovereign individual not as a given entity but as 'a particular product of historically specific practices of social regulation' (Henriques *et al.*, 1984: 12; see also Foucault, 1977b). To insist that the sovereign individual is a fiction is not to argue that it is purely illusion, since not only does this discourse of individualism interpellate the subject as a sovereign individual but it is also written into social practices of organization and regulation (Hirst and Woolley, 1982). In challenging the ontological foundations of the concept of 'the sovereign individual', post-structuralist/non-humanist theorists have sought to transgress the dividual–society dichotomy and to retheorize 'the person' in terms of decentred subjectivity because

> Theories of the social agent cannot conceive individuals as necessarily unitary subjects centred in a determinative consciousness if the results of ethnography and cultural analysis, revealing other modes of conceiving and specifying social agents, and of psychoanalysis, challenging the view of the subject as self-possessed by consciousness, are to be taken into account.
>
> (Hirst and Woolley, 1982: 133)

The Lacanian psychoanalytic theorization of (gender) identity as a Symbolic subject position, and the Foucauldian theorization of discourses (and discursive practices) as constituting rather than reflecting their objects and as constituting fields of power/knowledge, provide a theoretical framework within which to question the ontological status of the sovereign individual and to retheorize subjectivity as discursively produced through multiple and often contradictory subject positions (see also Chapter 1). As Foucault argues,

> I do not refer the various enunciative modalities [subject positions] to the unity of the subject . . . instead of referring back to *the* synthesis or *the* unifying function of *a* subject, the various enunciative modalities manifest his [*sic*] dispersion. To the various statuses, the various sites, the various positions that he can occupy or be given when making a discourse. To the discontinuity of the planes from which he speaks.
>
> (Foucault, 1972: 54)

Humanistic discourse and the fiction of the sovereign, unitary individual appear to be of limited efficacy in countering the cultural pressures on women to be thin and eat less. Indeed, in idealizing the self-governing 'inner self' this discourse produces many of the same problems encountered in the discourse of individualism discussed above. By exploring a retheorization of 'the person' as fragmented and multiply constituted in discourse, we might find a more effective strategy with which to resist the dominant cultural construction and regulation of our experiences of eating and not eating, of subjectivity, embodiment and gender.

CONCLUSION

In this chapter I have explored some of the multiplicity of contending constructions of 'anorexia', analysing the shifting relationships between the speaking subject and this plural category. In analysing discursive constructions of anorexia and identity, the chapter has examined the construction of anorexia as an identity that simultaneously signifies a lack of/in identity. It focused on a discourse of individualism which produces the idealized subject position of self-governing individual and which constitutes identity in terms of topographical metaphors such as body boundaries, internality, externality, superficiality and depth. This metaphorical space, it was argued, is a profoundly gendered space, which constructs identity as something internal and which constructs (superficial) femininity as an antithesis to this deep internality. In producing the self-governing individual as an ideal, this discourse also curtails socio-political explanations of women's desire to be thin. It dictates that women explain wanting to be (or failing to be) thin in terms of internal (psychopathological) rather than external (political) factors. By idealizing the self-governing individual, this discourse might have offered a site in which women could resist the discourses and discursive practices that require women to conform to an idealized thinness. Instead, however, it seems to interpellate the woman who is concerned with appearance as trivial and superficial. Individualistic and humanistic discourses seem to do little to undermine the disciplinary power of those discourses that compel women to be thin, yet they also produce a whole series of discursive dilemmas for women who want to be (or fail to be) thin. The non-humanism of feminist post-structuralism might, it was argued, provide a more effective theoretical space in which to address the problematics of contemporary femininity, subjectivity and embodiment.

8

DISCURSIVE SELF-PRODUCTION AND SELF-DESTRUCTION

As we have seen, a variety of different discourses converge upon the thin/anorexic body, constituting that body in numerous often conflicting ways so that it signifies a multiplicity of diverse subjectivities. The discursive productions of 'anorexia' are inextricably tied up with the discursive productions of identity and the problematics of feminine subjectivity (see Chapter 7). From this perspective 'anorexia' can be read as a form of self-production. The material and discursive production of the female body as an 'anorexic' body simultaneously produces a range of particular subjectivities for the thin or 'anorexic' woman. And, indeed, 'anorexia' may be explicitly construed as a means of producing identity (see Chapter 7): self-starvation may be explicitly constituted as a form of self-production. Yet such 'anorexic' practices are also quite clearly associated with profound psychological distress and are in themselves damaging and self-destructive. 'Anorexia' can thus be understood as a material and discursive process of producing an identity for oneself and simultaneously of destroying oneself both literally and metaphorically. And it is this tension, this paradoxical construction of 'anorexia' as both self-producing and self-annihilating, that I shall explore in this chapter.

NEGATIVE CONSTRUCTIONS OF THE SELF

'Anorexia nervosa' has frequently been interpreted as a 'self-pathology' (Geist, 1989) characterized by 'diffuse ego-boundaries' or a lack of sense of self as well as poor self-image and low self-esteem (e.g. Bruch, 1973). The discursive construction of 'anorexia' as an identity which simultaneously signified a lack of (or in) identity (see Chapter 7) clearly converges in part with this interpretation. And, indeed, the women I talked to frequently articulated such negative constructions of themselves associated with profound psychological distress and self-loathing.

LYNN: I thought: ooh I I'm worthless. Everybody hates me and, you know, I just felt I'm *nothing* you know, didn't know why I existed all the time /H: right/ and often felt like suicidal. Thought: well it'll be the best way out

and people wouldn't miss me anyway you know. /H: mm/ I used to feel
like that a lot.

Such denigrated subject positions suffused the women's accounts of their experiences and were articulated in a multiplicity of ways. For instance, discursive constructions of the anorexic body as a rejection of (heterosexually attractive) femininity or of adulthood were often associated with constructions of 'the self' as not good enough to fulfil these 'roles'.

PENNY: I don't think I'm worth having, you know, being told I look nice or
/H: right/ stuff like that [. . .] But um (.) it {being an adult} is responsibility and actually having to do things for yourself I think. And feeling I'm not good enough. I can't do that. So let's just hu /H: right/ stop now and then we won't have to get there.

'Anorexia' thus becomes a means of avoiding the responsibilities of adulthood that Penny describes herself as 'not good enough' to take on. Similarly, within the context of dualist discourse (see Chapter 6) 'the self' was often construed as 'failing' to exert sufficient control, whilst food and body weight were frequently presented as the *only* arena in which one could exert control.

DENISE: I didn't like myself so (.) I saw myself as a failure, can't do
anything right. /H: right/ And in in a way (laughing) that losing weight or having troubles around food was sort of saying: well I can do this. /H: right/ You know I'm in control of *this*.

Whilst Denise construes herself as 'in control' of food and body weight, she also portrays herself as a failure in all other areas of her life. Dualistic discourse also provides the positively construed subject position of the mind/self dissociated from an eruptive, bad body. However, when this mind/body dichotomy is collapsed, as it is in the extracts below, 'the self' too becomes negative: hatred of the body becomes hatred of oneself.

NICKI: I think it's to do with the lower self-esteem /H: right/ and just, I
mean I think I separated my mind from my body. /H: mm/ But also I must have, like if I hated my body really I was hating myself [. . .] And I think I was going against myself /H: mm/ or my body which was how I saw and my, I didn't like myself either /H: right/ but /H: mm/ and I just wanted to like starve.

ZOE: I felt like such a loser because I felt like *I couldn't control my weight because*
I was overweight. /H: right/ So there *must* be something wrong with me.

The body is negatively construed here as hateful, evil and uncontrollable. However, in contrast with those extracts discussed in Chapter 6 the mind/body dichotomy is collapsed so that 'the self' too is bad and hated.

Within the discourse of Cartesian dualism self-starvation was frequently construed as a technique of self-production, a means of achieving a defined and

160

powerful identity. Yet dualistic constructions of body management also involve moralistic and penitential themes which may conversely produce very negative self-constructions. In the extracts below, for example, Emma's hatred of her body and her desire to eradicate its fat is construed in terms of past transgressions and a subsequent need for penitent reparation (see also p. 129).

EMMA: It's just, it's just the fat. I just hate it [...] And I feel to a certain extent that something I did a few years ago has forced it to be there and now I've got to force it to go away again /H: right/ you know.

Through the deployment of a penitential theme, body fat becomes 'proof' of past transgression so that 'the self' is construed negatively as transgressive and not eating becomes a necessary atonement. As Foucault (1988) argues in his discussion of technologies of the self, Christian asceticism can be distinguished from Stoicism by its concern with the renunciation of the self as well as the flesh. Penitence of sin serves not to establish identity but to refuse the self. That is, when read in the context of a penitential rather than a Stoic theme, control/denial of the body through food refusal can be understood as refusal of a (sinful) self, as self-destructive rather than self-productive.

Similarly the self may be negatively construed as undeserving of food. In the dualistic construction of 'food' as temptation (see Chapter 6) the construction of food as simultaneously desired and feared is paralleled by a construction of the self as both sufficiently strong to resist this debasing temptation and as undeserving of this desired object.

LAYLA: I felt as if I'd nothing to do in my life. (.) I mean the things that I had been doing like the school (.) didn't mean anything to me /H: right/ (.) so which meant that I didn't deserve the food.

CATHY: I was so angry with myself. I wouldn't buy myself anything. You know, I /H: mm/ wouldn't buy myself even a drink. I wouldn't buy myself a *magazine*. I c' /H: right/ I wouldn't buy anything (.) um and that was because I was so angry with myself and I didn't feel I deserved it.

NICKI: You'd eat if you like yourself [...] I didn't like myself either /H: right/ but /H: mm/ and I just wanted to like starve.

In these extracts the self is constituted very negatively as undeserving of food. Nicki's use of the word 'starve' rather than 'diet', and the inclusion of magazines as well as food and drink in Cathy's self-deprivation, both function to emphasize that food refusal is not only about weight loss. It also serves to mark one's self-dislike and lack of worth.

Further negative subjectivities emerge in a 'discourse of self-improvement'. In the extract below, for example, this discourse constitutes Michelle as entirely flawed and thereby produces the need for self-improvement.

MICHELLE: Although there was (.) every single thing about me that I want to change some things you can change and some things you can't. /H: right/ (.) And um (.) that one thing, my weight, I can change pretty easily /H: right/ if people will let me. (laughs) /H: (laughing) right/ And um (.) it just makes me feel I can do something to improve myself (.) so I'm getting a step closer to being happy I suppose. I mean I I know /H: mm/ this is unreasonable but (.) this is the kind of thinking that goes (.) /H: right/ behind everything that I do.

The discourse of self-improvement deployed here constructs 'an imperfect self' which can be worked upon and improved. A constant striving for perfection will bring one closer to happiness. This is a discourse that is found not only in talk about body management but also in the more general context of a late capitalist, (post-)Thatcherite ethos that asserts that all is within our grasp if only we strive hard enough to attain it. It is a narrative that interpellates the subject as lacking in some way, suggesting that one will not be happy until a perfect body weight or shape, a better education, a larger salary, a bigger house or higher social/class status, has been achieved. That Michelle reflexively evaluates this discourse as 'unreasonable' does not prevent her from being interpellated by it as lacking and defective.

ANOREXIA AS SELF-PUNISHMENT

The numerous discourses that converge upon the anorexic body produce, then, a multiplicity of negative as well as positive 'anorexic' subjectivities. 'Anorexic' practices such as self-starvation are associated with constructions of 'the self' as defective, transgressive or undeserving, and are often construed in terms of self-punishment. In the two extracts below, for example, losing weight is discursively construed as *burning* fat, a construction that emphasizes the aggressive, self-destructive significations of 'dieting' and exercise.

LYNN: I used to do exercise like /H: mm/ mad. I used to think all that *fat burnt* [. . .] I'd exercise like hell.

JANE: I just wanted to burn off the fat /H: mm/ and lose as much weight as I could and you know, you know not to sort of look feminine or anything. It was basically to kill myself.

In these extracts losing weight is explicitly dissociated from a desire to look attractive. Rather, it is about burning up fat, destroying one's body and thereby oneself, so that 'anorexia' becomes a process of total self-annihilation: 'It was basically to kill myself.' This profoundly disturbing aspect of 'anorexia' is further emphasized when not eating is discursively (and materially) contextualized as one of many self-damaging behaviours.

NICKI: It's not just eating. I think it's everything, /H: mm/ just harming yourself, cos I used to like cut myself. I used to make myself really cold [. . .] I just went on this rampage of like being hungry /H: mm/ which felt wonderful [. . .] And it was like a matter of life and death. /H: mm/ And it was the only way of being able to feel on top of things.

CATHY: My favourite *day*, although it was tough, was like to have um school all day and then come home, do 5,000 sit-ups, two other hours of exercise and all this without even a piece of water, without anything [. . .] And sometimes I mean I have to confess that sometimes I did all the exercise and I was crying because I was thinking: Why are you doing this to yourself? /H: mm/ You know: Why am I treating myself like this?

In these extracts the self is implicitly construed so negatively that 'it' deserves starvation, cutting, cold, excessive exercise, long, slow, painful punishment, and even death. Not eating becomes just one of many ways of inflicting self-harm. Its primary signification and function is self-destruction.

JANE: I wanted to harm myself and sort of kill myself /H: right/ um and then it got to the stage when I really got into it [. . .] Initially it started cos I hated myself so much. /H: mm/ I used to cut myself up and everything.

As part of a wider strategy of self-punishment and self-destruction, food refusal thus serves to mark one's lack of worth, just as other forms of self-harming like cutting up or making oneself cold also do. Yet, whilst this self-punishment is associated with painfully negative self-constructions, it is simultaneously construed as pleasurable. Cathy describes a day of gruelling exercise and self-deprivation as her 'favourite day' and Nicki construed her 'rampage' of hunger as feeling 'wonderful'. This ambivalence might be interpreted in relation to a dual signification of 'self-starvation': perhaps the pleasure is associated with the more positive self-producing significations of 'anorexia'.

EMMA: I know it sounds crazy but the anorexic episodes are the good ones [. . .] That's assertion of control and you feel really together that. And every time you feel your stomach rumbling you ignore it and when you go to bed and your stomach quite hurts and you ignore it you feel really good.

As Emma's extract illustrates, stomach pain may be construed as 'really good' because it signifies that one has successfully asserted control as well as because it hurts. And, as Foucault argues in his discussion of penitence, 'The acts by which he [*sic*] punishes himself are indistinguishable from the acts by which he reveals himself. Self-punishment and the voluntary expression of the self are bound together' (1988: 42). 'Self-starvation' construed as self-punishment may be indistinguishable from 'self-starvation' construed as the expression, the physical and discursive production, of the self (see also Chapter 6).

However, the construction of self-punishment as pleasurable might also be interpreted as masochistic; that is, in terms of 'a tendency which has self-destruction as its aim' (Freud, 1933a: 136), 'in which satisfaction is conditional upon suffering physical or mental pain' (Freud, 1905: 71). And within psychoanalytic theory masochism has frequently been associated with feminine sexuality. Freud, for example, described masochism as 'truly feminine' (1933c: 149). Helen Deutsch (1944), taking up Freud's term 'feminine masochism', argued that narcissism, passivity and masochism constituted the three essential traits of femininity, and that masochism was normal, desirable and necessary for female psychosexual development. In the extract below, Emma construes a comparable relationship between women and masochism, producing a similarly naturalizing explanation of self-damaging behaviour in women.

EMMA: I think very much that it's you know sex characteristics /H: mm/ for men to turn their aggression out, whatever the root of their aggression is and for women to tend to turn it in. /H: right/ It's a lot, it's a lot more easy I think for women to control themselves because of the physical disadvantage than it is to go out and /H: right/ you know go to the pub and stab someone or go and mug an old woman or something (laughter) you know. /H: right/ You just don't have the physical characteristics to be able to do it. /H: right/ So if you want to inflict some serious damage (laughing) then the safest option is to do it on yourself (laughter) you know cos at least then you know what you're doing.

In this extract both men and women are construed as aggressive. But men 'turn their aggression out' whereas women are construed as tending to turn their aggression upon themselves, a discursive construction which can be read in terms of Freud's conceptualization of secondary masochism as 'an extension of sadism turned round upon the subject's own self' (Freud, 1905: 71–72).[1] Emma explains this 'feminine masochism' in terms of women's supposed 'physical disadvantage'; in terms of a natural rather than a social cause. 'Women' are too physically weak to damage others and must therefore express their aggression through self-injury. Her description of 'inflict{ing} some serious damage' on oneself as 'the safest option' is accompanied by laughter and perhaps suggests that the tensions in this argument are uncomfortably apparent.

Whilst Deutsch conceptualizes masochism as an essential trait of femininity, other psychoanalytic theorists have disputed her assertion of the normality of masochism in mature femininity, arguing, for example, that she had wrongly equated feminine passivity with masochism (Gardiner, 1955), that masochism is a caricature rather than an essential trait of femininity (Waelder, in Panel, 1956) or that masochism is associated with *impaired* object relations rather than with 'normal' feminine development (Blum, 1976). The way in which one conceptualizes the relationship between 'femininity' and 'masochism' depends upon one's concept of femininity itself. But it is clearly problematic to equate the two terms, to invoke concepts such as masochism in a simplistic reductionism that reduces 'femininity' to a set of traits such as masochism, passivity or penis envy (Blum, 1976). Indeed, Freud's theorization of 'feminine masochism' was far more complex than that offered by Deutsch. First, his assertion that masochism is often found in men (1933c) indicates the problematic nature of any simple equation of women with femininity or 'feminine masochism'. Second, Freud associated masochism and sadism with femininity and masculinity *indirectly* via the concepts of passivity and activity:

> The term masochism comprises any passive attitude towards sexual life and the sexual object, the extreme instance of which appears to be that in which satisfaction is conditional upon suffering physical and mental pain at the hands of the sexual object.
>
> (Freud, 1905: 71)

Masochism can thus be understood as feminine in that 'femininity' is associated with passivity (Nagera, 1969). Yet, as Freud (e.g. 1933c: 147–148) repeatedly argued, these associations are highly problematic. For Freud, masculinity and femininity are combined in bisexuality and 'sadism and masochism are habitually found together in the same person'. And although:

> when you say 'masculine' you mean as a rule 'active' and when you say 'feminine' you mean 'passive' . . . [e]ven in the sphere of human sexual life, one soon notices how unsatisfactory it is to identify masculine behaviour with activity and feminine with passivity . . . The further you go from the sexual field, in the narrower sense of the word, the more apparent it becomes that the two ideas do not coincide.
>
> (Freud, 1905: 73)

Thus, the relationship of femininity to masochism becomes problematized since there is no easy equation between women and femininity, nor between femininity, passivity and masochism: ' . . . pure masculinity and femininity remain theoretical constructs of uncertain content' (Freud, 1925: 258). Moreover, in conceptualizing masochism as an essential trait of femininity Deutsch failed to address our cultural ideologies of gender in which 'devoted sacrifice', a clearly masochistic position, is frequently elevated as a feminine ideal (Blum, 1976). And, as Freud (1933c) acknowledged, social conventions tend to prohibit female aggression, forcing women into passive situations so that, he argued, 'The repression of their aggressiveness, which is imposed upon women by their constitution and by society, favours the development of strong masochistic impulses, which have the effect of binding erotically the destructive tendencies which have turned inwards' (Freud, 1933c: 149). Whilst masochism may be feminine, the concept of femininity does not coincide with woman. Nor is 'feminine masochism' a natural category since, he argues, society plays a part in its development. 'Femininity' and 'feminine masochism' are problematic socially constructed categories.

The discursive construction of self-starvation as self-punishing, evidenced in the extracts above, might thus be read in terms of a psychoanalytic theory of masochism, as articulating a desire for punishment and suffering and as constituting a 'femininely masochistic' self. Yet, as we have seen, the relationship between masochism and femininity is both complex and problematic. It would be a simplistic reductionism to interpret these extracts as evidence of an essentially feminine masochism. Constructions of anorexia as self-punishing and of 'the anorexic' as 'femininely masochistic' might be best viewed not as expressions of individuals' 'feminine masochism' but rather as interpellations of (female) subjects within the already existing discourses and discursive practices which produce woman as masochistic.

(UN)COMFORTABLY NUMB: PURGING, PURITY AND EMPTINESS

These themes of masochism, self-punishment and self-destruction pervade discursive constructions of purging as well as self-starvation. Like food refusal, bingeing, vomiting and laxative abuse clearly manifest self-destructive elements, both physically and emotionally.

LAYLA: I know that bulimia is not the right way to do it. /H: mm/ It cost me *a lot* (.) /H: yeah/ physically and emotionally. (.) It was just another mechanism to pull me down, to destroy my (.) feelings of self-worth or whatever.

NICKI: I think some of my friends who I went round with, I think some of them sort of, you know, started taking laxatives and things which I felt really bad about, /H: mm/ which I, you know, like with close friends /H: mm/ but and I was like really unsociable anyway.

Nicki's account of feeling 'really bad' when her friends started to copy her laxative abuse implies a construction of laxative abuse as damaging and self-destructive. She 'felt really bad' because she is the 'cause' of their self-destructive behaviour. It is a construction of purging which differs significantly from those in other parts of her transcript where she construes her own laxative abuse positively as a means of purifying and cleansing herself.

NICKI: Even I mean like if, I don't like to say, you take laxatives, and you take strong ones and you can lose like a stone from being sick or whatever. /H: right/ Then even though I knew that I hadn't lost any fat /H: mm/ or if I had a drink it would all come back, it was still good. It was pure and it would just be focused on the scales and weight and whatever [. . .] Like if you binge /H: yeah/ then everything's gone and then if you take, then after if you like clean yourself then you can begin to feel relieved.

Like self-starvation, purging is discursively constituted ambivalently. It is negatively construed as self-destructive but is also simultaneously construed positively as a cleansing and purifying process.

CATHY: After I ended up in hospital for a heart condition I said that I wouldn't take them {laxatives} again. And yet I did straight away. /H: mm/ I mean I don't think I will ever give them up. They're too much of a comfort. /H: right/ Even if I have a drink I have to have some, some tablets because uhm (.) I feel better. I feel more clean. That's it, I feel clean [. . .] I look at these things {indicating a Ribena carton} as being poison and I don't want poison in my body and I want to be cleansed inside.

As Cathy's account of laxative abuse illustrates, this construction of purging as self-purifying is double-edged. Purging is positively construed here as bringing relief and comfort and Cathy is positively produced as 'cleansed inside'. Yet 'she' is also thereby implicitly constituted as having been contaminated (particularly by food) and in need of purification. The explicit construction of the self as purified by purging contains a subtextual construction of self as impure and dirtied. And a similar negative subtext can also be read in the construction of purging itself. Whilst purging is construed as purifying it may also, paradoxically, be construed as shameful. Nicki, for example, did not like to say that she takes laxatives and avoided using the word. She also avoided any detailed description of their effects – they make you 'sick or whatever' – and both her and Cathy's construal of their effects as cleansing might be read as concealing their defecation-inducing properties.

Discursive constructions of purging thus parallel those of 'self-starvation' in that purging is represented both positively – as producing a purified self – and negatively – as self-punishing and self-destructive. In the extracts below, this tension between self-production and self-destruction pivots around a desire to be empty.

LAYLA: I used to feel like that I'm pure (.) because /H: right/ I was refusing to eat. /H: mm/ I'm not, to *know* that my stomach was *empty* gave me such a good feeling.

EMMA: It's a lot easier to make yourself sick when you've eaten vast amounts than it is when you've only eaten a little bit. /H: yeah/ So it's much better to just let it run its course and get it out of your system /H: mm/ than to stop it halfway through and then worry about not being able to get it all out again.

ELAINE: I wanted just starve myself [. . .] the empty feeling /H: right/ felt good (.) for a while.

Purging is construed here as a means of getting food out of one's body. The ideal is to have nothing inside, to be empty. Whilst this might be viewed as simply an aspect of weight control the desire to be empty can also be read as symbolically (and physically) self-destructive. Within the framework of a discourse of individualism (see Chapter 7) identity is produced as something internal, and 'purging' obliterates this internality, producing an emptied, voided self; a subjectivity that resonates with those constructions (discussed above) of the self as an identity-less, empty shell.

Like purging, the 'anorexic' focus on weight and food can also be read as self-destructive, producing an emptied and numbed 'self', evacuated of all emotion and meaningful 'internality'.

NICKI: It made me able to cope, block out lots of things. It was something to focus on. I didn't like myself either /H: right/ but /H: mm/ and I just wanted to like starve and also um like you become numb, /H: mm/ emotionally detached. And like if like you don't, now I could cry about something if I was upset but if I wasn't eating then I'd sort of be numb to the feelings [. . .] it would just be focused on the scales and weight and whatever.

Focusing only 'on the scales and weight' blocks out Nicki's painful 'internality'; her thoughts and feelings; her subjectivity so that this 'anorexic' focus becomes a means of coping. Painful thoughts and feelings and traumatic memories are covered over, suppressed and replaced by numbers on weighing scales.

JANE: I was abused when I was a child (.) and I know now that it was trying to cover that up because /H: right/ by having anorexia I didn't have to face and think about that /H: mm/ because (.) everything inside me was concentrated on anorexia [. . .] It was all I thought about. It was all I could concentrate on /H: mm/ and just everything else went out of my head. /H: right/ I couldn't think about anything else.

In Jane's account of being abused as a child focusing on 'anorexia' becomes a way of coping. But this coping is achieved only through self-destruction, through obliterating all thoughts and feelings, becoming 'emotionally detached' and 'numb', so that 'anorexia' becomes a means of coping *through* self-destruction.

LAURA: It helped me deal with with worry and fear [. . .]

PENNY: Yeah for me too, like to cover up feelings, /H: right/ feelings of fear, anger, any feelings. I mean it to suppress that because I just didn't want to feel it.

H: Right, was there anything particular that you felt sort of fear of or angry about?

PENNY: Um (.) hu (.) well it's kind of (.) /H: I don't/ Anger and the fear were kind of just (.) of being Penny I think, of being me /H: right/ which was quite difficult, but um (.) just being me cos I hadn't been, you know I thought no one liked me. I did everything wrong so I think it

was a fear of being me totally [. . .] I didn't have to feel. I didn't feel. I
felt I was stoned all the time. /H: right/

LAURA: You feel numb.

In this extract Penny and Laura powerfully articulate the profound distress that
many women experience in relation to eating and not eating, in relation to
gender, subjectivity and embodiment. 'Anorexia' figures not only as a means of
avoiding painful thoughts and feelings. In producing 'numbness' it also becomes
an avoidance of subjectivity: 'of being Penny I think, of being me . . . which was
quite difficult'.

The psychoanalytic concept of schizoid fragmentation (Bion, 1967) further
elucidates this self-destructive theme. By focusing on the minutiae of one's life,
emotionally significant or threatening meanings can be warded off, fragmented
into an array of seemingly meaningless details. Sayers, for example, describes
how a client focused on 'the minutiae of the calories and grammes' that he ate
and weighed until he

> felt he was nothing but the grains of muesli he ate . . . Having defensively
> fragmented his life, David could then only pedantically regale me with its
> 'agglomerated' (Bion, 1967) details till I found myself as emotionally
> numbed as he sought to be himself.
>
> (Sayers, 1994: 3–4)

The 'anorexic' focus on the seemingly meaningless details of calories, grammes
and kilogrammes can thus be read as an attempt to erase meaning from one's
life, as an (a)voidance of any meaningful subjectivity.

'DISCIPLINE AND PUNISH': DETAILING INDIVIDUALITY[2]

There is, then, a continual shifting between the multiple discursive constructions
of anorexia as a signifier of numerous subjectivities, as a resistance to various
subject (im)positions and as a search for others, as simultaneously signifying identity and lack of identity, as an emptying of one's internality, and as an erasure of
meaning or identity. It is discursively constructed both as self-productive and self-
destructive. The discursive construction of 'anorexia' as a fragmentation of one's
life into seemingly meaningless details, as an expunging of feelings, memories
and thoughts, can be read as discursive self-obliterating and self-destruction.
However, this focus on detail might contrarily be interpreted as self-productive.
From a Foucauldian perspective modern individuality is produced precisely
through the exact observation and detailed examination of the body and the self
(Foucault, 1977b) that is exemplified in 'anorexia' (see also Malson and Ussher, in
press). Detail can be understood as producing as well as obliterating individuality.

Foucault (1977b) argues that the Classical Age (the seventeenth and eighteenth centuries) saw previous regimes of domination (such as slavery or
'service') being displaced by a political anatomy of power that 'produces

subjected and practised bodies, "docile" bodies' (ibid.:138) through detailed observation. 'The Classical Age discovered the body as the object and target of power' (ibid.: 136) and what was new here was

> the scale of the control: it was a question not of treating the body, *en masse*, 'wholesale', as if it were an indissociable unity, but of working it 'retail', *individually*; of exercising upon it a subtle coercion, of obtaining holds upon it at the level of the mechanism itself – movements, gestures, attitudes, rapidity: an infinitesimal power over the active body.
>
> (ibid.: 136–137, my emphasis)

That is, a 'new micro-physics of power', a 'political anatomy of detail' (ibid.:139) has emerged which functions through a multiplicity of minor processes of domination; through supervision, observation, surveillance, examination and the accumulation of detailed knowledge of the individual rather than the social body. It is through detailed surveillance and knowledge rather than violent physical coercion that human bodies are disciplined; are made intelligible, docile and useful.

> A meticulous observation of detail, and at the same time a political awareness of these small things, for the control and use of men [*sic*], emerge through the Classical Age bearing with them a whole set of techniques, a whole corpus of methods and knowledge, description, plans and data. And from such trifles, no doubt, the man of modern humanism was born.
>
> (Foucault, 1977b:141)

Discipline is exercised, then, through 'a meticulous observation of detail', through techniques of description and examination and through the accumulation of detailed knowledge, assessing and documenting the individual rather than the social body *en masse*. And, as Foucault argues, this infinitesimal control is not simply a repression. Rather 'discipline "makes" individuals' (ibid.:170):

> The individual is no doubt the fictive atom of an 'ideological' representation of society, but he [*sic*] is also a reality fabricated by this specific technology of power that I have called 'discipline'. We must cease once and for all to describe the effects of power in negative terms: it 'excludes', it 'represses', it 'censors', it 'abstracts', it 'masks', it 'conceals'. In fact, power produces; it produces reality, it produces domains of objects and rituals of truth. The individual and the knowledge that may be gained of him belong to this production.
>
> (Foucault, 1977b: 194)

Prior to the Classical Age everyday individuality 'remained below the threshold of description' (ibid.: 171). Since the emergence of modern discipline, however, the individual has become subjected (constituted and regulated) through detailed observation and description. Discipline individualizes. It produces the individual (as individual) as the effect and object of power and knowledge.

170

The 'anorexic' focus on the details of the pounds one weighs, the calories consumed or on the precise details of one's exercise regime can be viewed as an exemplar of this discipline. The self-observation, examination and documentation of such minutiae can be read as the exertion of a meticulous control and simultaneously as the constituting of oneself as an individual defined in its most minute detail, so that paradoxically this 'anorexic' focus on detail signifies a self-production as well as a self-destruction.[3] On the one hand it is constituted as a 'schizoid fragmentation' of 'the self' into seemingly meaningless details, as a numbing process of self-destruction. On the other it may be construed as self-producing, as a disciplinary process of detailed (self-)observation, examination and documentation that not only controls but also produces individuated subjects.

THE VISION THING: PANOPTICISM AND THE DISCIPLINED INDIVIDUAL

> I don't exist when you don't see me
> I don't exist when you're not here
> what the eye don't see won't break the heart
> you can make believe when we're apart
> but when you leave I disappear
> when you don't see me . . .
>
> (Sisters of Mercy, 1990)

In *Discipline and Punish* (1977b) Foucault argues that 'the examination' plays a central role in the exercise of discipline, in the process of producing disciplined individuals. It

> introduces individuality into the field of documentation. The examination leaves behind it a whole meticulous archive . . . [It] places individuals in a field of surveillance . . . it engages them in a whole mass of documents that capture and fix them.
>
> (Foucault, 1977b: 189)

The examination simultaneously constitutes and dominates the individual as an individual by meticulously documenting, i.e. discursively constituting, him or her. It links 'a certain type of the formation of knowledge' to 'a certain form of the exercise of power' (ibid.: 187). But it exercises power not only through documenting detail but also, necessarily, through observation, through placing the individual in 'a field of surveillance'.

> The examination transformed the economy of visibility into the exercise of power . . . In discipline, it is the subjects who have to be seen. Their visibility assures the hold of the power that is exercised over them. It is the fact of being constantly seen, of being able always to be seen, that maintains the disciplined individual in his subjection.
>
> (Foucault, 1977b: 187)

171

Through the examination, 'the economy of visibility' becomes an exercise of disciplinary power. 'It is a normalizing gaze, a surveillance that makes it possible to qualify, to classify and to punish' (ibid.: 184). In this next extract the economy of visibility is discursively constituted in precisely this Foucauldian way as a disciplinary, normalizing gaze:

LYNN: I thought people must look at me and and think I'm, that person's mental uh like, you know. Like sort of you might walk round the town and you'll see someone who's schizophrenic, you know, with all the homeless people and everything. And I'd think they'd look at me and they'd think I'm like that /JANE: mm/ so I stopped going out /H: mm/ so that people wouldn't see me. They must think: well she's mentally ill, that woman. /H: right/ And I think, you know, people'd think I was mental. I'd stay away from people, wouldn't even look at people. I'd walk up the road and keep my head down (.) /H: mm/ so that people wouldn't notice me.

In Lynn's extract she gives an account of how she stopped going out so that people wouldn't see her. The public's gaze is disciplinary and normalizing. It observes and categorizes her, judging whether or not she deviates from 'the norm', as 'mentally ill', 'schizophrenic' and 'homeless people' do. Hence, she attempts to become less visible in order to avoid this disciplinary 'field of surveillance'. Mandy construes medical intervention in a similar way.

MANDY: I think doctors pay far too much attention on the weight side of it. /H: right/ And um I mean I had to go through um sort of weighing and this kind of thing and it, all it does is um make you focus more on that. /H: mm/ If if a doctor is standing there and weighing you up and down and saying /H: yeah/ this, that and the other /H: yeah/ it makes you focus on it.

In her account Mandy is primarily concerned to argue that the attention doctors give to her weight is counterproductive as 'all it does is um make you focus more on that'. However, her construction of medical intervention as 'weighing you up and down' might be read as amalgamating the phrases 'weighing you', 'weighing you up' and 'looking you up and down'. It suggests a disciplinary theme of surveillance in which Mandy is subjected to an 'observational hierarchy' and a 'normalizing judgement' that measures and assesses her, comparing her with a norm. It is indeed a disciplinary technique that characterizes medical, psychiatric and psychological practices as a whole in terms of their procedures of observation, measurement and categorization and normalization (Foucault, 1977b; see also Ussher, 1991). It is also a technique that suffuses everyday life; the 'male gaze' at women (see Coward, 1984) for example. And the widespread attention that many girls and women (both those diagnosed as anorexic and others) give to the details of their food and body weight can similarly be understood in terms of a normalizing gaze, as critical *self*-examination, as a process that disciplines through *self*-surveillance, measurement and comparison with a norm or, rather, with a fictive norm, an 'ideal'.

After their emergence in the Classical Age techniques of individualizing discipline developed, so that by the nineteenth century procedures of observation, documentation, surveillance and examination were combined with procedures of exclusion (Foucault, 1977b). Discipline involved a 'constant division between the normal and the abnormal', an exclusion of the abnormal in asylums, prisons and hospitals and an individualizing of the excluded through constant surveillance.

Bentham's invention, the 'Panopticon' – a building in which a central observation tower is surrounded by an annular building divided into cells, each of which can be seen from the tower – represents 'the architectural figure of this composition'. 'All that is needed, then, is to place a supervisor in a central tower and to shut up in each cell a madman, a patient, a condemned man, a worker or a schoolboy' (ibid.: 200). In this way the inmate never knows when she (or he) is watched, but knows that she may always be watched. As Foucault argues,

> he who is subjected to a field of visibility, and who knows it, assumes responsibility for the constraints of power; he makes them play spontaneously upon himself; he inscribes in himself the power relations in which he simultaneously plays both roles; he becomes the principle of his own subjection.
>
> (Foucault, 1977b: 202)

The Panopticon thus represents an exemplar of discipline, producing disciplined individuals by making them constantly visible. It formed an important element of political technology, not only because it is 'polyvalent in its applications' (ibid.: 205) but also because it 'automatizes' and makes power anonymous, whilst individualizing its inmates. In the Panopticon 'power has its principle not so much in a person as in a certain distribution of bodies, surfaces, lights, gazes; in an arrangement whose internal mechanisms produce the relations in which individuals are caught up' (ibid: 202). And this principle of Panopticism is not only manifested as a disciplinary technique of institutions such as prisons, hospitals and schools. It is also a generalizable principle, a means by which power relations have come to permeate our everyday lives. Panopticism, the principle of a constant (or continually possible) surveillance and normalizing gaze, has become 'a new political anatomy' of disciplinary power, 'destined to spread throughout the social body; its vocation was to become a generalized function' (ibid.: 207). Foucault's discussion of Panopticism thus makes clear the significance of 'the economy of visibility' in the political anatomy of discipline. Surveillance (or its possibility) and the normalizing gaze are techniques of individualization and control. It is by being visible that one is constituted as a (disciplined) individual.

VISIBILITY AND THE THIN/ANOREXIC BODY

As we have seen, the anorexic body may be discursively constituted in a number of different ways. As a small body, for example, it may be construed as femininely petite (see Chapter 5). Alternatively through a discourse of Cartesian dualism it may be construed as a controlled body, signifying an idealized non-body and a powerful and independent subjectivity (see Chapter 6). And, in relation to Foucault's theory of Panopticism, the thin/anorexic body may be read differently again. For, as that body becomes progressively smaller, it also (in a sense) becomes less visible and may thus signify an evasion of the disciplinary gaze that both controls and individualizes (Malson and Ussher, 1997). Anorexia may be construed as both an exemplar of discipline and as a resistance to the individuality that discipline produces. In the extracts below, anorexia is constituted in precisely this way as an attempt to become less visible.

MANDY: I think um a lot of doctors tend to just focus on: somebody looks that thin, they're actually *wanting* somebody to see what's going on. /H: right/ But I think it's, it starts off with the control over eating which is the important thing [. . .] And the actual um, the physical appearance is much more to do with um *not* wanting wanting to be seen in in some ways, um. There's sort of a a feeling there of wanting to sort of just fade into the background literally.

PENNY: It's kind of (.) /H: I don't/ anger and the fear were kind of just (.) of being Penny I think, of being me /H: right/ which was quite difficult, but um, just being me cos I hadn't been, you know I thought no one liked me. I did everything wrong so I think it was a fear of being me /H: mm/ totally [. . .] I just wanted to fade away (inaud.)=

=LAURA: I avoided being me. I didn't want to know what me really was so I thought that if I just sort of (.) you know go along like this, just sort of hiding, I think I was just sort of hiding from myself.

In these extracts 'anorexia' is constituted as a means of becoming progressively less visible (Malson and Ussher, in press). 'Getting smaller' is not so much about being femininely petite as about fading away, hiding and avoiding 'being me'. Because Penny had a total 'fear of being me' she 'just wanted to fade away'. In Princess Diana's widely publicized speech to the International Eating Disorders Conference (cited in EDA, 1993: 3) she similarly portrayed disordered eating as 'a compulsion to dissolve like a Disprin and disappear'. Fading into the background, disappearing, becoming less visible can be read as evading the 'economy of visibility' in which the (disciplined) individual is constituted. Fading away is about self-destruction, because not wanting to be seen is also about not wanting to be (a disciplined individual). In becoming less visible the 'anorexic' body thereby becomes less individualized. But 'disappearing' also involves a physical destruction of the body. To become impossibly small is literally suicidal.

NICKI: It's just a way of like trying to disappear [. . .] You just want to get smaller and smaller [. . .] I mean I just wanted to die anyway /H: mm/ so not eating, becoming smaller is very relevant to that.

To disappear is both discursively and physically self-destructive. It signifies an evasion of (disciplined) individuality. But becoming ever smaller is also eventually fatal, so that fading away figures as the ultimate avoidance of an individualizing gaze through total (physical) self-destruction (Malson and Ussher, 1997).

Paradoxically, however, this ever-diminishing body also becomes more noticeable, more visible as it becomes increasingly subject to both social and medical scrutiny.

MANDY: It's the way of conforming and it is a way actually um not being individual. /H: right/ Um you, you can ac', you can literally fade into the background and and /H: mm/ and in, it's a bit sort of um (.) somehow it's it's not quite right. I mean on the one hand you can say that; you can fade away into the background but then on the other hand you can't because if you're that thin /H: mm/ then people will notice you anyway.

As Mandy argues, being 'that thin' may make you *more* rather than *less* noticeable (both to the public and to the medical profession). Her discussion illustrates how describing the thin/anorexic body as fading away or disappearing is a discursive construction. Whilst it is *physically* getting smaller it may equally be *discursively* construed as becoming more as well as less visible, so that, from a Foucauldian perspective, we can understand the anorexic body as both courting and evading the individualizing disciplinary gaze (Malson and Ussher, 1997); as both resisting and conforming to social control; as both self-destructive and self-productive.

VISIBILITY AND PSYCHOANALYTIC THEORIZATIONS OF SUBJECTIVITY AND GENDER

The importance of 'the economy of visibility' in the production of 'the individual' is indicated not only in Foucauldian theory but also in psychoanalytic theory (Malson and Ussher, 1997). Visibility plays a part in 'the mirror stage as formative of the function of the I' (Lacan, 1949) and in Oedipal development or the entry of the subject into the Symbolic order (see Chapter 1).

During the mirror stage the infant's identification with her mirror image 'situates the agency of the ego, before its social determination in a fictional direction' (Lacan, 1949: 2). The infant gazes at, and identifies with her, own reflection. She takes up a 'specular I' which prefigures 'the social I' of the Symbolic order 'in a primordial form':

This jubilant assumption of his [*sic*] specular image by the child at the *infans* stage, still sunk in his motor incapacity and nursling dependence, would seem to exhibit in an exemplary form, before it is objectified in the dialectic of identification with the other, and before language restores to it, in the universal, its function as subject.

(Lacan, 1949: 2)

The infant's misrecognition of herself as her specular image represents a primordial form of identity. It prefigures both 'the mental permanence of the I' and 'its alienated destination' (ibid.). As Lemaire (1981: xix, my emphasis) notes, the ego emerges 'through the necessary mediation of the *perceived image*'.[4]

Visibility also plays a part in psychoanalytic theorizations of later psycho-sexual development of gender identity. For Freud, the *sight* of the other sex's genitals is central to the development of masculine and feminine sexuality. Boys' conviction that both sexes have a penis 'is obstinately defended against the contradictions which soon result from *observation*, and is only abandoned after severe internal struggles (the castration complex)' (Freud, 1905: 113, my emphasis):

> *The observation* which finally breaks down his unbelief (in the threat of castration) is the *sight* of the female genitals . . . With this, the loss of his own penis becomes imaginable, and the threat of castration takes its deferred effects.
>
> (Freud, 1924a: 317–318, 319, my emphasis)

Feminine sexuality similarly develops when a girl compares her own genitals with a boy's and '*perceives* that she has "come off badly" and she feels this as a wrong done to her and as a ground for inferiority' (ibid.: 320, my emphasis).

The development of both masculine and feminine sexual identity is, then, for Freud, predicated in part on an economy of visibility in which male and female genitals are observed and compared with each other and, more significantly, with the phallic 'norm' of having a penis so that 'femininity' emerges as a *perceived* lack. Clearly, then, this perception, 'this phallic contempt and derision of women' is a socially (symbolically or discursively) constructed perception (see Blum, 1976: 169). Girls and women cannot be lacking in the real, since 'there is nothing missing in the real' (Lacan, 1982e: 113). We can only be *seen* as lacking in relation to a preconstituted (phallic) hierarchy of values:

> The phallus . . . indicates the reduction of difference to an instance of visible perception, a *seeming* value. Freud gave the moment when boy and girl child saw that they were different the status of a trauma in which the girl is seen to be lacking . . . But something can only be *seen* to be missing according to a pre-existing hierarchy of values . . . What counts is not the perception but its already assigned meaning – the moment therefore belongs in the symbolic.
>
> (Rose, 1982: 42)

As Lacanian rereadings of Freud emphasize, this 'instance of visible perception' can only be *significant* because it is already Symbolic. The girl is perceived as lacking only because that perception is located within a preconstituted field of vision, the Symbolic order. And this perception, like the disciplinary individualizing gaze, can be understood as 'an exercise of power' (see Foucault, 1977b: 187), which constitutes (gendered) subjectivity within an already-structured (phallic) field of vision.

Lacan has often been criticized for asserting that the status of the phallus as the privileged signifier within the Symbolic order stems from its visibility (Rose, 1982: 42); that the phallic nature of the Symbolic order can itself be understood in terms of the visibility of the penis (the real). Arguably, however, it is precisely this 'order of the visible, the apparent, the seeming that is the object of his attack' (Rose, 1982: 42). To assert that the phallus is the privileged signifier within the Symbolic because of its visibility is *not* an explanation of the origins of the Symbolic in terms of the real because the (fraudulent) vision of the phallus is *always* already located within a preconstituted Symbolic (Rose, 1982). From a Lacanian perspective gender-identities are constituted in an order of visibility whose ordering is always already Symbolic rather than real.

In short, psychoanalytic theory, like Foucauldian theory, asserts the importance of visibility in constituting subjectivity. It is 'the order of the visible' which privileges the visibility of the phallus, which renders meaningful the Oedipal 'instance of visible perception' and which constitutes femininity as a seeming lack. Lacan's 'order of the visible' constitutes gendered subjectivities in relation to the pre-existing phallic norm of the Symbolic order. And, as Foucault's 'economy of visibility' is located within a socio-historically specific politics of discipline which constitutes individuals, so too is Lacan's 'order of the visible' located in a Symbolic order within which masculine or feminine subject positions are constituted. And for both Lacan and Foucault these economies or orders of visibility always pre-exist the individual and always constitute as well as reveal their objects. And, like the metaphorical space of personhood produced by the discourse of individualism (see Chapter 6), these fields of visibility are spaces in which power/knowledge operates (see Foucault, 1977b).

Within the framework of both Lacanian and Foucauldian theories, the discursive construction of the thin/anorexic body as fading away or disappearing can thus be read as a resistance to disciplined or gendered individuality. The paradoxical construction of this body as one that is both less and more visible, as a body that *appears* to *disappear*, can be read as signifying an ambivalence towards, a simultaneous courting and evasion of, the disciplining, individualizing and gendering effects of these fields of vision which are always already located within socio-historically specific forms of power/knowledge.

ANOREXIA, DEATH, THE MOTHER AND THE ETHEREAL WOMAN

The thin/anorexic body may, then, signify both an evasion and a courting of a disciplining, individualizing and gendering gaze. Fading away involves a theme of self-destruction as well as self-production at both a discursive and a physical level. This theme of physical self-destruction of suicide and dying emerges sporadically in the different discourses which converge on the thin/anorexic body (see also Malson and Ussher, 1997). It is a theme evoked by the dualistic ideal of a non-body and one that also emerges as an extreme of self-punishment and self-destruction. In the following extract, for example, Jackie offers a profoundly disturbing account in which self-starvation is harrowingly presented as a particularly punishing form of self-destruction.

JACKIE: I mean it's only lately that I've felt maybe I want to live. /H: right mm/ Most of the time the result (.) of doing what I've done to myself is (.) just really wanting to kill myself.

H: Right, through starvation or=

=JACKIE: Yeah *definitely.* /H: right/ I've always had, always thought (.) the only way I wanted to die was to starve myself.

H: Oh right. Why was that? (.) I mean why that form rather than (.) another form? (.)

JACKIE: I don't know. I quite like (.) I *did* like the idea of it being a punishment. (.) /H: right (.) mm/ (.) And it was long and slow as well.

H: Right, so it was particularly painful.

JACKIE: Yeah, I used to get a kick out of that, /H: right/ (.) of the punishment part of it (.) and the pain.

Jackie's account graphically illustrates not only the extreme anguish and distress associated with 'anorexia' but also thereby the appalling damage done by the many discourses that converge to constitute and regulate women's experiences of themselves, of eating and not eating and of gender, subjectivity and embodiment. For Jackie, pain, self-punishment and death feature as highly prominent aspects of her experience. And self-starvation is produced as the apparent 'solution' to her wish to die just as it is produced in other discursive contexts as an apparent 'solution' to many of the other dilemmas that women face in relation to issues of gender, subjectivity and embodiment. In the extracts below, this self-destructive theme is again made explicit in women's accounts of their near-fatalities.

CATHY: I started feeling very ill and everything and my mother called my nurses and they said: bring her in, we'll run some tests. This was a Sunday uhm and I was brought in and I was actually on the verge of having a heart attack. My potassium levels were sky high.

JANE: Like because of my abuse (.) it helped me to face that. Um (.) I don't know (.) uh because I'd come so close to dying /H: right/ like quite a couple of times.

As recent studies demonstrate, mortality rates for anorexia remain alarmingly high (see Introduction). The dying anorexic body has a very real extra-discursive reality. Discursive-material 'anorexic' practices have physically hazardous and possibly fatal consequences. The ways in which these consequences are discursively constituted, however, does vary. The 'anorexic' woman may, for example, be construed as being passively 'taken to death'.

LAYLA: I think in a way it's more self-destructive than any other kind of depression /H: mm yeah/ unless it's suicide /H: right/ because in a way it takes you to death.

Whilst 'anorexia' is presented here as (possibly) fatal it is not construed as 'deliberate' suicide. It is 'the anorexia' rather than the woman herself that 'takes you to death': the self-destruction is passive. In other extracts, however, the 'anorexic' woman is construed as actively seeking death, as more actively self-destructive.

RACHEL: It's like a slow method, a slow method of killing yourself. P'raps men would maybe go from their car and put a hosepipe round.

JANE: I think with me it was hating myself so much. /H: right/ Um basically I just wanted to, initially I wanted to harm myself and sort of kill myself.

'Anorexia' is presented here as a form of suicide, as an extreme of 'deliberate', active self-destruction. Rachel, for example, constructs anorexia as 'a slow method of killing yourself', comparing it with another form of suicide, carbon monoxide poisoning. In contrast with this latter form, 'anorexic' suicide is construed as slower and as implicitly feminine. As with constructions of anorexia as a form of self-punishment, the construction of anorexia as suicide is associated with a very negative construction of the self as hated.

The discourses around death and dying also inevitably produce the 'anorexic' subject as a dying subject.

JANE: I've wasted so much of my life /H: mm/ you know. I spent eight months like in hospital and I was just (.) /H: mm/ half dead.

LAYLA: I was dying and I couldn't stop it and I was much too unhappy to do anything about it and I hated the way I was but I couldn't change the way I was.

In these extracts the dying self is construed very negatively and is associated with self-hatred, unhappiness and a regrettable wasting of life. In Elaine's extract below, this misery is emphasized through understatement:

ELAINE: I think when I lose weight I get happier but that doesn't normally work /H: mm/ out cos you know when I've been (.) you know

virtually dying (half laughing) I haven't been happy at all. /H: right/ (.)
You know I couldn't say I was exactly (.) (laughing) cheerful when I
came in here [. . .] I mean I just wanted to die.

Through understatement Elaine's account serves both to emphasize her distress
and represent this distress as an everyday aspect of her life. And by contrasting
her misery in 'virtually dying' of starvation with a construction of losing weight
as a key to happiness, promulgated by the diet and fashion industries, her
account graphically highlights the pernicious deception of these discourses that
induce women to eat less and lose weight.

This theme of death and dying is consolidated through the juxtaposition of
'anorexic' suicide with constructions of anorexia as an attempt to fade away. As we
have seen, fading away can be read as both symbolically and physically self-destructive, as the ultimate (symbolic) avoidance of an individualizing gaze through the
total (physical) destruction of the self. In other extracts this theme of death emerges
in association with a discursive construction of anorexia as a sometimes fatal form
of self-punishment (Malson and Ussher, 1997); a constellation of themes that again
highlights the extreme distress associated with 'anorexia'. In Jackie's extract above
(see p. 178), for example, death through self-starvation was construed as a long,
slow and painful punishment. Her account continues, contextualizing her wish for
self-punishment and death in an account of her mother's death:

H: Was there anything that you felt you were punishing yourself for
or? (.)

JACKIE: Um (.) I think I was very guilty about my mum's death. /H: right/
And (.) I don't know, my, I had um my childhood was quite difficult
[. . .] also my mum died of an illness which meant she lost an awful lot
of weight. (.) /H: oh right/ Yeah and so that, I think there's probably
some (.) significance with that. (.) /H: mm/ It's the fact that she was
really, she was six foot and she was uh seven stone something when she
died. (.) So she was very underweight. /H: mm/ (.) And so I think
there's probably some sort of parallel with the way I've been going, (.)
/H: right/ wanting to be thin like she was.

Jackie's troubled and troubling account allows for several explanations of her
suicidal feelings, one of which is her guilt about her mother's death. There is an
implication here that Jackie's own death would constitute an appropriate punishment or atonement for her mother's death. However, in addition to its
explanatory function, this extract also functions to produce death as a point of
identification between Jackie and her mother (Malson and Ussher, 1997). Just as
her mother died, so she is also dying. And, like her mother, Jackie would die after
losing 'an awful lot of weight'. Both mother and daughter would die very thin.

Amongst the women I interviewed this autobiographical association between
'anorexic' death and the mother's death was particular to Jackie and Teresa, and
illustrates the necessity of exploring the specificities as well as the commonalities

in discursive constructions of 'anorexia'. Whilst a number of common significations, themes and discourses have been explicated from the interview transcripts, there are also many specificities both within and across transcripts, in this case associated with the autobiographical diversity of the women. Yet, despite this specificity, the discursive relationship between 'anorexic' death and the mother's death is also of wider significance because in these autobiographical accounts the trope of 'the dead mother' is associated with themes of identity, resistance and escape; themes which, as we have seen, frequently emerge in the discourses surrounding 'anorexia', gender, subjectivity and embodiment.

In this next extract Teresa's account of her mother's death functions, like Jackie's, to produce an identification between mother and daughter (Malson and Ussher, 1997).

TERESA: It {anorexia} was also linked to the fact that I compulsively cared for my family /H: right mm/ and (.) and my mother's death [. . .] A couple of days before she died I went round to give her this present and things. And I was very, I remember my relationship with my mother as being much more as friends /H: mm/ and *me* worrying about looking after *her*.

Teresa explicitly relates her anorexia to her mother's death. This relationship does not focus on a suicidal aspect of anorexia or on a substantive similarity with her mother's death as Jackie's did. In this case the identification is constituted when Teresa is herself interpellated by the discourse in which she construes her mother and her mother's death. She takes up a 'maternal' position associated with her dead or dying mother. It is *she* who 'compulsively cared' for her family and who worried about looking after her mother. And it is her mother's death that is in some way associated with her anorexia. In the extract below this discursive relation between Teresa and her mother becomes more complex. Teresa describes how she chose a career 'that was the complete opposite and anathema to what {her} mother was', thus effecting an ostensibly categorical distinction between them. However, this distinction soon collapses into a further identification that pivots on self-destruction and sacrifice.

TERESA: I chose to do something that was the complete opposite and anathema to what my mother was. /H: right/ Uhm and that destroyed me too /H: mm/ because there was nothing of the identity that I had in relationship to what I could say was me. But also that the two things that they had in common was that my mother sacrificed herself as a mother and I was sacrificing myself as a nurse.

The extract produces an ambivalence in Teresa's relationship to her mother. There is a discursive shifting between separation and identification and both of these relationships involve self-destruction. Being a nurse, distinguishing herself from her mother, destroyed her 'because there was nothing of the identity that {she} had in relationship to what {she} could say was {herself}'. But her identification with her mother also involves destruction through self-sacrifice (Malson and Ussher, 1997). In this next extract this theme of sacrifice is again linked with Teresa's mother, with her anorexia and with themes of identity and escape.

TERESA: In our society mothers are not meant to have desires, to be angry, to be powerful, to be selfish. They're meant to like /H: mm/ completely orientate themselves and nurture /H: mm/ other people and I suppose I saw that destroy my mother. /H: mm/ And looking after us meant (.) that she had to kind of give up (.) had to be this sacrificial. /H: right/ She became very religious and sort of became this, I think she transcended it all by her religion. It was an escape. /H: mm/ And I'm, I'm very angry with her for that. Um (.) /H: mm/ but uh yeah definitely that was to do with my anorexia. And also it was an identification with her because she was a very elusive figure, my mother /H: yeah/ in a lot of ways.

Here Teresa provides a critique of a dominant ideology of motherhood in which 'the mother' should be completely oriented to others' needs and is therefore devoid of any desire or subjectivity of her own. Teresa's argument thus illustrates the wider cultural relevance of this trope of the dead mother. For this dominant patriarchal ideology produces 'the mother' as a function without subjectivity; 'her' subjective desire is sacrificed to others. As Irigaray (1988: 156) argues, 'when fathers took the power they had already annihilated the mother', barring 'her' subjectivity. Teresa's account emphasizes this matricidal theme when she describes her mother being destroyed by, and sacrificed to, this 'role'. Not only is Teresa's mother construed as sacrificed to motherhood, but this 'role' is itself construed as sacrificial. And sacrifice is constituted as a point of identification between mother and daughter.

However, Teresa's mother is also discursively produced as 'always escaping her life as a wife and mother because it was just so awful'.

TERESA: I always felt that she wanted to die /H: right/ because, you know, she was always escaping from her life as a wife and mother because it was just so awful [. . .] she never fitted in. I mean she just wore odd clothes and spent the whole of, collecting for Oxfam and working politically and, and as I said sitting up trees /H: mm/ painting pictures and writing poetry. I mean she didn't do the things that a wife and mother should [. . .] and she seemed very, very eccentric. /H: right/ But also she was completely trapped [. . .] I mean there were always routes out for her. /H: yeah/ And she used to write a lot of poetry about death and um I was always convinced that she wanted to die so when she did /H: mm/ I just felt angry about it.

Teresa's mother's 'eccentricity', her religious transcendence and her death all constituted 'routes out', ways of escaping 'her life as a wife and mother'. As an eccentric she is portrayed as 'sitting up trees' writing poetry about death rather than doing 'the things that a wife and mother should'. Ultimately, however, Teresa construes her mother as having to escape her life in order to escape 'her life as a wife and mother'. Her 'mother' is produced here as artistic, spiritual, ethereal and elusive, and as a figure whose escapes are closely associated with death (Malson and Ussher, 1997): 'she was a very elusive figure, my mother, . . . in a lot of ways.'

This construction of an elusive mother not only discursively consolidates a specific autobiographical relationship between the mother and death; it also constitutes a second point of identification between Teresa and her mother. In these extracts the mother–daughter relationship is again construed ambivalently: Teresa is 'very angry with her' for escaping, but 'escape' is also constructed as precisely a focus of further identification between mother and daughter. And it is 'escape' and the 'elusive figure' that are produced as the links between Teresa's anorexia and her mother's death. It is her mother's multiple elusiveness which is construed both as 'an identification with her' and as 'definitely . . . to do with {her} anorexia'. The implication is that in 'being anorexic' Teresa, like her mother, is a 'very elusive figure'.

This discursive construction of 'the anorexic woman' as elusive converges with the construction, discussed above, of anorexia as fading away or disappearing (Malson and Ussher, 1997). From a Foucauldian perspective 'anorexia' can be read as signifying an avoidance or evasion of an individualizing gaze. In Teresa's account, however, the elusive figure is not anonymous but is constituted as subject position in itself; at once signifying an identity and an escape from (maternal) identity. It is perhaps in this figure of the elusive woman that the opposing themes of self-production and self-destruction collide most dramatically. For this elusiveness is in part effected through death. The elusive figure is construed as dead (the dead mother who escaped her allotted life by dying), as thoroughly destroyed. Yet 'she' is also a particular subject position, an ethereal figure who is spiritual and other-worldly rather than bodily and mundane. In the extract below Tricia construes anorexia/thinness in precisely this way.

H: Were there any particular kind of (.) characteristics or (.) something that you associated with with this thin ideal?

TRICIA: I s'pose this sort of ethereal sort of fairy creature (.) /H: right/ that never quite landed on Earth, /H: yeah/ didn't really want to be here at all. /H: yeah, yeah/ I think that's some of the reason in a sort of quotes spiritual sense. There's (.) part of me just didn't really want to (.) to be here at all [. . .] I mean at one time I remember feeling (.) I was so up really *out* of my body /H: mm/ that I remember sort of (.) looking in the mirror and being actually surprised that I saw a form in the mirror /H: right/ and not just a nothingness.

In contrast with the harrowing accounts of 'anorexia' as a painful and possibly fatal form of self-punishment, Tricia articulates an almost dreamy version of 'anorexia' in which 'being anorexic' signifies an 'ethereal sort of fairy creature' and is associated with being 'up really *out* of my body'. In its emphasis on a disembodied subjectivity and out-of-body experience, the account evokes a theme of death or dying. Yet this deathly figure is construed quite positively as an 'ethereal sort of fairy creature . . . that never quite landed on Earth'. Like Teresa's dead mother this figure is elusive, spiritual, other-worldly and artistic. 'She' might sit up trees writing poetry about death to escape from mundane life. It is, in addition, a gendered subject position. Tricia's use of the word 'fairy' and Teresa's constructions of a 'maternal' death both produce this ethereal, elusive and deathly figure as feminine. Death and femininity converge here to produce dying as a perversely, dangerously appealing scenario (Malson and Ussher, 1997).

'Death' thus appears in the transcripts as a further example of a signifier of unfixed meaning. It is an ultimate form of punishing self-destruction associated with extreme psychological distress. But the 'deathly' figure of 'the elusive, ethereal woman' is positively construed as a spiritual disembodied 'fairy creature' who escapes *above* the mundanity of her allotted role. The meanings of the female body, the thin body, the anorexic body and the dying body continually shift, slipping through the multiplicity of discourses that converge to regulate women's experiences of eating and not eating, of gender, subjectivity and embodiment and of death, so that our experiences tumble from one dangerous fiction to the next.

This appeal of the elusive, deathly woman is not, then, a distortion particular to pathologized individuals. Rather, it is an effect of the many discourses and discursive practices in which women's subjectivities and experiences are constituted and regulated, for there are long-standing cultural associations between 'woman' and 'death' (Bronfen, 1992) upon which these extracts draw (Malson and Ussher, 1997). De Beauvoir (1953), for example, discusses a variety of mythological female figures of sirens, sorceresses, mothers and mistresses in which death is in one way or another associated with 'woman'. 'Woman', she writes, 'is not fully integrated into the world of men; as the other, she is opposed to them'. And in

> seeking to appropriate the Other . . . [man] plunges into the depths of fleeting and deadly waters. The Mother dooms her son to death in giving him life; the loved one lures her lover on to renounce life and abandon himself to the last sleep . . . Born of flesh, the man in love finds fulfilment as flesh, and the flesh is destined to the tomb. Here the alliance between Woman and Death is confirmed; the great harvestress is the inverse aspect of the fecundity that makes the grain thrive. But she appears, too, as the dreadful bride whose skeleton is revealed under her sweet, mendacious flesh.
>
> (de Beauvoir, 1953: 197)

A cultural fascination with death and femininity is also apparent in the prevalence of pictorial representations of dead women such as Delaroche's *La Jeune*

Martyre, Millais' *Ophelia* or G.F. Watts' *Found Drowned* (Bronfen, 1992). Lichtenstein's *Drowning Girl* or Phillippe Halsman's *Salvador Dali – in voluptate mors* (in which a skull is depicted formed out of seven naked female bodies) constitute more recent examples. The culturally embedded connection between 'woman' and 'death' is similarly evident in poetry (in the works of Plath and Poe, for example); in opera (e.g. *Carmen*); literature (e.g Emily Brontë's *Wuthering Heights*, Wilkie Collins' *The Woman in White*, Anne Rice's *The Queen of the Damned* or Toni Morrison's *Beloved*); film (e.g. *Dracula*, *The Hunger*, or countless films revelling in the violent murder of women) and fashion (in grainy black-and-white fashion shots of young women whose collar-bones protrude above designer clothes).

There is undoubtedly a misogynistic element to this long-standing association of death and femininity (Bronfen, 1992). Edgar Allan Poe's assertion that 'the death of a beautiful woman is, unquestionably, the most poetic topic in the world' has been roundly criticized by feminists as damaging to women (Bronfen, 1992: 59). And clearly the discursive production(s) of the dying or dead woman as an icon of femininity has facilitated a suppression and greater marginalization of woman as Other (Bronfen, 1992).

Yet the aestheticized image of the dead woman as an ethereal and elusive figure also seems to entail (perhaps perversely) positive aspects (Malson and Ussher, 1997). Cultural representations such as *Ophelia* are not only aesthetically 'appealing', they are also liminal. They are at once feminine and beyond/above (mundane) femininity. Representations of 'deathly' women such as Emily Brontë's Catherine Earnshaw, Bram Stoker's or Coppola's Lucy or the female vampire of *The Hunger* provide a construction of 'woman' that, whilst 'feminine', is also powerful and independent of the external world. Their liminality allows them to transgress social regulations, particularly those associated with their gender.

Discursive constructions of 'deathly women' thus provide subject positions which are both 'feminine' and liminal or subversive. It is perhaps such figures that inform the personal as well as the societal experience of the female body emaciated through 'anorexic' self-starvation. For discursive constructions of 'the anorexic woman' as deathly, ethereal, elusive and disembodied can be read as re-presentations of these culturally prevalent figures of deathly women.

This physical and discursive construction of woman as deathly is undoubtedly dangerous, sometimes resulting in actual death. Yet the figure of 'the deathly woman' signifies a positively construed subject position which is very 'feminine' and yet which, through 'her' liminality, eludes and subverts the (im)positions of femininity. In a socio-cultural context, in which the dominant ideal of 'femininity' is an ever-decreasing thinness, the ethereal, elusive, deathly significations of the thin/anorexic body may appear as a perfect, though double-edged and sometimes fatal, solution to the many culturally constituted dilemmas that women face in relation to issues of gender, subjectivity and embodiment (Malson and Ussher, 1997).

PENNY: Cos I always wanted to be the perfect anorexic, but I know the perfect anorexic's a dead one basically.

In short, the construction of the thin/anorexic body as deathly, ethereal, elusive and disembodied converges, in its (extreme) thinness with dominant constructions of feminine beauty; in its frailty with constructions of feminine fragility and sickness; in its smallness with constructions of the feminine as childlike; in its 'androgyny' as a masculine ideal. In denying the body almost to the point of death, it converges with the dualistic ideal of the non-body and pure consciousness that transcends the (gendered) body. The discursive construction of 'the anorexic' as an ethereal, elusive and deathly figure appears to provide a 'solution' to the always socio-historically specific problem of feminine subjectivity. The deathly thin body signifies a point of closure, the fiction of a fixed identity (see Wetherell, 1991). As the following extract illustrates, the discourses which converge upon the thin/anorexic body have very powerful real effects (see Walkerdine, 1986) in constituting and regulating women's experiences of gender, subjectivity and embodiment.

JACKIE: I mean god if I was going to write a book I think I'd have to write a lot about the misery of what it's actually like /H: right mm/ because you even forget yourself. (.) /H: right/ Because for this time I got to my target weight and I'd been losing and (.) I'd been delighted at losing (.) /H: mm/ until I just hit a point where I've been getting really down (.) again /H: right/ because you forget all of the (.) /H: mm/ you know, it's not a solution (.) /H: right/ unless you you actually kill yourself.

CONCLUSION

In Chapters 7 and 8 I have explored how subjectivity is discursively constituted in relation to 'anorexia' and the thin/anorexic body. In Chapter 7 I sought to illustrate the multiplicity of constructions of 'anorexia', analysing how 'anorexia' may be constituted as an identity that simultaneously constitutes a lack of/in identity. This chapter has continued the theme of subjectivity, focusing on the mutually conflicting, but profoundly related, themes of self-production and self-destruction. After examining some of the very negative self-constructions evidenced in the transcripts, the analysis explored how anorexia could be construed as self-punishing and self-destructive and yet simultaneously self-producing. 'Anorexia', I have argued, can be read as a multiple and ambiguous technology of the self whose meanings are multiple, shifting and contradictory. It can be read as a discursive (and material) practice which is paradoxically both self-productive and self-destructive. As a body that is fading away and disappearing, 'the anorexic body' simultaneously evades and courts a disciplinary, individualizing and gendering gaze. From a Foucauldian perspective, 'fading away' may signify a resistance to a number of socially available subject (im)positions. Yet, in evading an individualizing gaze, 'fading away' can also be understood as literally and discursively self-annihilating. At its most extreme this self-annihilation was articulated in terms of death and dying. Inevitably the discursive and material production of anorexia as a fatal process are associated with profound psychological distress and emotionally harrowing accounts of the self. But death may also be constituted as a site of mother–daughter identification and as the site of an elusive and transgressive feminine subjectivity. And as a point of closure death may also figure as the site of a (fictively) fixed identity (see Wetherell, 1991). This extreme and paradoxical convergence of self-destruction and self-production can thus be understood within the context of cultural re-productions of the deathly woman. The thin/anorexic is discursively and materially constituted as a process of self-annihilation. Yet it simultaneously signifies a multiplicity of positive as well as negative subjectivities produced in the pre-existing discourses and discursive practices which constitute and regulate women's experiences of eating and not eating, of gender subjectivity and embodiment.

CONCLUSIONS

'Anorexia nervosa' seems to crystallize many contemporary complex socio-cultural concerns and conflicts surrounding gender, subjectivity and embodiment. It is expressive of societal preoccupations as well as personal distress. It is saying something about what it means to be a woman in late twentieth-century Western society. But what is 'anorexia nervosa'? Most people are now familiar with what are now regarded as the central characteristics of 'anorexia' and will often see it as, in some way, a feminine disorder: 'anorexia' is something that afflicts today's young women. As a diagnostic category, 'anorexia' has existed since the late nineteenth century and yet it also seems to be a pecu-liarly modern 'disorder'. Whilst interpretations of epidemiological data are always contentious (see Brumberg, 1986) it does seem that increasing numbers of girls and women are being diagnosed as anorexic. And 'disordered' eating is clearly an important, troubling, aspect of many womens' lives (Bruch, 1978) and appears to be affecting ever younger girls (Hill and Robinson, 1991). Compared with many other 'disorders', 'anorexia' also has a high profile both in the media and in academic and clinical literature, suggesting a cultural fascination with all things 'anorexic'.

'Anorexia nervosa' is also the object of an increasing array of medical and psychological knowledges each of which constructs 'anorexia' in different and sometimes contradictory ways (see Chapters 3 and 4). These perspectives cannot be easily judged right or wrong: 'As one walks around a sculpture or any other three-dimensional object, the views one obtains are all, in some sense, equally valid. However, this in no way implies that they are all equally useful or insightful' (Edley and Wetherell, 1995: 206).

Like visual perspectives, each particular theoretical perspective on 'anorexia nervosa' – be it biomedical, cognitive, psycho-dynamic, feminist, or whatever – produces its own image and its own lacunae. In constructing 'anorexia nervosa' in one way rather than another a field of knowledge thereby also constrains the kinds of questions that can (legitimately) be asked about the distress that many girls and women in contemporary Western society experience around eating and not eating, around losing and gaining weight, being fat or thin, around being a woman. And one lacuna common to the majority of mainstream perspectives on 'anorexia' is gender. Despite the fact that many more women than men have been diagnosed as 'anorexic', issues of gender are often marginalized and/or undertheorized in much of the literature. Indeed, 'femininity' may even feature implicitly or explicitly as an explanation of women's propensity to disordered eating, just as it did in nineteenth-century accounts of anorexia hysterica/nervosa (see Chapter 3). Today, body-dissatisfaction and dieting amongst women has become an accepted norm (Polivy and Herman, 1987): 'Women like to diet. Women expect to diet. Women are accustomed to diet. Women have a tendency to fat. Women are vain. Women are always so self-involved' (Orbach, 1993: xxiii), so *naturally* women get eating disorders. There is so much literature on anorexia nervosa seemingly from so many perspectives. Yet the lack of adequate attention to, and theorization of, gender in the mainstream suggests that 'the anorexic sculpture' is being viewed only from certain (patriarchally) prescribed sites.

And, unlike the different perspectives on a sculpture, these different perspectives on 'anorexia' cannot be simply tacked together to produce a fuller, more 'objective' picture. Each of these different fields of knowledge about anorexia constitutes its object differently and each entails their own metatheoretical assumptions, their own sometimes incompatible criteria for what constitutes valid knowledge about 'anorexia' and 'anorexic' women. It is, for example, difficult to imagine how one could coherently combine a biomedical construction of 'anorexia' as biological dysfunction with a feminist construction of 'anorexia' as one of many effects of patriarchal oppression. Indeed, from most feminist perspectives explanations of women's distress in terms of supposed dysfunctions of their bodies (despite the lack of satisfactory supporting evidence) can only be seen as part of that patriarchal oppression.

Moreover, the very notion of producing a fuller, more objective knowledge of 'anorexia' is itself profoundly problematic. It assumes that an objective knowledge, an absolute Truth of 'anorexia', is possible. And it assumes a priori that 'anorexia nervosa' exists as a distinct clinical entity independently of the various scientific and clinical discourses in which it is constituted and treated. Yet positivist notions of objectivity and (scientific) Truth have been shown to be highly problematic (see Chapter 1); for, like other discourses, scientific and clinical discourses about 'anorexia' do not simply describe or reflect their objects more or less accurately. They are social practices that 'systematically form the objects of which they speak' (Foucault, 1972: 49), and each of these fields of knowledge brings with it a correlative set of power relations (see Foucault, 1977b). Each discourse on 'anorexia' positions girls and women (both those diagnosed as 'anorexic' and those not) in particular ways and has particular effects on women's lives. Discourses as social practices have very 'real' effects, legitimating particular practices, particular forms of authority, constituting particular 'truths' about 'reality' and positioning and constituting people in particular ways so that the possibility exists for fiction to function in truth, for fictional discourse to induce effects of truth, and for bringing it about that a true discourse engenders or 'manufactures' something that does not as yet exist, that is, 'fictions' it.

(Foucault, 1980: 193)

It is these 'facts, fictions and fantasies' (see Walkerdine, 1990) about 'anorexia' and about 'woman' that I have been concerned with in this book. For the very concept 'anorexia nervosa' circumscribes only particular constructions of girls' and women's experiences around eating, food and body weight, dictating that these experiences and behaviours be constituted in terms of *individual* pathology. For, whilst explanations of 'anorexia' vary, the validity of medical or quasi-medical conceptions of 'anorexia nervosa' itself remain largely unchallenged. Are there not other ways of understanding the distress that many girls and women in contemporary Western society experience around eating and not eating, around losing and gaining weight, being fat or thin, around being a woman?

By drawing on feminist post-structuralist and psychoanalytic theory I have sought in this book to develop a theoretical and methodological framework which is critically opposed to mainstream positivist and quasi-medical conceptions of 'anorexia' as a distinct *individual* clinical entity. Within this framework I have sought instead to elucidate the discursively constituted nature of 'anorexia nervosa' and to explore those discourses and discursive practices that converge upon the female body and the 'anorexic' body, interpellating girls and women in particular ways, constituting and regulating their/our experiences of eating and not eating, of losing and gaining weight, of being fat or thin, of gender, subjectivity and embodiment.

Hence, after setting out this theoretical and methodological framework (Part I) I was concerned in Part II with producing a genealogy of 'anorexia nervosa', exploring how women's self-starvation came to be constituted as a medical rather than theological matter, and then looking at how 'anorexia nervosa' first emerged within medical discourse as a distinct clinical entity. I was concerned with analysing the 'surface of emergence' (Foucault, 1972), the socio-cultural conditions that made it possible for 'anorexia' to be formulated as a distinct diagnostic category. The emergence of 'anorexia nervosa' I argued was a discursive event made possible by the gaps *in*, and the relationships *between*, the developing medical discourses of the Georgian and Victorian era. Georgian and Victorian society was already preoccupied with sickness and 'nerves' and with gender, preoccupations that were epitomized in the medical concepts of hypochondria and hysteria. In continual dialogue with the wider culture, medical discourses constituted the body as nervous and simultaneously feminized nervous disorder. In the concept of hypochondria nervousness was associated with gastric disorder, whilst 'hysteria' epitomized the feminization of nervousness and the pathologization of 'woman'. The already-existing medically and culturally entrenched concerns with nervousness, gastric disorder and pathologized femininity thus converged in the medical formulation of 'anorexia nervosa'. That is, 'anorexia' first emerged at an interface of medical and cultural discourses on hypochondria, hysteria and femininity and was constituted as a feminine nervous disorder at a time when 'the nervous woman' was already a significant cultural figure (see Ehrenreich and English, 1974), when explanations of female nervous debility were shifting (see Rousseau, 1991) and when woman's social status and rights as well as her nature were being hotly contended (see Sayers, 1982). In these initial texts on 'anorexia', 'femininity' figured as a causal explanation of pathology in and of itself. Hence this newly emerging category functioned as a political as much as a medical forum in which to debate and therefore constitute and reconstitute feminine nervousness. In the nineteenth-century medical journal articles on 'anorexia' the concepts of femininity and pathology were merged to produce a profoundly gendered (anorexic) subject whose very nature required the existence of a medical (masculine) authority.

Clearly institutional discursive constructions of 'anorexia nervosa' have changed substantially since the late nineteenth century. Chapter 4 therefore took this genealogy of 'anorexia nervosa' up to the present day, exploring the wide array of academic and clinical discourses in which 'anorexia' is now constituted. Each of these discourses, located in various disciplines and institutional sites, constitutes 'anorexia' in different often conflicting ways so that we now have a multiplicity of truths about 'anorexia', a multiplicity of anorexias. And, as noted above, in constituting universalistic, homogenizing and pathologizing truths about 'anorexia' and about 'anorexic' women, these (mainstream) fields of knowledge have real effects on women's lives. They *fiction* truths by circumscribing how we should understand the experiences of girls and women around eating, food and body weight; by positioning girls and women in particular ways and thereby constituting certain power relations.

In this book I have been concerned with the discursive construction of 'anorexia' and women's 'anorexic' experiences rather than with the therapies and clinical treatments of eating disorders *per se*. Yet clearly our knowledges of 'anorexia' have implications for the ways in which those diagnosed as 'anorexic' are treated. The discourses on anorexia and the discursive practices of treatment and therapy are clearly inextricably entwined (see Jarman, 1996). The location of 'anorexia' in its socio-historically specific discursive contexts and the elucidation of the gender power relations, the 'micro-processes of domination' in which 'anorexia' is constituted, imply that clinicians might usefully work within a framework that questions the medical model of 'anorexia', that acknowledges its socio-cultural context and acknowledges the discursively constituted nature of women's experiences and practices surrounding eating and not eating, gaining and losing weight, being fat or thin; surrounding gender, subjectivity and embodiment.

In Part III I therefore turned my attention from the institutional discourses in which 'anorexia' is (multiply) constituted as a clinical entity towards the popular discourses that surround 'anorexia', femininity, subjectivity and the body and which thereby constitute and regulate women's lives. Thus in Chapter 5 I examined how the thin/anorexic body sustains a multiplicity of meanings and how different discourses gender that body in different, often conflicting ways. In Chapter 6 I was concerned with analysing how the thin/anorexic body is discursively constituted as a controlled body, locating this construction within a discourse of Cartesian dualism which produced the body as eruptive, alien and threatening to the mind/self. This culturally entrenched discourse thus produced the necessity of exercising control over the body and constructed the thin/anorexic body as proof of such control. The thin/anorexic body was produced as a signifier of an idealized non-body and of an independent, disembodied and therefore genderless subjectivity. Yet, whilst this subject position appears genderless, gender is nevertheless imbricated in this discourse for it consolidates a polyvalent figure of 'woman' as bodily, excessive, uncontrolled, dangerous and alien, as other. It compounds as much as it alleviates the (discursively produced) problem of female embodiment.

The thin/anorexic body has thus been shown to signify a multiplicity of subjectivities. Hence, the production and maintenance of this body can be understood as a management of subjectivity. Yet 'anorexia' is also painfully self-destructive. In Chapters 7 and 8 I therefore explored these mutually conflicting but profoundly related themes of self-production and self-annihilation. Chapter 7 was concerned with different discursive relationships between the speaking subject and 'anorexia', focusing on the construction of 'anorexia' as an identity that simultaneously signifies a lack of or in identity. It also explored how constructions of 'the self' resist other potential identities and examined how identity is constituted within a discourse of individualism. In Chapter 8 I examined a multiplicity of negative constructions of 'the self' and focused on the discursive production of 'anorexia' as a form of self-punishment and self-destruction. In particular I explored how constructions of self-starvation, purging and a detailed attention to food and body weight simultaneously signified the annihilation of a very negative 'self' but also, paradoxically, the production of positively construed subjectivities. Similarly, constructions of the thin/anorexic body as disappearing and as dying could be read in terms of both self-production and self-destruction. I explored how the themes of visibility, of death and of femininity, were imbricated in the discursive construction of the thin/anorexic body. The paradoxical construction of the thin/anorexic body as a signifier of both self-production and self-destruction could, I argued, be located within the pre-existing discourses and discursive practices, within the 'micro-processes of domination' that converge on the thin/anorexic body, constituting and regulating women's subjectivities, femininities and our bodies in their socio-historical specificities.

The pernicious effects of the diet and fashion industries on many girls' and women's lives (and deaths) cannot be underestimated. But, in exploring the discourses and discursive practices which constitute and regulate women's experiences of gender, subjectivity and embodiment, I have sought to illustrate that contemporary Western culture is also much more deeply and complexly imbricated in these very damaging and distressing 'anorexic' practices that pervade so many women's lives.

APPENDIX

The analysis of the discourses surrounding 'anorexia' and the female 'anorexic' body (Chapters 5–8) is based on a series of interviews that I conducted with 23 women, 21 of whom had been diagnosed as anorexic and 2 of whom were self-diagnosed. The women were asked about their experiences of, and ideas about, 'anorexia' and 'femininity'. Following Marshall and Wetherell (1989), the emphasis was on maintaining an informal, conversational style. I also wanted to discuss issues that the women considered important as well as covering my own agenda. However, the following interview schedule was used as a guide to discussion.

INTERVIEW SCHEDULE

1 Often it is whilst we are teenagers that we first start to think of ourselves as becoming adult women, as feminine. Is that your experience? Do you remember any particular times or events when you first began to think of yourself as a woman?
2 How was this different to feeling like a child or a girl?
3 Did you have a particular idea of an ideal woman, someone that you would like to be like as a woman? What was it that made you want to be like her? Is that something you still feel or do you have different ideas now?
4 What about other girls, your friends – did they have similar ideas?
5 There are a lot of images in the media, in magazines and newspapers and on TV of so-called 'perfect' men and women. How would you describe these images or stereotypes?
6 What do you feel are the important differences between these ideas of how men and women 'should' be? Do these differences come naturally or do we have to work at becoming 'masculine' or 'feminine' people?
7 Do you think it is difficult being a girl or a woman? How is it difficult? Have you felt any pressure to conform to particular ideas about how girls and women 'should' be?
8 What about the media, magazines, our families or schools? Do you feel they

194

affect our experiences as girls and women and as people with eating problems?

9 As I am sure you already know, far more girls and women are diagnosed as anorexic than boys and men. Why do you think this is? Why is it that some women become anorexic and others do not? Is there a particular sort of person that becomes anorexic?

10 When you first became 'anorexic', how did you feel? How did you feel about yourself, about your body, about food?

11 How did you react when you were diagnosed as anorexic or as having 'anorexic' eating problems? *or*

11 What was it that made you decide that you were 'anorexic' or having 'anorexic' eating problems? Was it your decision?

12 A lot of people who write about anorexia describe it as a pseudo-solution, meaning it is a troubled way of trying to sort things out or deal with a problem. Did you feel being 'anorexic' would help you in some way?

13 What sort of things did food, not eating, losing weight and being thinner mean to you?

14 What would you say being anorexic means (to you) now? How is it different from not being anorexic? Is this a different experience from when you first became 'anorexic'?

15 Is this how other people – other 'anorexic' people, family, friends, doctors, the media – see anorexia?

16 Do you think there are ways in which anorexics are similar to each other and different from non-anorexics?

17 If you were going to write a book about anorexia, what sort of things would you want to say in it?

18 A lot of people have pointed out that there has been an increase in anorexia in the last twenty years. Why do you think this is? Do you think it has anything to do with the ideas we were talking about earlier, about being girls and women?

19 Is there anything that we could change in society or in our families to stop this increase, or not? What sort of things do you feel contributed towards you becoming 'anorexic' or developing 'anorexic' eating problems, and towards 'recovering'?

20 Are there any other things that we have not talked about that you feel are important?

Where possible, a copy of the interview schedule was sent to participants beforehand and before starting each interview I gave a brief explanation of the study and assured participants of the confidentiality of the interviews. I also reminded the women that they could terminate the interview at any point and that they need not answer any questions they chose not to. It was very probable that distressing issues would be covered, and although I did not ask any direct questions about past traumas several of the women disclosed particularly disturbing experiences. It was, therefore, particularly important to remind the women at certain times during the interviews that they could terminate the interview or not answer questions if they wished.

Each interview lasted between twenty minutes and two hours, with most lasting about an hour. All the interviews were audiotaped and transcribed verbatim. Following Marshall and Wetherell (1989), the transcription conventions outlined on page xiv stress readability rather than the detailing of speech features such as intonation or lengths of pauses or overlaps (see also Potter and Wetherell, 1987), since these were not considered in the analyses. The transcripts were then analysed using a discourse analytic methodology.

NOTES

INTRODUCTION

1 All names and identifying details have, of course, been changed in these and all the other extracts from interviews used in this book. In these extracts I have omitted my interjections to make the women's texts more readable. In Part III, where I analyse the interview transcripts, I have included my own contributions for the sake of completeness. The transcription conventions are provided on page xiv.

2 Susan Sontag, for example, discusses TB, cancer (1978) and HIV/AIDS (1989) in terms of cultural metaphor.

1 THEORIZING WOMEN: DISCOURSING GENDER, SUBJECTIVITY AND EMBODIMENT

1 Psychoanalytic theory posits that sexual difference is created only in relation to the phallus. Phallocentrism refers to this privileging of the masculine over the feminine, to the setting up of the male body as the norm against which the female body is viewed as lacking (a penis). See Mitchell and Rose (1982) for a more detailed discussion.

2 See Brennan's (1989) edited collection of this title.

3 Psychoanalysis theorizes gender identity not as natural, stable and coherent givens but as the precarious and problematic consequence of a process of interpretation of the body (Sayers, 1982). And this process of interpretation is profoundly phallocentric (see note 1). Our idealization of the masculine ideal, our beliefs in the coherence of our identity and in the security of our gender identity, are thereby shown to be illusory (see Sayers, 1994, 1995 for a fuller discussion).

4 The term 'bisexuality' refers to the idea that 'the boy has a bit of the female, the girl a bit of the male', but also to 'the very uncertainty of sexual division itself' (Mitchell, 1982: 12; see also Benvenuto and Kennedy, 1986).

5 See Freud (1905) and Mitchell (1974) for a more detailed discussion of infantile sexuality and psychosexual development.

6 See Sayers (1982), Mitchell (1974), Freud (1905) and Nagera (1969) for more detailed discussions of psychosexual development.

7 Until this time the father has been absent from the mother–child dyad. The Oedipus complex represents 'the original exogamous incest taboo' (Mitchell, 1974: 377) in which 'the law of the Father' prohibits the child's (now phallic) desire for its mother. For boys, this prohibition is experienced (unconsciously) as a threat of castration by the father. Hence, the boy perceives his father as an Oedipal rival for

his mother. However, recognizing the law of the Father, he renounces his Oedipal desires for his mother and understands that he will later be able to take up the privileged masculine position currently occupied by his father. See Freud (1924a) for a more detailed discussion of the Oedipus complex. The Oedipus complex has been interpreted by structuralist and Lacanian theorists (e.g. Althusser, 1971) as the moment at which the child enters the Cultural or the Symbolic order (Sayers, 1982). This interpretation is discussed in further detail below.

8 See Lacan (1949) and Sarup (1988) for further discussion of 'the mirror stage'.

9 For Lacan, this is not an 'alienation' from some pre-existing 'identity', but is rather a 'lack-in-being' of the profound splitting of subjectivity (Rose, 1982: 40).

10 For Lacan, language, the Symbolic, 'stands in' for objects. 'The real' refers therefore to 'the moment of impossibility' (Rose, 1982: 31), describing 'that which is lacking in the symbolic order'. 'The real in its "raw" state . . . may only be supposed' (Sheridan, 1977: x). This ontological stance thus corresponds with the 'critical realist' stance discussed below.

11 Whilst Lacan adopts the epistemological framework of Saussurean linguistics he also transposes Saussure's 'fraction of sign = signified/signifier' (Walkerdine, 1988: 3–4).

12 Lacan refers the phallus to the function of 'veiling', indicating that it 'covers over the complexity of the child's early sexual life with a crude opposition in which that very complexity is refused or repressed. The phallus thus indicates the reduction of difference to an instance of visible perception, a seeming value' (Rose, 1982: 42).

13 Freud similarly argued that

> what is at issue for him [throughout the moment of castration] is the mode of representation of a lack from which the subject finds himself suspended in his traumatic relation to desire: whence the traumatic, unbearable character of this perception and of the profound fissure in which it establishes the subject.
>
> (Lacan, 1982e: 113)

14 See Sayers (1988, 1991) for a fuller discussion of this shift towards a focus on the mother in feminist psychoanalysis.

15 For more detailed accounts of feminist post-structuralist theorizations of 'woman', see Riley (1988), Jardine (1985), Poovey (1988) and Walkerdine (1993).

16 Cf. Freud (1925: 342), who argued that in 'girls the motive for the demolition of the Oedipus complex is lacking' because castration 'has already had its effect'. Because for the girls there can be no 'castration anxiety' there will be less cause to resolve the Oedipus complex, to take up the feminine position to the same extent as boys will take up the masculine position.

17 Hence Foucault's genealogies of discourses and discursive practices stress discontinuity as much as continuity (Foucault, 1977a). Foucault's post-structuralist theory of discourse is discussed in the following section of this chapter.

18 The shift from structuralism to post-structuralism clearly produces some tensions between the works of Foucault and Lacan. However I would argue that these theories are nevertheless epistemologically compatible. Both adopt Saussurean or post-Saussurean linguistics as an epistemological or metatheoretical framework, viewing the relationship between signifier and signified as arbitrary. Hence meaning, and therefore knowledge, is constituted *within* language. Both Lacan and Foucault must thus contest the notion of absolute, objective, empirically verifiable 'truth'. Further, both transgress the 'traditional' individual–society dichotomy, theorizing a decentred, non-humanist subject, constituted outside of itself in discourse or the Symbolic. However, as Walkerdine (1986: 64–65) notes, Foucault does not (until his most recent work) address 'the problem of subjectivity directly, but rather skirts

around it'. It is therefore important to retain Lacan's insights into the phallic nature of signification and his theorization of desire and gendered subjectivity within the post-structuralist perspective that Foucault provides.

19 For further discussion of language as constitutive rather than reflective of reality see Potter and Wetherell (1987), Burman and Parker (1993), Henriques *et al.* (1984) or Walkerdine (1988).

20 'Ennuciative modality' refers to the positions in discourses from which the subject speaks and is spoken. The concept thus refers to the rules of what can and cannot be said, how things can be said and what power-relations pertain in any particular position within discourse (see Foucault, 1972).

2 DISCOURSE, FEMINISM, RESEARCH AND THE PRODUCTION OF TRUTH

1 See Henwood and Pidgeon (1992), Kitzinger (1987), Harre and Secord (1972) and Tseelon (1991) for more detailed critiques of positivist research. For further discussion of philosophies of science, see also Bechtel (1988).

2 See Fee (1981), Jordanova (1989), Harding (1987), Bleier (1984), Ussher (1992c) and Griffin (1986) for feminist discussions of positivistic science and psychology.

3 See, for example, Potter and Wetherell (1991) Potter *et al.* (1990) and Antaki (1988) for further discussions of different approaches to 'discourse analysis'.

3 A GENEALOGY OF 'ANOREXIA NERVOSA'

1 See Ussher (1991) and Showalter (1985) for further discussion of the relationship(s) between women and madness.

2 Whilst the validity of this claim is generally accepted, Porter (1987) asserts that prior to the mid-nineteenth century more men than women were admitted to asylums. Busfield (1994) similarly argues that neither the statistics on insanity nor the cultural representations of women provide much evidence of a notable affinity between women and madness.

3 This case is discussed in great detail by Bell (1985). Numerous other historical cases of women's self-starvation are discussed by Bynum (1987) and Brumberg (1988).

4 See, for example, Robinson (1893), anon (1881a), Sutherland (1881) and Salter (1868).

5 See Showalter (1985), Veith (1965), Brumberg (1982) and Ehrenreich and English (1974) for further discussion of 'female maladies'.

6 See Salter (1868), Lasegue (1873b), Robinson (1893) and Sutherland (1881), for example.

7 See Vandereycken and Van Deth (1989) for a further discussion of Gull's claims to priority over Lasegue and of the politics of the issue.

8 See Potter and Edwards (1990), who discuss 'consensus warranting' as a rhetorical resource for producing an account as 'factual'. That is, the apparent 'factuality' of an account may be increased by its being consensually agreed upon.

9 For example, Collins (1894), Marshall (1895), anon (1895a), anon (1895b) and Taylor (1904).

10 See Ehrenreich and English (1974) and Veith (1965) for discussions of femininity as a class-specific concept.

11 See Ehrenreich and English (1974), Showalter (1985) and Ussher (1989) for further accounts of such medical treatments.

12 See also de Berdt Hovell (1888a; 1888b) and Mackenzie (1888).

4 DISCOURSING ANOREXIAS IN THE LATE TWENTIETH CENTURY

1 See Malson (1995b) for a more detailed review of these literatures.
2 In terms of biomedical research, Schweitzer et al. (1990), for example, found that those anorexic participants evidencing HPA-axis dysfunction were no more severely depressed than those without such dysfunction. Similarly, whilst some genetic studies have found higher rates of affective disorders in relatives of anorexics (see Rivinus et al., 1984), findings vary across studies and there is as yet no evidence that anorexia is more common in relatives of those with affective disorders than would be expected if there were a genetic relationship between the two disorders (Rutter et al., 1990).
3 Minuchin et al. (1978) assert that the family system comprises a number of different subsystems, such as spouse, parental and sibling subsystems. They argue that the boundaries and transaction patterns between these form a 'matrix' for the psychological development of family members.
4 Sayers (1988) provides a detailed critical discussion of this focus on the mother in recent psychoanalytic theory and therapy.
5 This research most commonly involves 'pre-load' experiments in which college students are categorized as either restrained or unrestrained eaters on the basis of a restraint scale. In a typical experiment, half of the participants are then given a pre-load (usually one or two milkshakes) and half are not, before a taste-test (often of ice cream) in which the quantity eaten is measured. See Ruderman (1986) for a review of such studies.
6 See, for example, Broverman et al. (1970) whose study illustrates how 'adult femininity' is equated by psychology professionals with mental ill health, while 'adult masculinity' corresponds with conceptualizations of 'the healthy adult'.
7 See Ussher (1992b) for discussions of parallel developments in research and therapy in depression, schizophrenia and PMS.

5 THE THIN/ANOREXIC BODY AND THE DISCURSIVE PRODUCTION OF GENDER

1 Further details of this interview study are provided in the Appendix. All names and identifying details of the women involved have, of course, been changed. Parts of these analyses are to be found in Malson (1995a, forthcoming) and Malson and Ussher (1996a, 1996b, 1997).
2 A phrase of Barthes used by Jardine (1985) in her discussion of femininity.
3 See also Adams (1986), who describes children's fairy stories as 'conspiring' to regulate the readers' subjectivity and emotions within particular cultural frameworks. Such texts, he argues (1986: 4), 'conspire with language to direct readings which are appropriate to the culture'. See also Wetherell (1991) for a discussion of romantic discourse.
4 Indeed, anorexia has been interpreted as a retreat from adulthood (Plaut and Hutchinson, 1986; Crisp, 1970).
5 Squire (1983: 49) similarly argues that, for Lacan, 'tropic relations of unconscious signifiers must continue indefinitely and never be completely tied down', since such relations are grounded in the Symbolic in an absent, unidentifiable signified.

6 SUBJECTIVITY, EMBODIMENT AND GENDER IN A DISCOURSE OF CARTESIAN DUALISM

1 If the past event to which Emma refers physically causes her to gain weight then the delay in its effects seems inexplicable. When asked what this event might have been, she replied, 'I don't know. I don't know whether it's a change in eating behaviour or what it was [. . .] or whether just you know hitting a certain age changed my metabolism.' Both the vagueness surrounding the nature of this past transgression and the reference to 'hitting a certain age' suggest that the transgression may have been becoming a woman. Orbach (1993: 44) has similarly argued that 'Since women must not eat they know not how to eat or what they wish to eat. They live in the shadow of Eve. They have all sinned.'

2 Christian asceticism is also still evidenced in religious practices. A devout Christian student recently died whilst fasting in an attempt to grow nearer to God (*South Today News*, BBC1, 6.30pm, 21 October1993).

3 As Bynum (1987: 216) notes from the medieval 'Sayings of the Fathers', 'As the body waxes fat, the soul grows thin; and as the body grows thin, the soul by so much waxes fat.' Whilst not wishing to suggest that the ascetic fasting of medieval female saints can be retrospectively diagnosed as 'anorexic' (see Chapter 3), I would argue that dualistic discourse represents a site of partial convergence between the two phenomena.

4 The figure of the vulnerable sexual woman as a food-like commodity is, I would argue, exemplified in a bizarre incident, documented in *Witness: Excuse Me for Living* (Channel 4, 9.00pm, 21 November 1993). A Japanese student in Paris, Issei Sagawa, killed, dismembered and ate a Dutch woman who was, significantly, misidentified as his 'girlfriend'. French courts declared the man insane, dropped the prosecution and after three years returned him to Japan, where he was released after a year and has since become a media celebrity, 'lionised by the Japanese avant-garde'. He wanted to know how the flesh of a beautiful white woman would taste (*Guardian Guide*, 20 November 1993, 16).

7 ANOREXIA AND THE DISCURSIVE PRODUCTION OF THE SELF

1 This construction of 'anorexia' as a creature surviving in the body might also be interpreted as an image of pregnancy, relating to the psychoanalytic interpretations of anorexia as a fear of oral impregnation (see Chapter 4).

2 This discursive relationship between body boundaries and identity is also evidenced in discursive constructions of menstruation (see Chapter 5) and eating (see Chapter 6), as threatening to the integrity of the self in that they transgress the body's physical boundaries.

3 Discursive constructions of 'anorexia' as a 'slimmer's disease', for example, imply that it is a superficial issue of feminine vanity rather than a 'deeper', and therefore more serious, issue.

8 DISCURSIVE SELF-PRODUCTION AND SELF-DESTRUCTION

1 In 1924, Freud added a footnote to his discussion of masochism in *The Sexual Aberrations* (1905), in which he drew a distinction between primary and secondary masochism, writing that:

My opinion of masochism has been to a large extent altered by later reflection . . . I have been led to distinguish a *primary* or *erotogenic* masochism, out of which the later forms, *feminine* and *moral* masochism, have developed. Sadism which cannot find employment in actual life is turned round upon the subject's own self and so produces a *secondary* masochism, which is superadded to the primary kind.

(Freud, 1905: 71–72)

2 This section takes part of its title from Foucault's *Discipline and Punish: the birth of the prison* (1977).

3 See also Gutman's (1988) discussion of Rousseau's *Confessions* (1765), in which he argues that 'Rousseau constituted the self as subject by objectivizing the speaking subject in language' (Gutman, 1988: 117). In the *Confessions*, Rousseau develops a technology of the self through which the individuated subject emerges 'as a subject of observation and description', constituted through an examination and written confession that stresses 'the inclusion of every detail' (Gutman, 1988: 116–117).

4 The notion of 'reflection' is also apparent in other psychoanalytic theories of development. Winnicott (1967), for example, describes the mother as mirroring the child to itself. His conceptualization of 'reflection' does, however, differ significantly from Lacan's.

REFERENCES

anon (1873a) Clinical Society, Friday 24 October, *Medical Times and Gazette*, 2, 8 November, 534–536.

——(1873b) Clinical Society of London, Friday 24 October, *British Medical Journal*, 2, 527–529.

——(1873c) Foreign Gleanings: hysteric anorexia, *Lancet*, 12 July, 49.

——(1874) Abstract of the introductory lectures delivered at the various medical schools of London at the opening session 1874–1875. Guy's Hospital, introductory lecture by Sir William Gull, *Lancet*, 3 October, 485.

——(1881a) A mirror of hospital practice, British and foreign: Middlesex Hospital: Hysterical vomiting of eight months' duration, *Lancet*, 19 February, 291–292.

——(1881b) Clinical Society of London, report of the committee on excision of the hip-joint in childhood – aortic aneurism – anorexia nervosa – antiseptic osteotomy of the tibia, *Lancet*, 21 May, 826–828.

——(1885) Medical Society of London: Gastric ulcers, *Lancet*, 5 December, 1048–1049.

——(1888) Editorial, *Lancet*, 24 March, 581–584.

——(1895a) Emsworth Cottage Hospital: Case of anorexia nervosa; necropsy, *Lancet*, 5 January, 31–32.

——(1895b) Northumberland and Durham Medical Society: Exhibition of cases and specimens, *Lancet*, 19 October, 987–988.

——(1896) A case of anorexia nervosa, *The Northumberland and Durham Medical Journal*, 7–8.

Adaire, G. (1993) *Death of the Author*, Minerva, London.

Adaire, J.M. (1790) *Essays on Fashionable Diseases*, Bateman, London.

Adams, J. (1888) Sir W. Gull on anorexia nervosa (letter), *Lancet*, 24 March, 597.

Adams, J. (1986) *The Conspiracy of the Text: the place of narrative in the development of thought*, Routledge, London.

Althusser, L. (1971) Freud and Lacan, in *Lenin and Philosophy and Other Essays* (trans. B. Brewster), New Left Books, London.

——(1977) *Lenin and Philosophy and other Essays* (trans. B. Brewster, 2nd edition), NLB, London.

American Psychiatric Association (APA) (1980) *Diagnostic and Statistical Manual of Mental Disorder* (3rd edition), American Psychiatric Association, Washington DC.

——(1987) *Diagnostic and Statistical Manual of Mental Disorder* (3rd edition, revised), American Psychiatric Association, Washington DC.

Andersen, A.E. (1987) Contrast and comparison of behavioural, cognitive-behavioural and comprehensive treatment methods for anorexia nervosa and bulimia nervosa, *Behaviour Modification*, 11(4), 522–543. Special issue: Behavioural and cognitive-behavioural treatments of anorexia nervosa and bulimia nervosa.

REFERENCES

Andreasen, N.C., Endicott, J., Spitzer, R.L. and Winokur, G. (1977) The family history method using diagnostic criteria: reliability and validity, *Archives of General Psychiatry*, 34, 1229–1235.

Antaki, C. (ed.) (1988) *Analyzing Everyday Explanations: a casebook of methods*, Sage, London.

Appels, A. (1986) Culture and disease, *Social Science and Medicine*, 23(5), 477–483.

Austen, J. (1811) *Sense and Sensibility* (1992 reprint), Wordsworth Editions Limited, Hertfordshire.

Austin, J.L. (1962) *How to Do Things with Words*, Clarendon Press, Oxford.

Bardwick, J. (1971) *Psychology of Women: a study of bio-chemical cultural conflicts*, Harper and Row, New York.

Bayne, R. (1994) The 'big five' versus the Myers-Briggs, *The Psychologist*, 7(1), 14–16.

de Beauvoir, S. (1953) *The Second Sex* (trans. J. Cape, 1984 edition), Penguin, London.

Bechtel, W. (1988) *Philosophy of Science: an overview of cognitive science*, Erlbaum, Hillsdale, NJ.

Beglin, S. and Fairburn, C.G. (1992) Women who choose not to participate in surveys on eating disorders, *International Journal of Eating Disorders*, 12(1), 113–116.

Bell, R.M. (1985) *Holy Anorexia*, University of Chicago Press, Chicago.

Bemis, K.M. (1979) Current approaches to the etiology and treatment of anorexia nervosa, *Annual Progress in Child Psychiatry and Child Development*, 486–523. Reprinted from *Psychological Bulletin*, 85, 593–617.

——(1983) A comparison of functional relationships in anorexia nervosa and phobia, in P.L. Darby, P.E. Garfinkel, D.M. Garner and M. Olmsted (eds) *Anorexia Nervosa: recent developments in research*, pp. 403–415, Alan Liss, New York.

Benjamin, J. (1985) *A Desire of One's Own: psychoanalytic feminism and intersubjective space*, Centre for Twentieth Century Studies, Working Paper no. 2, Fall, University of Wisconsin, Milwaukee.

——(1990) *The Bonds of Love*, Virago, London.

Bentall, R.P. (1990) *Reconstructing Schizophrenia*, Routledge, London.

Benvenuto, B. and Kennedy, R. (1986) *The Works of Jacques Lacan: an introduction*, Free Association Books, London.

de Berdt Hovell, D. (1873) Hysteria simplified and explained, *Lancet*, 20 December, 872–874.

——(1888a) Anorexia nervosa (letter), *Lancet*, 12 May, 949.

——(1888b) Sir W. Gull on anorexia nervosa (letter), *Lancet*, 24 March, 597.

Bernheimer, C. and Kahane, C. (eds) (1985) *In Dora's Case: Freud, hysteria, feminism*, Virago, London.

Bhaskar, R. (1978) *A Realist Theory of Science* (2nd edition), Harvester, Brighton.

Billig, M. (1991) *Ideologies and Beliefs*, Sage, London.

Billig, M., Condor, S., Edwards, D., Gane, M., Middleton, T. and Radley, A. (1988) *Ideological Dilemmas: a social psychology of everyday thinking*, Sage, London.

Bion, W.R. (1967) *Second Thoughts*, Heinemann, London.

Birksted-Breen, D. (1989) Working with an anorexic patient, *International Journal of Psychoanalysis*, 70, 29–39.

Bleier, R. (1984) *Science and Gender: a critique of biology and its theories on women*, Pergamon Press, New York.

Bliss, E. (1982) History of anorexia nervosa, in M. Gross (ed.) *Anorexia Nervosa*, pp. 5–7, Collamore Press, Toronto.

Bliss, E.L. and Branch, C.H. (1960) *Anorexia Nervosa: its history, psychology and biology*, Paul B. Hoeber, New York.

Blum, H. (1976) Masochism, the ego-ideal and the psychology of women, *Journal of the American Psychoanalytic Association*, 24, 157–191.

Bordo, S. (1990) Reading the slender body, in M. Jacobus, E. Fox Keller and S. Shuttleworth (eds) *Body/Politics: women and the discourses of science*, pp. 83–112, Routledge, London.

——(1992) Anorexia nervosa: Psychopathology as the crystalization of culture, in H. Crowley and S. Himmelweit (eds) *Knowing Women: feminism and knowledge*, Polity Press in association with Open University Press, Cambridge and Oxford.

Boris, H. (1984) The problem of anorexia nervosa, *International Journal of Psychoanalysis*, 65, 315–322.

Boskind-Lodahl, M. (1976) Cinderella's step-sisters: a feminist perspective on anorexia nervosa and bulimia, *Signs*, 2 (2), 342–356.

Bowlby, J. (1969) *Attachment and Loss*, vol. 1, Basic Books, New York.

——(1973) *Separation and Loss*, Basic Books, New York.

Bowlby, R. (1989) Still crazy after all these years, in T. Brennan (ed.) *Between Feminism and Psychoanalysis*, pp. 40–59, Routledge, London.

Bracher, M. (1993) *Lacan, Discourse and Social change: a psychoanalytic cultural criticism*, Cornell University Press, Ithaca.

Branch, C.H. and Eurman, L.J. (1980) Social attitudes towards patients with anorexia nervosa, *American Journal of Psychiatry*, 137(5), 631–632.

Brennan, T. (ed.) (1989) *Between Feminism and Psychoanalysis*, Routledge, London.

Brinded, P.M., Bushnell, J.A., McKenzie, J.M. and Wells, J.E. (1990) Body image distortion revisited: temporal instability of body image distortion in anorexia nervosa, *International Journal of Eating Disorders*, 9(6), 695–701.

Bronfen, E. (1992) *Over Her Dead Body: death, femininity and the aesthetic*, Manchester University Press, Manchester.

Broverman, I.K., Broverman, D.M., Clarkson, F.E., Rosenkrantz, P.S. and Vogel, S.R. (1970) Sex-role stereotypes and clinical judgments of mental health, *Journal of Consulting and Clinical Psychology*, 34(1), 1–7.

Bruch, H. (1973) *Eating Disorders*, New York, Basic Books.

——(1974) *Eating Disorders: obesity and anorexia nervosa and the person within*, Routledge, London.

——(1978) *The Golden Cage: the enigma of anorexia nervosa*, Harvard University Press, Cambridge, MA.

——(1982) Anorexia nervosa: therapy and theory, *American Journal of Psychiatry*, 139, 1531–1538.

——(1985) Four decades of eating disorders, in D.M. Garner and P.E. Garfinkel (eds) *Handbook of Psychotherapy for Anorexia Nervosa and Bulimia*, pp. 7–18, Guildford Press, New York.

Brumberg, J. (1982) Chlorotic girls, 1870–1920: a historical perspective on female adolescence, *Child Development*, 53, 1468–1477.

——(1986) Fasting girls: reflections on writing the history of anorexia nervosa, *Monograph of the Society for Research in Child Development*, 50 (4–5), 93–104.

——(1988) *Fasting Girls: the emergence of anorexia nervosa as a modern disease*, Harvard University Press, Cambridge, MA.

Buchan, W. (1769) *Domestic Medicine, or a treatise on the prevention and cure of diseases by regimen and simple medicines*, Balfour, Auld and Smellie, Edinburgh.

Burman, E. (1990) Differing with deconstruction: a feminist critique, in I. Parker and J. Shotter (eds) *Deconstructing Social Psychology*, Routledge, London.

Burman, E. and Parker, I. (eds) (1993) *Discourse Analytic Research: repertoires and readings of texts in action*, Routledge, London.

Burton, F. and Carlen, B. (1979) *Official Discourse: on discourse analysis, government publications, ideology and the state*, Routledge, London.

Busfield, J. (1994) The female malady? Men, women and madness in nineteenth century Britain, *Sociology*, 28(1), 259–277.

Butler, N.M., Slade, P.D. and Newton, T. (1990) Attitudes towards anorexia nervosa and bulimic disorders: experts and lay opinions, *British Review of Bulimia and Anorexia Nervosa*, 4(2), 61–69.

Bynum, C.W. (1987) *Holy Feast and holy Fast: the religious significance of food to medieval women*, University of California Press, Berkeley.

Caplan, P.J. and Hall-McCorquodale, I. (1985) The scapegoating of mothers: a call for change, *American Journal of Orthopsychiatry*, 55(4), 610–613.

Caplan, P.J. (1990) Making mother-blaming visible: the emperor's new clothes, *Women and Therapy*, 10(1–2), 61–70. Special issue: Motherhood: a feminist perspective.

Cash, T.F. and Brown, T.A. (1987) Body image in anorexia nervosa and bulimia nervosa: A review of the literature. Special issue: Behavioural and cognitive-behavioural treatments of anorexia nervosa and bulimia nervosa, *Behavioural Modification*, 11 (4), 487–521.

Caskey, N. (1989) Interpreting anorexia nervosa, in S.R. Suleiman (ed.) *The Female Body in Western Culture*, pp. 175–189, Harvard University Press, Massachusetts.

Casper, R.C. (1983) On the emergence of bulimia nervosa as a syndrome, *International Journal of Eating Disorders*, 2, 3–16.

Casper, R.C., Eckert, E.S., Halmi, K.A., Goldberg, S.C. and Davis, J.M. (1980) Bulimia: its incidence and clinical importance in patients with anorexia nervosa, *Archives of General Psychiatry*, 37, 1030–1035.

Cavafy, J. (1874) A case of male hysteria, *Lancet*, 26 December, 899.

Channon, S., Hemsley, D. and de Silva, P. (1988) Selective processing of food words in anorexia nervosa, *British Journal of Clinical Psychology*, 27, 259–260.

Charcot, J.M. (1889) Lecture XVII: Isolation in the treatment of hysteria, in *Clinical lectures on diseases of the nervous system, delivered at the infirmary of La Salpetrière by Professor J.M. Charcot*, vol. 3 (trans T. Savill), pp. 207–219, The New Sydenham Society, London. Reprinted (1991) in R. Harris (ed.) *Clinical Lectures on Diseases of the Nervous System. A translation of* Leçons sur les maladies du système nerveux, Tavistock/Routledge, London.

Chernin, K. (1981) *The Obsession: reflections on the tyranny of slenderness*, Harper and Row, New York.

——(1983) *Womansize: the tyranny of slenderness*, Women's Press, London.

——(1986) *The Hungry Self*, Virago, London.

Chesler, P. (1972) *Women and Madness*, Doubleday, New York.

Chiappelli, F., Gwirtsman, H.E., Loey, M., Gormley, G., *et al.* (1991) Pituitary-adrenal-immune system in normal subjects and in patients with anorexia nervosa: the number of circulating helper T lymphocytes (CD4) expressing the homing receptor Leu is regulated in part by pituitary-adrenal products, *Psychoneuroendocrinology*, 16(5), 423–432.

Chipley, W.S. (1859) Sitomania: its causes and treatment, *American Journal of Insanity*, 16 (July), 1–42.

Chodorow, N. (1978) *The Reproduction of Mothering*, University of California Press, Berkeley.

Cixous, H. and Clément, C. (1975) *La Jeune Née*, Paris, Bibliothéque 10/18, English translation (1986) *The Newly Born Woman*, Manchester University Press, Manchester.

Clark, D.A., Feldman, J. and Channon, S. (1989) Dysfunctional thinking in anorexia nervosa and bulimia nervosa, *Cognitive Therapy and Research*, 13(4), 377–387.

Collins, W.J. (1894) Anorexia nervosa (letter), *Lancet*, 27 January, 202–203.

Concise Oxford Dictionary of Current English (1984) 7th edition, (ed. J.B. Sykes), Clarendon Press, Oxford.

Cools, J., Schotte, D.E. and McNally, R.J. (1992) Emotional arousal and overeating in restrained eaters, *Journal of Abnormal Psychology*, 101(2), 348–351.

Cooper, Z., Cooper, P.J. and Fairburn, C.G. (1985) The specificity of the Eating Disorders Inventory, *British Journal of Clinical Psychology*, 24, 129–130.

Couzens Hoy, D. (1986) Power, repression, progress: Foucault, Lukes and the Frankfurt school, in D. Couzens Hoy (ed.) *Foucault: a critical reader*, pp. 123–147, Basil Blackwell, Oxford.

Coward, R. (1984) *Female Desire: women's sexuality today*, Paladin, London.

Coward, R., Lipshitz, S. and Cowie, E. (1976) Psychoanalysis and patriarchal structure, in *Papers on Patriarchy* (Patriarchy Conference, 1976, London), Women's Publishing Collective, Brighton.

Cox, O. (1989) Saussure and psychoanalytic feminism – a made match, *Irish Journal of Psychological Medicine*, 6(2), 100–102.

Crisp, A.H. (1970) Anorexia nervosa: feeding disorder, nervous malnutrition or weight phobia?, *World Review of Nutrition and Diet*, 12, 452–504.

——(1980) *Anorexia Nervosa: let me be*, Academic Press, London.

Crisp, A.H. and Kalucy, R.S. (1974) Aspects of the perceptual disorder in anorexia nervosa, *British Journal of Medical Psychology*, 47, 349–361.

Crisp, A.H. and Stonehill, E. (1971) Relationships between aspects of nutritional disturbance and menstrual activity in primary anorexia nervosa, *British Medical Journal*, 3, 149–151.

Crisp, A.H., Harding, B. and McGuinness, B. (1974) Anorexia nervosa. Psychoneurotic characteristics of parents: relationship to prognosis. A quantitive study, *Journal of Psychosomatic Research*, 18, 167–173.

Crisp, A.H., Palmer, R.L. and Kalucy, R.S. (1976) How common is anorexia nervosa? A prevalence study, *British Journal of Psychiatry*, 128, 549–554.

Crisp, A.H., Callender, J.S., Halek, C. and Hsu, L.G. (1992) Long term mortality in anorexia nervosa: a 20 year follow up study of the St George's and Aberdeen cohorts, *British Journal of Psychiatry*, 161, 104–107.

Crisp, A.H., Hsu, L.K.G., Harding, B. and Hartshorn, J. (1980) Clinical features of anorexia nervosa, *Journal of Psychosomatic Research*, 24, 179–191.

Crowley, H. and Himmelweit, S. (eds) (1992) *Knowing Women: feminism and knowledge*, Polity Press/Open University Press, Cambridge/Oxford.

Dally, P. and Gomez, J. (1979) *Anorexia Nervosa*, Heinemann, London.

Daly, M. (1984) *Pure Lust: elemental feminist philosophy*, Women's Press, London.

Darby, P., Garfinkel, P.E., Garner, D.M. and Olmsted, M. (eds) (1983) *Anorexia Nervosa: recent developments in research*, Alan Liss, New York.

De Groot, J.M., Kennedy, S., Rodin, G. and McVey, G. (1992) Correlates of sexual abuse in women with anorexia nervosa and bulimia nervosa, *Canadian Journal of Psychiatry*, 37(3), 516–518.

DeJong, W. and Kleck, R.E. (1986) The social psychological effects of overweight, in C.P. Herman, M.P. Zanna and E.T. Higgins (eds) *Physical Appearance, Stigma and Social Behaviour: the third Ontario Symposium in personality and social psychology*, pp. 65–88, Erlbaum, Hillsdale, NJ.

Derrida, J. (1976) *Of Grammatology*, Johns Hopkins Press, Baltimore.

Deutsch, H. (1944) *The Psychology of Women*, vol. 1, Grune and Stratton, New York.

Dewberry, C. and Ussher, J.M. (1994) Restraint and perception of body weight among British adults, *Journal of Social Psychology*, 134(5), 609–619.

van Dijk, T.A. (1983) Discourse analysis: its development and application to the structure of the news, *Journal of Communication*, 33(2), 20–43.

Dinicola, V.F. (1990) Anorexia multiforme: self-starvation in historical and cultural context. Part 1: Self-starvation as a historical chameleon, *Transcultural Psychiatric Research Review*, 27, 165–196.

Dinnerstein, D. (1987) *The Rocking of the Cradle and the Ruling of the World*, Women's Press, London.

Dolan, B. (1991) Cross-cultural aspects of anorexia nervosa and bulimia: a review, *International Journal of Eating Disorders*, 10(1), 67–78.

Dolan, B., Lacey, J.H. and Evans, C. (1990) Eating behaviour and attitudes to weight and shape in British women from three ethnic groups, *British Journal of Psychiatry*, 157, 523–528.

Douglas-Wood, A. (1973) 'The fashionable diseases': women's complaints and their treatment in nineteenth century America, *Journal of Interdisciplinary History*, 4(1), 25–52.

Dowse, S.T. (1881) Anorexia nervosa, *Medical Press and Circular*, 32, 3 August, 95–97.

Drewnowski, A. and Yee, D.K. (1987) Men and body image: are males satisfied with their body? *Psychosomatic Medicine*, 49, 626–634.

Drummond, D.A. (1896) A case of anorexia nervosa, *The Northumberland and Durham Medical Journal*, 4, 7–8.

Eating Disorders Association (EDA) (1993) *Annual report* (including reprint of speech given by Princess Diana to the International Conference on Eating Disorders, 1993), EDA, Norfolk.

Edge, A.M. (1888) A case of anorexia nervosa, *Lancet*, 28 April, 818.

Edley, N. and Wetherell, M. (1995) *Men in Perspective: practice, power and identity*, Prentice Hall, Hemel Hempsted.

Edwards-Hewitt, T. and Gray, J.J. (1993) The prevalence of disordered eating attitudes and behaviour in Black-American and White-American College Women: ethnic, regional, class and media differences, *Eating Disorders Review*, 1(1), 41–54.

Ehrenreich, B. and English, D. (1974) *Complaints and Disorders: the sexual politics of sickness*, Glass Mountain Pamphlet no. 2, Compendium, London.

Eichenbaum, L. and Orbach, S. (1983) *Understanding Women: a feminist psychoanalytic approach*, Basic Books, New York.

Elliott, L.S. (1985) Genetic factors in anorexia nervosa in females, *Southern Psychologist*, 2(3), 19–21.

Ellis, H. (1897) *Sexual Inversion: studies in the psychology of sex*, vol. 2 . Reprinted (1927) F.A. Davis, Philadelphia.

Esquivel, L. (1993) *Like Water for Chocolate*, Black Swan, London.

Evans, C. and Thornton, M. (1991) Fashion, representation, femininity, *Feminist Review*, 38, 48–66.

Fairburn, C.G. (1987) *The uncertain status of the cognitive approach to bulimia nervosa*, paper presented at the Symposium on the Psychobiology of Bulimia Nervosa, Ringberg Castle, Germany.

Fairclough, N. (1989) *Language and Power*, Longman, London.

Fee, E. (1981) Is feminism a threat to scientific objectivity, *International Journal of Women's Studies*, 4, 378–392.

Feighner, J.P., Robins, E. and Guze, S.B. (1972) Diagnostic criteria for use in psychiatric research, *Archives of General Psychiatry*, 26, 57–63.

Ferguson, M. (1983) *Forever Feminine: women's magazines and the cult of femininity*, Heinemann, London.

Fichter, M.M., Meister, I. and Koch, H.J. (1986) The measurement of body image distortion in anorexia nervosa: experimental comparison of different methods, *British Journal of Psychiatry*, 148, 453–461.

Fischer, N. (1989) Anorexia nervosa and unresolved rapprochement conflicts: a case study, *International Journal of Psychoanalysis*, 70, 41–54.

Fischer-Homberger, E. (1972) Hypochondriasis in the eighteenth century – neurosis of the present century, *Bulletin of the History of Medicine*, 46, 391–401.

Flax, J. (1987) Post-modernism and gender relations in feminist theory, *Signs*, 12, 621–643.

Foucault, M. (1967) *Madness and Civilization: a history of insanity in the age of reason* (1985 edition), Tavistock, London.

——(1972) *The Archeology of Knowledge and the Discourse on Language* (trans. A. Sheridan), Pantheon Books, New York.

——(1977a) Nietzsche, genealogy, history, in D.F. Bouchard (ed.) *Language, Counter-Memory, Practice: selected essays and interviews*, pp. 139–164, Cornell University Press, New York.

——(1977b) *Discipline and Punish: the birth of the prison* (1987 edition), Penguin, London.

——(1979) *The History of Sexuality*, vol. 1, *An introduction* (1990 edition), Penguin, London.

——(1980) *Power/Knowledge: selected interviews and other writings 1972–1977* (ed. C. Gordon), Harvester Wheatsheaf, London.

——(1988) Technologies of the self, in L.H. Martin, H. Gutman and P.H. Hutton (eds)*Technologies of the Self: a seminar with Michel Foucault*, University of Massachusetts Press, London.

Fowler, R. (1871) *A complete history of the case of the Welsh fasting girl (Sarah Jacob) with comments thereon and observations on death from starvation*, Henry Renshaw, London.

Fraenkel, L. and Leichner, P.P. (1989) Relationship of body image distortion to sex-role identifications, irrational cognitions, and body weight in eating disordered females, *Journal of Clinical Psychology*, 45(1), 61–65.

Franklin, J.S., Schiele, B.C., Brozek, J. and Keys, A. (1948) Observations on human behaviour in experimental starvation and rehabilitation, *Journal of Clinical Psychology*, 4, 28–45.

Freeman, R.J., Thomas, C.D., Solymon, L. and Miles, J.E. (1983) Body image disturbances in anorexia nervosa: a re-examination and a new technique, in P.L. Darby, P.E. Garfinkel, D.M. Garner and M. Olmsted (eds) *Anorexia Nervosa: recent developments in research*, pp. 117–127 Alan Liss, New York.

Freud, S. (1905) Three essays on the theory of sexuality, in *On Sexuality* (1984 edition), pp. 45–169, Penguin, London.

——(1914) *On Narcissism: an introduction*, SE vol.14, Hogarth Press/Institute of Psychoanalysis, London.

——(1917) *A Difficulty on the Path of Psychoanalysis*, SE vol.17, Hogarth Press/Institute of Psychoanalysis, London.

——(1920) *Beyond the Pleasure Principle*, SE vol.18, Hogarth Press/Institute of Psychoanalysis, London.

——(1923) *The Ego and the Id*, SE vol.19, Hogarth Press/Institute of Psychoanalysis, London.

——(1924a) The dissolution of the oedipus complex, in *On Sexuality* (1984 edition), pp. 313–322, Penguin, London.

——(1924b) *The Economic Problem of Masochism*, SE vol.19, pp. 157–170, Hogarth Press, London (1961).

——(1925) Some psychical consequences of the anatomical distinction between the sexes, in *On Sexuality* (1984 edition), pp. 323–343, Penguin, London.

——(1931) Female sexuality, in *On Sexuality* (1984 edition), pp. 367–392, Penguin, London.

——(1933a) Anxiety and instinctual life, in *New Introductory Lectures on Psychoanalysis* (trans. W.J.H. Sprott), The International Psychoanalytic Library, no. 24, pp. 107–143, Hogarth Press, London (1946).

——(1933b) Femininity, in *The Complete Introductory Lectures on Psychoanalysis* (ed. and trans. J. Stratchey), George Allen & Unwin, London (1971).

——(1933c) The psychology of women, in *New Introductory Lectures on Psychoanalysis* (trans. W.J.H. Sprott), The International Psychoanalytic Library, no. 24, pp. 144–174, Hogarth Press, London (1946).

——(1935) Letter to Carl Muller-Braunschweig, published as Freud and female sexuality: a previously unpublished letter, *Psychiatry*, (1971), 328–329.

Freud, S. and Breuer, J. (1895) *Studies on Hysteria* (1991 edition), Penguin, London.

Fries, H. (1977) Studies in secondary amenorrhea, anorectic behaviour and body image perception, in Vigersky, S. (ed.) *Anorexia Nervosa*, pp. 163–177, Raven Press, New York.

Frosh, S. (1994) *Sexual Difference: masculinity and psychoanalysis*, Routledge, London.

Gallop, J. (1985) Keys to Dora, in C. Bernheimer and C. Kahane (eds) *In Dora's Case: Freud, hysteria, feminism*, pp. 200–220, Virago, London.

Gardiner, M. (1955) Feminine masochism and passivity, *Bulletin of the Philadelphia Association of Psychoanalysis*, 5, 74–59.

Garfinkel, H. (1967) *Studies in Ethnomethodology*, Prentice-Hall, New York.

Garfinkel, P.E. and Garner, D.M. (1982) *Anorexia Nervosa: a multidimensional perspective*, Bruner Mazel, New York.

——(1983) The multidetermined nature of anorexia nervosa, in P.L. Darby, P.E. Garfinkel, D.M. Garner and M. Olmsted (eds) *Anorexia Nervosa: recent developments in research*, pp. 3–14, Alan Liss, New York.

Garfinkel, P.E., Moldofsky, H. and Garner, D.M. (1980) The heterogeneity of anorexia nervosa: bulimia as a distinct subgroup, *Archives of General Psychiatry*, 37, 1036–1040.

Garfinkel, P.E., Garner, D.M., Rose, J., Darby, P., Brandes, J., O'Hanlon, J. and Walsh, N. (1983) A comparison of characteristics in the families of patients with anorexia nervosa and normal controls, *Psychological Medicine*, 13, 821–828.

Garner, D.M. and Garfinkel, P.E. (1979) The eating attitudes test: an index of the symptoms of anorexia nervosa, *Psychological Medicine*, 9, 273–279.

——(1980) Socio-cultural factors in the development of anorexia nervosa, *Psychological Medicine*, 10, 647–656.

Garner, D.M., Garfinkel, P.E. and Bemis, K.M. (1982) A multidimensional psychotherapy for anorexia nervosa, *International Journal of Eating Disorders*, 1, 3–64.

Garner, D.M., Olmsted, M.P. and Polivy, J. (1983a) Development and validation of a multi-dimensional eating disorders inventory for anorexia nervosa and bulimia, *International Journal of Eating Disorders*, 2, 15–34.

Garner, D.M., Garfinkel, P.E. and Olmsted, M.P. (1983b) An overview of sociocultural factors in the development of anorexia nervosa, in P. Darby, P.E. Garfinkel, D.M. Garner and M. Olmsted (eds) *Anorexia Nervosa: recent developments in research*, pp. 65–82, Alan Liss, New York.

Garner, D.M., Garfinkel, P.E., Rockert, W. and Olmsted, M.P. (1987) A prospective study of eating disturbances in the ballet, *Psychotherapy and Psychosomatics*, 48(1–4), 170–175.

Garner, D.M., Garfinkel, P.E., Schwartz, D. and Thompson, M. (1980) Cultural expectations of thinness in women, *Psychological Reports*, 47, 483–491.

Garner, D.M., Olmsted, M.P., Polivy, J. and Garfinkel, P.E. (1984) Comparison between weight-preoccupied women and anorexia nervosa, *Psychosomatic Medicine*, 46, 255–266.

Garry, T.G. (1888) Anorexia nervosa (letter), *Lancet*, 19 May, 1002.

Gavey, N. (1989) Feminist post-structuralism and discourse analysis: contributions to feminist psychology, *Psychology of Women Quarterly*, 13, 459–475.

Geist, R.A. (1989) Self psychological reflections on the origins of eating disorders. Special issue: Psychoanalysis and eating disorders, *Journal of the American Academy of Psychoanalysis*, 17(1), 5–27.

Gilbert, G.N. and Mulkay, M. (1984) *Opening Pandora's Box: A sociological analysis of scientists' discourse*, Cambridge University Press, Cambridge.

Gillberg, C. (1985) Autism and anorexia nervosa: related conditions? *Nordisk-Psykiatrisk Tidsskrift*, 39(4), 307–312.

Gilligan, C. (1982) *In a Different Voice: psychological theory and women's development*, Harvard University Press, Cambridge, MA.

Gilman, C.P. (1892) *The Yellow Wallpaper* (1988 reprint), Virago, London.

Goldner, V. (1985) Feminism and Family Therapy, *Family Process*, 24, 31–47.

——(1989) Generation and gender: normative and covert hierarchies, in M. McGoldrick, C.M. Anderson and F. Walsh (eds) *Women in Families: a framework for family therapy*, pp. 42–61, Norton, New York.

Goodsitt, A. (1985) Self-psychology and the treatment of anorexia, in D.M. Garner and P.E. Garfinkel (eds) *Handbook of Psychotherapy for Anorexia Nervosa and Bulimia*, Guildford Press, London.

Griffin, C. (1986) Qualitative methods and female experience: young women from school to the job market, in S. Wilkinson (ed.) *Feminist Social Psychology*, pp. 173–192, Open University Press, Milton Keynes.

Griffin, C. and Phoenix, A. (1994) The relationship between qualitative and quantitative research: lessons from feminist psychology, *Journal of Community and Applied Social Psychology*, 4, 277–298.

Gross, J. and Rosen, J.C. (1988) Bulimia in adolescents. Prevalence and psychosocial correlates, *International Journal of Eating Disorders*, 7(1), 51–61.

Grosz, E. (1990) *Jacques Lacan: a feminist introduction*, Routledge, London.

Grunewald, K.K. (1985) Weight control in young college women: who are the dieters? *Journal of the American Dietetic Association*, 85(11), 1445–1450.

Gull, W.W. (1868) Dr. Gull's address in medicine, *Lancet*, 8 August, 171–176.

——(1874) Anorexia nervosa (apepsia hysterica, anorexia hysterica), *Transactions of the Clinical Society*, 7(2), 22–28.

——(1888) Clinical notes: medical, surgical, obstetrical, and therapeutic: anorexia nervosa, *Lancet*, 17 March, 516–517.

Gutman, H. (1988) Rousseau's *Confessions*: a technology of the self, in L.H. Martin, H. Gutman and P.H. Hutton (eds) *Technologies of the Self: a seminar with Michel Foucault*, Tavistock, London.

Guttman, H.A. (1986) Family therapy of anorexia nervosa: a feminist perspective, *Family Therapy Collection*, 16, 102–111.

Habermas, T. (1989) The psychiatric history of anorexia nervosa and bulimia nervosa: weight concerns and bulimic symptoms in early case reports, *International Journal of Eating Disorders*, 8(3), 259–273.

Haggerty, J.J. (1983) The psychosomatic family: an overview, *Psychosomatics*, 24(7), 615–623.

Hall, A. and Brown, L. (1982) A comparison of attitudes of young anorexia nervosa patients and non-patients with those of their mothers, *British Journal of Medical Psychology*, 56, 39–48.

Hall, M. (1827) *Commentaries on some of the more important diseases of females*, London.

Hall, S. (1982) The rediscovery of 'ideology': returning to the repressed in media studies, in M. Gurevitch, T. Bennett, J. Curran and J. Woollacott (eds) *Culture, Society and the Media*, Methuen, London.

Halmi, K.A. (1983) Advances in anorexia nervosa, *Advances in Developmental and Behavioural Pediatrics*, 4, 1–23.

——(1987) Anorexia nervosa and bulimia, *Annual Review of Medicine*, 38, 373–380.

Halmi, K.A. and Falk, J.R. (1983) Behavioral and dietary discriminators of menstrual functioning in anorexia nervosa, in P. Darby, P.E. Garfinkel, D.M. Garner and M. Olmsted (eds) *Anorexia Nervosa: Recent developments in research*, pp. 323–329, Alan Liss, New York.

Halmi, K.A., Falk, J.R. and Schwartz, E. (1981) Binge eating and vomiting: A survey of a college population, *Psychological Medicine*, 11, 697–706.

Halmi, K.A., Struss, A. and Goldberg, S.C. (1978) Anorexia nervosa: an investigation of weights in the parents of anorexia nervosa patients, *Journal of Nervous and Mental Disease*, 166, 358–361.

Hammond, W.A. (1879) *Fasting Girls: their physiology and pathology*, Putnam, New York.

Harding, S. (1987) Is there a feminist methodology?, in S. Harding (ed.) *Feminism and Methodology: social science issues*, pp. 1–14, Open University Press, Milton Keynes.

Harre, R. (1979) *Social Being: a theory for social psychology*, Blackwell, Oxford.

——(1992) What is real in psychology: a plea for persons, *Theory and Psychology*, 2(2), 153–158.

Harre, R. and Secord, P.F. (1972) *The Explanation of Social Behaviour*, Basil Blackwell, Oxford.

Harris, M.B., Walters, L.C. and Waschull, S. (1991) Gender and ethnic differences in obesity-related behaviours and attitudes in a college sample, *Journal of Applied Social Psychology*, 21, 1545–1566.

Hartley, L.P. (1953) *The Go-Between*, Hamish Hamilton, London.

Hattersley, R. (1993) Sick and tired of the superficial beautiful life, *Guardian*, 3 May.

Hedley, W.S. (1893) The insomnia of neurasthenia, *Lancet*, 10 June, 1381–1382.

Heilbrun, A.B. and Friedberg, L. (1990) Distorted body image in normal college women: possible implications for the development of anorexia nervosa, *Journal of Clinical Psychology*, 46(4), 398–401.

Henriques, J., Hollway, W., Urwin, C., Venn, C. and Walkerdine, V. (1984) *Changing the Subject: psychology, social regulation and subjectivity*, Methuen, London.

Henwood, K.L. and Pidgeon, N.F. (1992) Qualitative research and psychological theorizing, *British Journal of Psychology*, 83, 97–111.

Hepworth, J. (1991) *A post-structuralist analysis of the late nineteenth century medical discovery of anorexia nervosa and contemporary discourses on anorexia nervosa used by health-care workers*, unpublished Ph.D. thesis, Birmingham University.

Herzog, D.B., Staley, J.E., Carmody, S., Robbins, W.M. *et al.* (1993) Childhood sexual abuse in anorexia nervosa and bulimia nervosa: a pilot study, *Journal of the American Academy of Child and Adolescent Psychiatry*, 32(5), 962–966.

Hill, A.J. and Robinson, A. (1991) Dieting concerns have a functional effect on the behaviour of nine year old girls, *British Journal of Clinical Psychology*, 30, 265–267.

Hirsch, M. (1989) *The Mother/Daughter Plot: narrative, psychoanalysis, feminism*, Indiana University Press, Bloomington.

Hirst, P. and Woolley, P. (1982) *Social Relations and Human Attributes*, Tavistock, London.

Hobbes, T. (1668) Letter, in S.J. Gee (ed.) *Medical Lectures and Clinical Aphorisms* (1908 reprint), Oxford University Press, London.

Hoek, H.W. (1993) Review of the epidemiological studies of eating disorders, *International Journal of Eating Disorders*, 5(1), 61–74.

Holland, A.J., Sicotte, N. and Treasure, J.L. (1988) Anorexia nervosa: evidence for a genetic basis, 31st Annual Conference of the Society for Psychosomatic Research, 1987, London, *Journal of Psychosomatic Research*, 32(6), 561–571.

Holland, A.J, Hall, A., Murray, R., Russell, G.F.M. and Crisp, A.H. (1984) Anorexia nervosa: a study of 34 twin pairs and one set of triplets, *British Journal of Psychiatry*, 145, 414–419.

Hollway, W. (1989) *Subjectivity and Method in Psychology: gender, meaning and science*, Sage, London.

——(1992) Gender difference and the production of subjectivity, in H. Crowley and S. Himmelweit (eds) *Knowing Women: feminism and knowledge*, pp. 240–274, Polity Press/Open University Press, Cambridge/Oxford.

Hooper, M.S.H. and Garner, D.M. (1986) Application of the Eating Disorders Inventory to a sample of black, white and mixed race schoolgirls in Zimbabwe, *International Journal of Eating Disorders*, 5(1), 161–169.

Horney, K. (1926) *The Flight from Womanhood*. Reprinted in J.B. Miller (ed.) *Psychoanalysis and Women* (1973), Penguin, Harmondsworth.

Hsu, L.K.G. (1980) Outcomes of anorexia nervosa: a review of the literature (1954–1978), *Archives of General Psychiatry*, 9, 1041–1046.

——(1984) The aetiology of anorexia nervosa, *Annual Progress in Child Psychiatry and Child Development, Part VII: Eating Disorders*, 26, 407–419.

——(1989) The gender gap in eating disorders: why are the eating disorders more common among women? *Clinical Psychology Review*, 9, 393–407.

Hudson, J.I., Pope, H.G., Jonas, J.M. and Yorgelun-Todd, D. (1983) A family study of anorexia nervosa and bulimia, *British Journal of Psychiatry*, 142, 133, 138.

Hughes, J. (1991) *An Outline of Modern Psychiatry* (3rd edition), John Wiley and Sons, Chichester.

Humphrey, L.L. (1986) Structural analysis of parent–child relationships in eating disorders, *Journal of Abnormal Psychology*, 95(4), 395–402.

Hunter, R. and Macalpine, I. (1963) *Three Hundred Years of Psychiatry 1535–1860*, Oxford University Press, London.

Huon, G. and Brown, B. (1984) Psychological correlates of weight control amongst anorexia nervosa patients and normal girls, *British Journal of Medical Psychology*, 57, 61–66.

Irigaray, L. (1977) *Ce Sexe qui n'en est pas un*, Minuit, Paris. English edition (trans. C. Porter and C. Burke, 1985) *This Sex Which is Not One*, Cornell University Press, Ithaca and New York.

——(1985) *Parler n'est jamais neutre*, Minuit, Paris.

——(1988) Luce Irigaray, in H.E. Baruch and L.J. Sorrono (eds) *Women Analyse Women: in France, England and the United States*, pp. 149–164, Harvester Wheatsheaf, New York.

Jackson, S. (1986) *Melancholia and Depression from Hippocratic Times to Modern Times*, Yale University Press, New Haven.

Jacobovits, C., Halstead, P., Kelly, L., Roe, D.A. and Young, C.M. (1977) Eating habits and nutrient intakes of college women over a thirty year period, *Journal of the American Dietetic Association*, 71, 405–411.

Jampala, V.C. (1985) Anorexia nervosa: a variant form of affective disorder?, *Psychiatric Annals*, 15(12), 698–704.

Jardine, A. (1985) *Gynesis: configurations of woman and modernity*, Cornell University Press, Ithaca.

Jarman, M. (1996) *Caretaking and redistributing power and control: clinicians' perspectives on the treatment of young people with anorexia nervosa*, paper presented at the Qualitative and feminist research in women and eating disorders conference, January, Sheffield University.

Jarman, M. and Walsh, S. (1995) *Understanding eating disorders: changing the perspective*, paper presented at the 1995 BPS Annual Conference, April, Warwick University.

Jones, A.R. (1985) Writing the body: towards an understanding of l'écriture féminine, in J. Newton and D. Rosenfelt (eds) *Feminism, Criticism and Social Change*, pp. 86–101, Methuen, London.

Jordanova, L. (1989) *Sexual Visions: images of gender in science and medicine between the eighteenth and twentieth centuries*, Harvester Wheatsheaf, London.

Kalucy, R.S., Crisp, A.H. and Harding, B. (1977) A study of 56 families with anorexia nervosa, *British Journal of Medical Psychology*, 50, 381–395.

Kaplan, A. and Woodside, B. (1987) Biological aspects of anorexia nervosa and bulimia nervosa, *Journal of Consulting and Clinical Psychology*, 55(5), 645–652.

Keys, A., Brozek, J., Henschel, A., Mickelsen, O. and Taylor, H. (1950) *The Biology of Human Starvation*, 2 vols, University of Minnesota Press, Minneapolis.

King, G.A., Polivy, J. and Herman, C.P. (1991) Cognitive aspects of dietary restraint: effects on person memory, *International Journal of Eating Disorders*, 10(3), 313–321.

Kirmayer, L.J. (1992) The body's insistence on meaning: metaphor as presentation and representation in illness experience, *Medical Anthropology Quarterly*, 6(4), 323–346.

Kitzinger, C. (1987) *The Social Construction of Lesbianism*, Sage, London.

Klein, M. (1934) A contribution to the psychogenesis of manic-depressive states, in M. Klein (1968) *Contributions to Psychoanalysis 1921–1945* (ed. J.D. Sutherland), Hogarth University Press, London.

——(1968) *Contributions to Psychoanalysis 1921–1945* (ed. J.D. Sutherland), Hogarth University Press, London.

Kog, E. and Vandereycken, W. (1985) Family characteristics of anorexia nervosa and bulimia: a review of the research literature, *Clinical Psychology Review*, 5, 159–180.

Kolata, G. (1986) Depression, anorexia, Cushing's link revealed, *Science*, 232, 1197–1198.

Kowalski, P.S. (1986) Cognitive abilities of female adolescents with anorexia nervosa, *International Journal of Eating Disorders*, 5(6), 983–997.

Krieg, J.C., Lauer, C. and Pirke, K.M. (1987) Hormonal and metabolic mechanisms in the development of cerebral pseudoatrophy in eating disorders, 9th World Congress of the International College of Psychosomatic Medicine, 1987, Sydney, Australia, *Psychotherapy and Psychosomatics*, 48(1–4), 176–180.

Kristeva, J. (1974) *La Femme, ce n'est jamais ça*, an interview in *Tel Qel*, 59 (Fall).

Lacan, J. (1949) The mirror stage as formative of the function of the I, in *Ecrits: a selection* (trans. A. Sheridan, 1992 edition), pp. 1–7, Routledge, London.

——(1958a) The signification of the phallus, in *Ecrits: a selection* (trans. A. Sheridan, 1992 edition), pp. 281–291, Routledge, London.

——(1958b) The directive of the treatment and the principle of its power, in *Ecrits: a selection* (trans. A. Sheridan, 1992 edition), pp. 226–280, Routledge, London.

——(1972–73) Encore: Le seminaire XX (1975 edition), Seuil, Paris.

——(1977) Agency of the letter in the unconscious or reason since Freud, in *Ecrits: a selection* (trans. A. Sheridan, 1992 edition), pp. 146–178, Routledge, London.

——(1982a) Feminine sexuality in psychoanalytic doctrine (trans. J. Rose), in J. Mitchell and J. Rose (eds) *Feminine Sexuality: Jacques Lacan and the école Freudienne*, pp. 123–136, Macmillan, Basingstoke.

——(1982b) God and the jouissance of The Woman: a love letter (trans. J. Rose), in J. Mitchell and J. Rose (eds) *Feminine Sexuality: Jacques Lacan and the école Freudienne*, pp. 137–161, Macmillan, Basingstoke.

——(1982c) Guiding remarks for a congress on feminine sexuality (trans. J. Rose), in J. Mitchell and J. Rose (eds) *Feminine Sexuality: Jacques Lacan and the école Freudienne*, pp. 86–98, Macmillan, Basingstoke.

——(1982d) The meaning of the phallus (trans. J. Rose), in J. Mitchell and J. Rose (eds) *Feminine Sexuality: Jacques Lacan and the école Freudienne*, pp. 74–85, Macmillan, Basingstoke.

——(1982e) The phallic phase and the subjective import of the castration complex (trans. J. Rose), in J. Mitchell and J. Rose (eds) *Feminine Sexuality: Jacques Lacan and the école Freudienne*, pp. 99–122, Macmillan, Basingstoke.

Laessle, R.G., Krieg, J.C., Fichter, M.M. and Pirke, K.M. (1989) Cerebral atrophy and vigilance performance in patients with anorexia nervosa and bulimia nervosa, *Neuropsychobiology*, 21(4), 187–191.

Laplanche, J. and Pontalis, J. (1973) *The Language of Psychoanalysis* (trans. D. Nicholson-Smith), Hogarth Press, London.

Lasegue, C. (1873a) De l'anorexie hystérique, *Archives générales de médicine*, 1 (April), 385–403.

——(1873b) On hysterical anorexia, *Medical Times and Gazette*, 2, 6/27 September, 265–266, 367–369.

Latour, B. and Woolgar, S. (1979) *Laboratory Life: the social construction of scientific facts*, Sage, London.

Lawrence, M. (1979) Anorexia nervosa: the control paradox, *Women's Studies International Quarterly*, 2, 93–101.

——(1984) *The Anorexic Experience*, Women's Press, London.

Lawson, H. (1985) *Reflexivity: the post-modern predicament*, Hutchinson, London.

Lemaire, A. (1981) *Jacques Lacan*, Routledge, London.

Littlewood, R. and Lipsedge, M. (1985) Culture-bound syndromes, in K. Granville-Grossman (ed.), *Recent Advances in Psychiatry 5*, Churchill-Livingstone, Edinburgh.

——(1987) The butterfly and the serpent: culture, psychopathology and biomedicine, *Culture, Medicine and Psychiatry*, 11(3), 289–335.

Lloyd, J.H. (1893) Hysterical tremor and hysterical anorexia (anorexia nervosa) of a severe type, *American Journal of Medical Science*, 106, 264–277.

Loevinger, J. (1978) *Scientific ways in the study of ego-development, vol. XII*, Hein Warner Lecture Series, Clark University Press, Worcester, MA.

Luepnitz, D. (1988) The Family Interpreted: feminist theory in clinical practice, Basic Books, New York.

Lyons, J. (1981) *Language and Linguistics: an introduction*, Cambridge University Press, Cambridge.

McAdams, D.P. (1992) The five-factor model in personality: A critical appraisal, *Journal of Personality*, 60, 329–361.

MacCannell, J.F. (1986) *Figuring Lacan: criticism and the cultural unconscious*, Croom Helm, Beckenham.

McGoldrick, M., Andersen, C.M. and Walsh, F. (eds) (1989) *Women in Families*, Norton, New York.

Mackenzie, S. (1888) On a case of anorexia nervosa vel hysterica, *Lancet*, 31 March, 613–614.

McNay, L. (1992) *Foucault and Feminism: power, gender and the self*, Polity Press, Oxford.

Malson, H. (1992) Anorexia nervosa: displacing universalities and replacing gender, in P. Nicolson and J. Ussher (eds) *The Psychology of Women's Health and Health Care*, pp. 62–91, Macmillan, Basingstoke.

——(1995a) Anorexia nervosa: discourses of gender, subjectivity and the body, *Feminism and Psychology*, 5(1), 87–93.

——(1995b) Discursive constructions of anorexia nervosa: gender, subjectivity and the body, unpublished Ph.D. thesis, University of London.

——(forthcoming) Anorexic bodies and the discursive production of feminine excess, in J. Ussher (ed.) *Body Talk: the material and discursive regulation of sexuality, madness and reproduction*, Routledge, London.

Malson, H. and Ussher, J. (1996a) Bloody women: a discourse analysis of amenorrhea as a symptom of anorexia nervosa, *Feminism and Psychology*, 6(4), 505–521.

——(1996b) Body poly-texts: discourses of the anorexic body, *Journal of Community and Applied Social Psychology*, 6, 267–280.

——(1997) Beyond this mortal coil: femininity, death and discursive constructions of the anorexic body, *Mortality*, 2(1), 43–61.

Manley, R.B., Tonkin, R. and Hammond, C. (1988) A method for the assessment of body image disturbance in patients with eating disorders, *Journal of Adolescent Health Care*, 9(5), 384–388.

215

Marce, L.-V.(1860) On a form of hypochondriacal delirium occurring consecutive to dyspepsia, and characterized by refusal of food, *Journal of Psychological Medicine and Mental Pathology*, 13, 264–266.

de Marinis, L., Mancini, A., D'Amico, C., Zuppi, P. *et al.* (1991) Influence of naloxone infusion on prolactin and growth hormone response to growth hormone-releasing hormone in anorexia nervosa, *Psychoneuroendocrinology*, 16(6), 499–504.

Markus, H., Hamill, R. and Sentis, K.P. (1987) Thinking fat: self-schemas for body weight and the processing of weight relevant information, *Journal of Applied Social Psychology*, 17, 50–71.

Marshall, C.F. (1895) Clinical notes: medical, surgical, obstetrical, and therapeutic: a fatal case of anorexia nervosa, *Lancet*, 19 January, 149–150.

Marshall, H. and Raabe, B. (1993) Political discourse: talking about nationalization and privatization, in E. Burman and I. Parker (eds) *Discourse Analytic Research: repertoires and readings of texts in action*, pp. 35–51, Routledge, London.

Marshall, H. and Wetherell, M. (1989) Talking about careers and gender identities: a discourse analysis perspective, in S. Skevington and D. Barker (eds) *The Social Identity of Women*, pp. 106–129, Sage, London.

Martin, L.H. (1988) Technologies of the self and self-knowledge in the Syrian Thomas tradition, in L.H. Martin, H. Gutman and P.H. Hutton (eds) *Technologies of the Self: a seminar with Michel Foucault*, Tavistock, London.

Martin, L.H., Gutman, H. and Hutton, P.H. (eds) (1988) *Technologies of the Self: a seminar with Michel Foucault*, Tavistock, London.

Martin, P. (1987) *Mad women in Romantic Writing*, Harvester, Sussex.

Merskey, H. (1980) *Psychiatric Illness* (3rd edition), Bailliere Tindall, London.

Micale, M.S. (1990) Hysteria and its historiography: the future perspective, *History of Psychiatry*, 1(1), 33–124.

Millett, K. (1971) *Sexual Politics*, Hart-Davis, London.

Mills, I.H. (1985) The neuronal basis of compulsive behaviour in anorexia nervosa, *Journal of Psychiatric Research*, 19(2–3), 231–235.

Milne, A.A. (1924) *When We Were Very Young* (1979 edition), Methuen, London.

Mintz, L.B. and Betz, N.E. (1988) Prevalence and correlates of eating disordered behaviour among under-graduate women, *Journal of Counselling Psychology*, 35(4), 463–471.

Minuchin, S., Rosman, B.L. and Baker, L. (1978) *Psychosomatic Families: anorexia nervosa in context*, Harvard University Press, Cambridge, MA.

Mischel, W. (1968) *Personality and Assessment*, Wiley, New York.

Mitchell, J. (1974) *Psychoanalysis and Feminism* (1990 edition), Penguin, London.

——(1982) Introduction 1, in J. Mitchell and J. Rose (eds) *Feminine Sexuality: Jacques Lacan and the école Freudienne*, pp. 1–26, Macmillan, Basingstoke.

——(1984) *Women: The Longest Revolution: essays in feminism, literature and psychoanalysis*, Virago, London.

Mitchell, J. and Rose. J. (eds) (1982) *Feminine Sexuality: Jacques Lacan and the école Freudienne*, Macmillan, Basingstoke.

Mitchell, J.J. and Eckert, E.D. (1987) Scope and significance of eating disorders, *Journal of Consulting and Clinical Psychology*, 55(5), 628–634. Special issue: Eating disorders.

Mitchell, S.W. (1877) *Fat and Blood: and how to make them*, J.B. Lippincott, PA.

——(1881) Lecture XII: Gastro-intestinal disorders of hysteria, in S.W. Mitchell, *Lectures on the diseases of the nervous system especially in women*, pp. 201–216, Henry C. Lea, Sons and Co, PA.

——(1888) *Doctor and Patient*, J.B. Lippincott and Co, PA.

Moi, T. (1985) Representation of patriarchy: sexuality and epistemology in Freud's Dora, in C. Bernheimer and C. Kahane (eds) *In Dora's Case: Freud, hysteria, feminism*, pp. 181–199, Virago, London.

Morgan, H.G. (1977) Fasting girls and our attitudes towards them, *British Medical Journal*, 2, 1652–1655.

Morton, R. (1689/1694) *Phthisiologica: or, a Treatise of Consumption*, Samual Smith, London.

Mottram, M.A. (1985) Personal constructs in anorexia nervosa, *Journal of Psychiatric Research*, 19, 291–295.

Mumford, D.B. and Whitehouse, A.M. (1988) Increased prevalence of bulimia nervosa amongst Asian schoolgirls, *British Medical Journal*, 297, 718.

Myrtle, A.S. (1888) Anorexia nervosa (letter), *Lancet*, 5 May, 899.

Nagera, H. (ed.) (1969) *Basic Psychoanalytic Concepts on the Libido*, vol. 1, George Allen & Unwin, London.

Naudeau, J. (1789) Observation sur une maladie nerveuse accompagnée d'un dégoût extraordinaire pour les aliments, *Journal de Medicine, Chirurgie et Pharmacologie*, 80, 197–200.

Nicolson, P. (1986) Developing a feminist approach to depression following childbirth, in S. Wilkinson (ed.) *Feminist Social Psychology*, pp. 135–149, Open University Press, Milton Keynes.

——(1992) Towards a psychology of women's health and health care, in P. Nicolson and J. Ussher (eds) *The Psychology of Women's Health and Health Care*, pp. 6–30, Macmillan, Basingstoke.

Nisbett, R.E. (1972) Hunger, obesity and the ventromedial hypothalamus, *Psychological Reviews*, 79, 433–453.

Orbach, S, (1979) *Fat is a Feminist Issue*, Hamlyn, Feltham.

——(1993) *Hunger Strike*, Penguin, London.

Othmer, E. and DeSouza, C. (1985) A screening test for somatization disorder (hysteria), *American Journal of Psychiatry*, 142(10), 1146–1149.

Outhwaite, W. (1987) *New Philosophies of Social Science: realism hermeneutics and critical theory*, Macmillan, London.

Palazidou, E., Robinson, P. and Lishman, W.A. (1990) Neurological and neuropsychological assessment in anorexia nervosa, *Psychological Medicine*, 20(3), 521–527.

Palazzoli, M.S. (1974) *Self-Starvation from the Intrapsychic to the Transpersonal Approach to Anorexia Nervosa*, Human Context Books, London.

Panel (1956) The problem of masochism in the theory and technique of psychoanalysis, *Journal of the American Psychoanalytic Association*, 4, 526–538.

Parker, I. (1989) *The Crisis in Modern Social Psychology, and How to End It*, Routledge, London.

——(1990a) Discourse: definitions and contradictions, *Philosophical Psychology*, 3(2), 189–204.

——(1990b) Real things: discourse, context and practice, *Philosophical Psychology*, 3(2), 227–233.

——(1992) *Discourse Dynamics: critical analysis for social and individual psychology*, Routledge, London.

Parlee, M. (1989) *The science and politics of PMS research*, paper presented at the association from the Women and Psychology Annual Research Conference, 10–12 March, Newport, Rhode Island.

Pembroke, L.R. (ed.) (1993) *Eating Distress: perspectives from personal experience* (2nd edition), Survivors Speak Out, Chesham.

Pervin, L. (1989) *Personality: theory and research* (5th edition), Wiley, New York.

Plaut, E.A. and Hutchinson, F.L. (1986) The role of puberty in female psychosexual development, *International Journal of Psychoanalysis*, 13, 417–432.

Playfair, W.S. (1888) Note on the so-called 'anorexia nervosa', *Lancet*, 28 April, 817–818.

Polivy, J. and Herman, C.P. (1985) Dieting and binging, *American Psychologist*, 40(2), 193–201.

——(1987) Diagnosis and treatment of normal eating, *Journal of Consulting and Clinical Psychology*, 55(5), 635–644. Special issue: Eating disorders.

Polivy, J., Garner, D.M. and Garfinkel, P.E. (1986) Causes and consequences of the current preference for thin female physiques, in C.P. Herman, M.P. Zanna and E.T. Higgins (eds) *Physical Appearance, Stigma and Social Behaviour: the Third Ontario Symposium in Personality and Social Psychology*, pp. 89–112, Erlbaum, Hillsdale, N.J.

Poovey, M. (1988) Feminism and deconstruction, *Feminist Studies*, 14(1), 51–65.

Pope, H.G., Hudson, J.I., Yurgelum-Todd, D. and Hudson, M.S. (1984) Prevalence of anorexia nervosa and bulimia in three student populations, *International Journal of Eating Disorders*, 3(3), 45–51.

Porter, R. (1987) *Mind-Forg'd Manacles*, Athlone, London.

Porter, R. and Porter, D. (1988) *In Sickness and in Health: the British experience 1650–1850*, Fourth Estate, London.

Potter, J. and Edwards, D. (1990) Nigel Lawson's tent: discourse analysis, attribution theory and the social psychology of fact, *European Journal of Social Psychology*, 20, 405–424.

Potter, J. and Wetherell, M. (1987) *Discourse and Social Psychology: beyond attitudes and behaviour*, Sage, London.

——(1991) Analysing Discourse, draft of chapter appearing in A. Bryman and R. Burgess (eds) (1994) *Analyzing Qualitative Data*, Routledge, London.

Potter, J., Wetherell, M. and Chitty, A. (1991) Quantification rhetoric – cancer on television, *Discourse and Society*, 2(3), 333–365.

Potter, J., Wetherell, M., Gill, R. and Edwards, D. (1990) Discourse: noun, verb or social practice, *Philosophical Psychology*, 3(2), 205–217.

Prince, M. (1895) Discussion of Putnam's paper on neurasthenia, *Boston Medical and Surgical Journal*, 132, 517.

Prior, L. (1989) *The Social Organization of Death: medical discourse and social practice in Belfast*, Macmillan, Basingstoke.

Pumariega, A.J. (1986) Acculturation and eating attitudes in adolescent girls: a comparative and correlational study, *Journal of the American Academy of Child Psychiatry*, 25(2), 276–279.

Pumariega, A.J., Edwards, P. and Mitchell, C.B. (1984) Anorexia nervosa in Black adolescents, *Journal of the American Academy of Child Psychiatry*, 23(1), 111–114.

Pyle, R.L., Mitchell, J.E. and Eckert, E.D. (1981) Bulimia: a report of 34 cases, *Journal of Clinical Psychiatry*, 42, 60–64.

Rakoff, V. (1983) Multiple determinants of family dynamics in anorexia nervosa, in P. Darby, P.E. Garfinkel, D.M. Garner and M. Olmsted (eds) *Anorexia Nervosa: recent developments in research*, pp. 29–40, Alan Liss, New York.

Ramas, M. (1985) Freud's Dora, Dora's hysteria, in C. Bernheimer and C. Kahane (eds) *In Dora's Case: Freud, hysteria, feminism*, pp. 149–180, Virago, London.

Raulin, J. (1758) *Traité des affections vaporeuses du sexe*, Paris.

Reynolds, J.A. (1669) *A Discourse on Prodigious Abstinence*, London.

Rice, A. (1988) *Queen of the Damned*, Futura, London.

Richardson, S.A., Hastort, A.H., Goodman, N. and Darnbush, S.M. (1961) Cultural uniformity in reaction to physical disabilities, *American Sociological Review*, 26, 241–247.

Riley, D. (1988) *Am I that Name? Feminism and the category of 'women' in history*, Macmillan, Basingstoke.

Riviere, J. (1929) Womanliness as masquerade, *International Journal of Psychoanalysis*, 10, 303–313.

REFERENCES

Rivinus, T.M., Biederman, J., Herzog, D.B., Kemper, K., Harper, G.P., Harmatz, J.S. and Houseworth, S. (1984) Anorexia nervosa and affective disorders: a controlled family history study, *American Journal of Psychiatry*, 141(1), 1414–1418.

Robinson, T. (1893) Sudden death in a case of hysterical vomiting, *Lancet*, 10 June, 1380–1381.

Rodin, J. (1981) Current status of the internal–external hypothesis for obesity: what went wrong?, *American Psychologist*, 36, 361–372.

Rose, J. (1982) Introduction II, in J. Mitchell and J. Rose (eds) *Feminine Sexuality: Jacques Lacan and the école Freudienne*, pp. 27–57, Macmillan, Basingstoke.

Rousseau, G. (1976) Nerves, spirits and fibres: towards defining the origins of sensibility; with a postscript, *The Blue Guitar*, 2, 125–153.

——(1991) Cultural history in a new key: towards a semiotics of the nerve, in J.H. Pittock and A. Wear (eds) *Interpretation and Cultural History*, pp. 25–81, Macmillan, Basingstoke.

Ruderman, A.J. (1986) Dietary restraint: a theoretical and empirical review, *Psychological Bulletin*, 99(2), 247–262.

Russell, G.F.M. (1970) Anorexia nervosa: its identity as an illness and its treatment, in J.H. Price (ed.) *Modern Trends in Psychological Medicine*, Butterworth, London.

——(1977) The present status of anorexia nervosa, *Psychological Medicine*, 7, 363–367.

——(1979) Bulimia nervosa: an ominous variant of anorexia nervosa, *Psychological Medicine*, 9, 429–448.

——(1984) The modern history of anorexia nervosa, *Aktuelle Ernahrung*, 9, 3–7.

——(1985) The changing nature of anorexia nervosa, *Journal of Psychiatric Research*, 19, 101–109.

——(1986) The changing nature of anorexia nervosa, in G.I. Szmukler, P.E. Slade, P. Harris, D. Benton and G. Russell (eds) *Anorexia Nervosa and Bulimic Disorders*, Pergamon Press, Oxford.

Rutter, M., Macdonald, H., Le Couteur, A., Harrington, R., Bolton, P. and Bailey, A. (1990) Genetic factors in child psychiatric disorders – II. Empirical findings, *Journal of Child Psychology and Psychiatry*, 3(1), 39–83.

Ryle, G. (1949) *The Concept of Mind* (1978 edition), Penguin, Harmondsworth.

Salisbury, J.J. and Mitchell, J.E. (1991) Bone mineral density and anorexia nervosa in women, *American Journal of Psychiatry*, 148(6), 768–774.

Salter, H. (1868) Clinical lecture on hysterical vomiting, *Lancet*, 4 July, 1–2, 37–38.

Sarup, M. (1988) *An Introductory Guide to Post-Structuralism and Post-Modernism*, Harvester Wheatsheaf, New York.

Saussure, F. de (1960) *Course in General Linguistics*, Peter Owen, London.

——(1974) *Cours de linguistique générale*, Paris, Payot, 1915 (1978 edition, ed. T. de Mauro). English translation, *Course in General Linguistics* (1974), Fontana, London.

Sawicki, J. (1991) *Disciplining Foucault: feminism, power and the body*, Routledge, London.

Sayers, J. (1982) *Biological Politics: feminist and anti-feminist perspectives*, Tavistock, London.

——(1986) *Sexual Contradictions: psychology, psychoanalysis and feminism*, Tavistock, London.

——(1988) Anorexia, psychoanalysis, and feminism: fantasy and reality, *Journal of Adolescence*, 11, 361–371.

——(1990) Psychoanalytic feminism: deconstructing power in theory and therapy, in I. Parker and J. Shotter (eds) *Deconstructing Social Psychology*, pp. 196–207, Routledge, London.

——(1991) *Mothering Psychoanalysis*, Penguin, London.

——(1994) Draft of Phallic illusions, feminist therapy: a Freudian story, *Clinical Psychology Forum*, 64, 31–34.

——(1995) Consuming male fantasies: feminist psychoanalysis retold, in A. Elliott and S. Frosh (eds), *Psychoanalysis in Context*, pp. 123–141, Routledge, London.

Schweitzer, I., Szmukler, G.I., Maguire, K.P., Harrison, L.C., Tuckwell, V. and Davies, B.M. (1990) The dexamethasone suppression test in anorexia nervosa: the influence of weight, depression, adrenocorticotrophic hormone and dexamethasone, *British Journal of Psychiatry*, 157, 713–717.

Scull, A. (1983) The domestication of madness, *Medical History*, 27, 233–248.

Selig, N. (1988) Seventeen, sexy and suicidal, *Changes*, 5(4), 411–415.

Shafter, R. (1989) Women and madness: a social historical perspective, *Issues in Ego Psychology*, 12(1), 77–82.

Sheppy, M., Friesen J.D. and Hakstian, A.R. (1988) Eco-systemic analysis of anorexia nervosa, *Journal of Adolescence*, 11, 373–391.

Sheridan, A. (1977) Translator's notes, in J. Lacan, *Ecrits: a selection* (1992 edition), pp. vii–xii, Routledge, London.

Shotter, J. (1975) *Images of Man in Psychological Research*, Methuen, London.

——(1984) *Accountability and Selfhood*, Blackwell, Oxford.

Showalter, E. (1985) *The Female Malady: women, madness and English culture, 1830–1980*, Virago, London.

Siltanen, J. and Stanworth, M. (eds) (1984) *Women and the Public Sphere: a critique of sociology and politics*, Hutchinson, London.

Silverman, J.A. (1988) Before our time: anorexia nervosa in 1888, *Lancet*, 23 April, 928–930,

——(1989) Louis-Victor Marce, 1828–1864: anorexia nervosa's forgotten man, *Psychological Medicine*, 19, 833–835.

Silverstein, B., Peterson, B. and Perdue, L. (1986) Some correlates of the thin standard of bodily attractiveness for women, *International Journal of Eating Disorders*, 5, 895–905.

Simmonds, M. (1914) Ueber embolische Prozesse in der Hypophysis, *Virchows Archiv (Pathologische Anatomie)* 217, 226–239.

Sinclair, J. and Coulthard, M. (1975) *Towards an Analysis of Discourse*, Oxford University Press, London.

Sisters of Mercy (1990) When you don't see me, recorded on *Vision Thing*, Merciful Release.

Smither, B. (1994) Who's who special: *Elle*'s top ten supermodels, *Elle*, September, 20–21.

Smith-Rosenberg, C. and Rosenberg, C. (1973–1974) The female animal: medical and biological views of woman and her role in nineteenth-century America, *Journal of American History*, 60, 332–356.

Snyder, M. and Ickes, W. (1985) Personality and social behaviour, in G. Lindzet and E. Arenson (eds) *Handbook of Social Psychology* vol. 2 (3rd edition), pp. 883–947, Addison-Wesley, Reading, MA.

Sohlberg, S., Norring, C., Homgren, S. and Rosmark, B. (1989) Impulsivity and long-term prognosis of psychiatric patients with anorexia nervosa/bulimia nervosa, *Journal of Nervous and Mental Disease*, 177(5), 249–258.

Sontag, S. (1978) *Illness as Metaphor*, Farrar, Straus and Giroux, New York.

——(1989) *AIDS and its Metaphors*, Farrar, Straus and Giroux, New York.

Sours, J.A. (1980) *Starving to Death in a Sea of Objects*, Jason Aronson, New York.

Spencer, H. (1896) *The Principles of Biology*, Appleton, New York.

Spender, D. (1980) *Man Made Language*, Routledge, London.

Squire, C. (1983) The problem of the subject in current psychoanalytic and post-structuralist theory: identity in pieces, unpublished Ph.D. thesis, Exeter University.

Stainbrook, E. (1965) Psychosomatic medicine in the nineteenth century, in M.R. Kaufman and M. Heiman (eds) *Evolution of Psychosomatic Concepts: anorexia nervosa: a paradigm*, pp. 6–35, Hogarth Press, London.

Stanley, L. and Wise, S. (1983) *Breaking Out: feminist consciousness and feminist research*, Routledge, London.

Steiger, H., Fraenkel, L. and Leichner, P. (1989) Relationship of body-image distortion to sex-role identification, irrational cognitions and body-weight in eating-disordered females, *Journal of Clinical Psychology*, 45(1), 61–65.

Strauss, J. and Ryan, R.M. (1988) Cognitive dysfunction in eating disorders, *International Journal of Eating Disorders*, 7(1), 19–27.

Strober, M. (1986) Anorexia nervosa: history and psychological concept, in K.D. Brownell and J.P. Foret (eds) *Handbook of Eating Disorders: physiology, psychology and treatment of obesity, anorexia and bulimia*, pp. 231–246, Basic Books, New York.

——(1991) Family-genetic studies of eating disorders, Annual Meeting of the American Psychiatric Association Symposium: recent advances in bulimia nervosa, 1991, New Orleans, *Journal of Clinical Psychiatry*, 52 (supplement), 9–12.

Strober, M. and Katz, J.L. (1987) Do eating disorders and affective disorders share a common etiology? A dissenting opinion, *International Journal of Eating Disorders*, 6(2), 171–180.

Strober, M., Morrell, W., Burroughs, J., Salkin, B. and Jacobs, C. (1985) A controlled family study of anorexia nervosa, *Journal of Psychiatric Research*, 19, 239–246.

Strober, M., Salkin, B., Burroughs, J., Morrell, W. and Sadjak, J. (1986) *A family study of anorexia nervosa in depression*, paper presented at the annual meeting of the American Psychiatric Association, May, Washington DC.

Strong, B.E. (1989) Foucault, Freud and French feminism: theorizing hysteria as theorizing the feminine, *Literature and Psychology*, 35(4), 10–26.

Strupp, B.J., Weingartener, H., Kaye, W. and Gwirtsman, H. (1986) Cognitive processing in anorexia nervosa: a disturbance in automatic processing, *Neuropsychobiology*, 15(2), 89–94.

Suematsu, H., Kuboki, T. and Ogata, E. (1986) Anorexia nervosa in MZ twins, *Psychotherapy and Psychosomatics*, 45(1), 46–50.

Sunday, S.R., Halmi, K.A., Werdann, L. and Levey, C. (1992) Comparison of body size estimation and eating disorder inventory scores in anorexia and bulimia patients with obese, restrained and unrestrained controls, *International Journal of Eating Disorders*, 11(2), 133–149.

Sutherland, H.A. (1881) A case of chronic vomiting in which no food was taken, except Koumiss, for sixteen months, *Transactions of The Clinical Society*, 14, 113–114.

Swartz, L. (1985a) Anorexia nervosa as a culture-bound syndrome, *Social Science and Medicine*, 20(7), 725–730.

——(1985b) Is thin a feminist issue?, *Women's Studies International Forum*, 8(5), 429–437.

Szmukler, G.I. (1982) Drug treatment of anorexic states, in T. Silverstone (ed.) *Drugs and Appetite*, Academic Press, London.

Taylor, S.A. (1904) A case of anorexia nervosa, *West London Medical Journal*, 9(2, April), 110–204.

Theriot, N.M. (1988) Psychosomatic illness in history: the 'green sickness' among nineteenth-century adolescent girls, *The Journal of Psychohistory*, 15(4), 461–479.

Thomas, J.P. and Szmukler, G.I. (1985) Anorexia nervosa in patients of Afro-Caribbean extraction, *British Journal of Psychiatry*, 146, 653–656.

Thompson, E.P. (1978) *The Poverty of Theory*, Merlin, London.

Tolstrup, K. (1990) Incidence and causality of anorexia nervosa in a historical perspective, *Acta Psychiatrica Scandinavica*, 82(361, supplement), 1–6.

Tomarken, A.J. and Kirschenbaum, D.S. (1984) Effects of plans for future meals on counter-regulatory eating: where have all the unrestrained eaters gone? *Journal of Abnormal Psychology*, 93, 458–472.

Tracy, S. (1860) *The Mother and her Offspring*, New York.

Trotter, T. (1807) *A View of the Nervous Temperament*, Longman, Hurst, Rees and Owen, London.

Tseelon, E. (1991) The method is the message: on the meaning of methods as ideologies, *Theory and Psychology*, 1(3), 299–316.

Turner, B.S. (1984) *The Body and Society: explorations in social theory*, Blackwell, Oxford.

——(1987) *Medical Power and Social Knowledge*, Sage, London.

——(1992) *Regulating Bodies: essays in medical sociology*, Routledge, London.

Unsworth, T. and Shattock, R. (1993) *Cosmo* survey results: your love hate relationship with food, *Cosmopolitan* (March), 90–95.

Ussher, J. (1989) *The Psychology of the Female Body*, Routledge, London.

——(1991) *Women's Madness: misogyny or mental illness*, Harvester Wheatsheaf, London.

——(1992a) Reproductive rhetoric and the blaming of the body, in P. Nicolson and J. Ussher (eds) *The Psychology of Women's Health and Health Care*, pp. 31–61, Macmillan, Basingstoke,

——(1992b) Research and theory related to female reproduction: implications for clinical psychology, *British Journal of Clinical Psychology*, 31, 129–151.

——(1992c) Science sexing psychology, in J. Ussher and P. Nicolson (eds) *Gender Issues in Clinical Psychology*, Routledge, London.

——(1994) *A limited script: men's accounts of heterosexual sex*, paper presented at the Women and Psychology Conference, July, Nottingham University.

Vandereycken, W. and Van Deth, R. (1989) Who was the first to describe anorexia nervosa: Gull or Lasegue?, *Psychological Medicine*, 19, 837–845.

Vandereycken, W. and Lowenkopf, E.L. (1990) Anorexia nervosa in 19th century America, *Journal of Nervous and Mental Disease*, 178(8), 531–535.

Veith, I. (1965) *Hysteria: the history of a disease*, University of Chicago Press, Chicago.

Vitousek, K.B. and Hollon, S.D. (1990) The investigation of schematic content and processing in eating disorders, *Cognitive Therapy and Research*, 14(2), 191–214.

Wakeling, A. (1985) Neuro-biological aspects of feeding disorders, *Journal of Psychiatric Research*, 19(2–3), 191–201.

Walkerdine, V. (1984) Developmental psychology and the child-centred pedagogy: the insertion of Piaget into early education, in J. Henriques, W. Hollway, C. Urwin, C. Venn, and V. Walkerdine (1984) *Changing the Subject: psychology, social regulation and subjectivity*, pp. 153–202, Methuen, London.

——(1986) Post-structuralist theory and everyday social practices: the family and the school, in S. Wilkinson (ed.) *Feminist Social Psychology*, pp. 57–76, Open University Press, Milton Keynes.

——(1988) *The Mastery of Reason: cognitive development and the production of rationality*, Routledge, London.

——(1990) Paper presented at the Discourse and Gender Conference, Birkbeck College, London.

——(1993) *Post-modernity and feminist research*, paper presented at Psychology of Women Conference, July, University of Sussex, Brighton.

Walkerdine, V. and Lucey, H. (1989) *Democracy in the Kitchen: regulating mothers and socializing daughters*, Virago, London,

Waller, G., Halek, C. and Crisp, A.H. (1993) Sexual abuse as a factor in anorexia nervosa: evidence from two separate case studies, *Journal of Psychosomatic Research*, 37(8), 873–879.

Walmsley, J. (1994) Roseanne Arnold, *Independent Magazine* (29 January), 46.

Walsh, B.T., Katz, J., Levine, J. *et al.* (1981) The production rate of cortisol declines during recovery from anorexia nervosa, *Journal of Clinical Endocrinology and Metabolism*, 53, 203–5.

Walsh, F. and Scheinkman, M. (1989) (Fe)male: the hidden gender dimension in models of family therapy, in M. McGoldrick, C.M. Andersen and F. Walsh *Women in Families*, pp. 16–42, Norton, New York.

Waltos, D.L. (1986) Historical perspectives and diagnostic considerations, *Occupational Therapy in Mental Health*, 6(1), 1–13. Special issue: The evaluation and treatment of eating disorders.

Wardle, J. and Beales, S. (1986) Restraint body image and food attitudes in children from 12–18 years, *Appetite*, 7, 209–17.

Wardle, J. and Marsland, L. (1990) Adolescent concerns about weight and eating: a social developmental perspective, *Journal of Psychosomatic Research*, 34, 377–391.

Wardle, J., Bindra, R., Fairclough, B. and Westcombe, A. (1993) Culture and body image: body perception and weight concern in young Asian and Caucasian British women, *Journal of Community and Applied Social Psychology*, 3(3), 173–181.

Waters, B.G., Beumont, P.J., Touyz, S. and Kennedy, M. (1990) Behavioural differences between twin and non-twin female sibling pairs discordant for anorexia nervosa, *International Journal of Eating Disorders*, 9(3), 265–273.

Weedon, C. (1987) *Feminist Practice and Post-Structuralist Theory*, Blackwell, Oxford.

Weeks, J. (1989) *Sex, Politics and Society: the regulation of sexuality since 1800*, Longman, London.

Weight, L. and Noakes, T. (1987) Is running an anolog of anorexia? A survey of the incidence of eating disorders in female distance runners, *Medicine and Science in Sport and Exercise*, 19(3), 213–217.

Weiner, H. and Katz,. J.L. (1983) The hypothalmic–pituitary–adrenal axis in anorexia nervosa: a reassessment, in P. Darby, P.E. Garfinkel, D.M. Garner and M. Olmsted (eds) *Anorexia Nervosa: recent developments in research*, pp. 249–270, Alan Liss, New York.

Wetherell, M. (1986) Linguistic repertoires and literary criticism: new directions for a social psychology of gender, in S. Wilkinson (ed.) *Feminist Social Psychology: developing theory and practice*, Open University Press, Milton Keynes.

——(1991) *Romantic discourse: analysing investment, power and desire*, text of paper presented at the Fourth International Conference on Language and Social Psychology, August, University of California, Santa Barbara.

——(1996) 'Fear of fat: interpretive repertoires and ideological dilemmas', in J. Maybi and N. Mercer (eds) *Using English: from conversation to canon*, Routledge: London.

Wetherell, M. and Potter, J. (1988) Discourse analysis and the identification of interpretive repertoires, in C. Antaki (ed.) *Analyzing Everyday Explanations*, Sage, London.

Wetherell, M. and White, S. (1992) Fear of fat: young women talk about eating, dieting and body image, unpublished manuscript, Open University.

Whitehouse, A.M., Freeman, C.P. and Annandale, A. (1988) Body size estimation in anorexia nervosa, Second Leeds Psychopathology Symposium: The Psychopathology of Body Image, 1986, Leeds, *British Journal of Psychiatry*, 153 (supplement 2), 23–26.

Whitford, M. (1989) Re-reading Irigaray, in T. Brennan (ed.) *Between Feminism and Psychoanalysis*, pp. 106–126, Routledge, London.

Whytt, R. (1767) *Observations on the nature, causes, and cure of those disorders which are commonly called nervous, hypochondriac or hysterric, to which is prefixed some remarks on the sympathy of the nerves*, Becket, DeHondt and Balfour, Edinburgh (first edition 1764).

Widdicombe, S. (1993) Autobiography and change: rhetoric and authenticity of 'Gothic' style, in E. Burman and I. Parker (eds) *Discourse Analytic Research: repertoires and readings of texts in action*, Routledge, London.

Widdicombe, S. and Wooffitt, R. (1990) 'Being' versus 'doing' punk: on achieving authenticity as a member, *Journal of Language and Social Psychology*, 9(4), 257–277.

Wilkinson, S. (ed.) (1986) *Feminist Social Psychology*, Open University Press, Milton Keynes.

Wilks, S. (1888) Anorexia nervosa (letter), *Lancet*, 31 March, 646–647.

Willan, R. (1790) A remarkable case of abstinence, *Medical Communications*, 2, 113–122.

Wilson, C.P., Hogan C.C. and Mintz, I.L. (1983) *Fear of Being Fat: the treatment of anorexia nervosa and bulimia*, Jason Aronson, New York.

REFERENCES

Winnicott, D.W. (1967) Mirror-role of mother and family in child development, in *Playing and Reality*, pp. 111–118, Tavistock, London (1971).

Wittig, M. (1979) *One is not born a woman*, text of the speech given at the City University of New York Graduate Centre, September.

Wolff, H., Bateman, A. and Sturgeon, D. (eds) (1990) *UCH Textbook of Psychiatry: an integrated approach*, Gerald Duckworth, London.

Wolpert, E.A. (1980) Major affective disorders, in H.I. Kaplan, A.M. Freedman and B.J. Sadock (eds) *Comprehensive Textbook of Psychiatry*, vol. 2 (3rd edition), Williams and Wilkins, Baltimore.

Woodiwiss, A. (1990) *Social Theory after Post-Modernism: rethinking production, law and class*, Pluto, London.

Woolf, N. (1990) *The Beauty Myth*, Chatto and Windus, London.

Woolgar, S. (1988) *Science: the very idea*, Ellis Horwood, Chichester.

World Health Organization (1992) *ICD-10: classification of mental and behavioural disorders: clinical descriptions and diagnostic guidelines*, World Health Organization, Geneva.

Yager, J. (1982) Family issues in the pathogenesis of anorexia nervosa, *Psychosomatic Medicine*, 44(1), 43–60.

INDEX